MONUMENTS OF MEDIEVAL ART

ROBERT G. CALKINS is a professor in the Department of the History of Art at Cornell University, where he has taught since 1966. He received his B.A. degree from the Woodrow Wilson School of Public and International Affairs at Princeton University and his M.A. and Ph.D. degrees in Art History from Harvard University. He has published articles on fifteenth-century manuscript illumination in *Scriptorium, Arte Lombarda, Gesta, Oud Holland,* and *The Art Bulletin.* His books include an exhibition catalogue, *A Medieval Treasury* (1968), a monograph on the Master of Catherine of Cleves (1979), *Illuminated Books of the Middle Ages* (1983), and *Programs of Medieval Illumination* (1984).

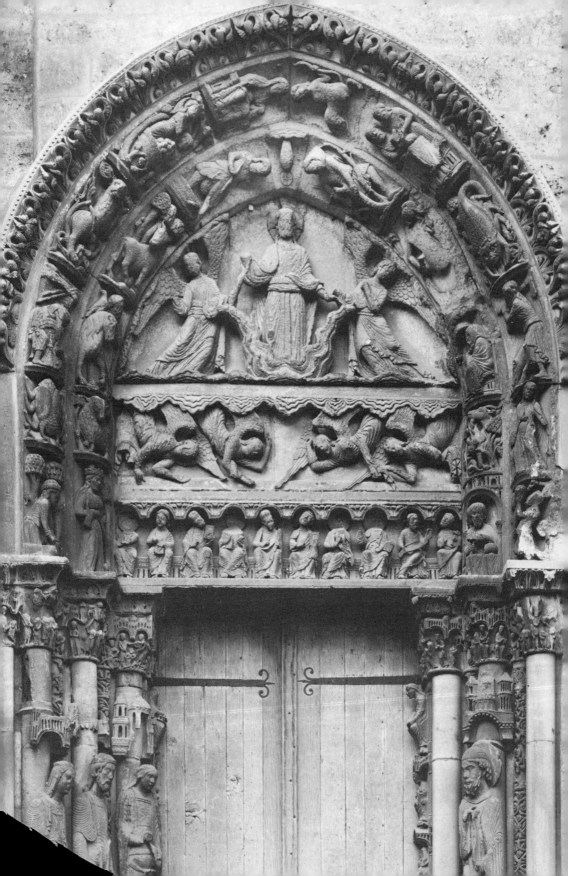

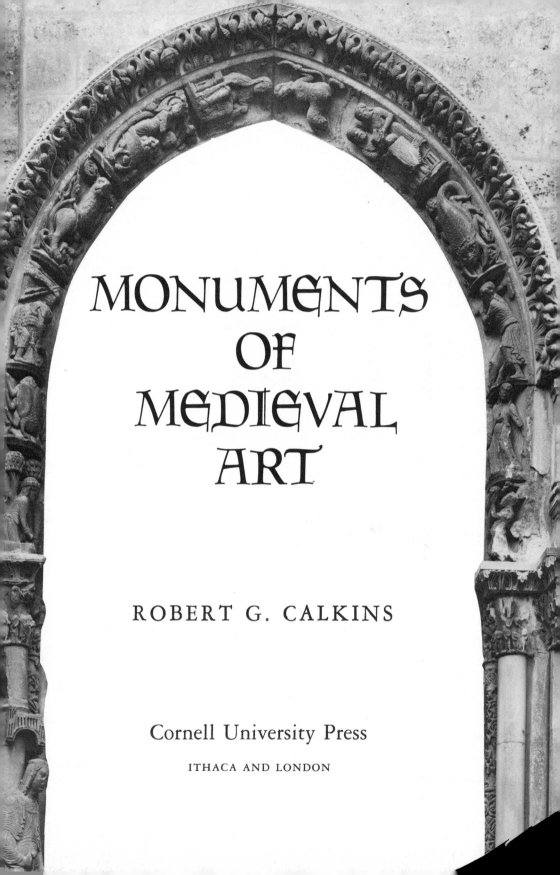

MONUMENTS OF MEDIEVAL ART

ROBERT G. CALKINS

Cornell University Press

ITHACA AND LONDON

For
ANN,
CAROLINE, RICHARD,
AND EDWARD

Contents

Illustrations

Preface

The following topical discussions are intended to serve as an introduction to the art and architecture of the Middle Ages. Although they are arranged more or less chronologically, at least in the first half of the book, they are not intended to present a complete survey of medieval art or to cover all the important works within a given medium, or even all of the relevant arts within a given historical period. Some of the representative examples of major art forms or developments have been selected to show how form and content or how architecture, decoration, and furnishings work together to make a particular artistic and cultural statement consistent with their larger historical context. The evolution of form and style is not a major concern here; rather, mature examples are discussed in the light of their immediate contexts. The titles of such sections as "The Romanesque Portal" or "The Gothic Cathedral" imply a greater degree of generalization than is warranted by the diverse forms and purposes of twelfth-century portals or thirteenth-century cathedrals. Yet, in a detailed examination of the sculptural ensemble at Moissac or of the structural and aesthetic effects of Chartres, the reader can extrapolate how similar monuments functioned in their particular circumstances and, in general, the nature of the cultural statement they embodied. The discussions of individual monuments and of the sources of their iconography are not exhaustive; they serve merely to introduce the reader to possible interpretations that can be followed more fully in the suggested Selected Bibliography. As the sections of this book are focused upon selected monuments, the Bibliography lists only those references that would extend the reader's investigations into the topics of these discussions.

I am grateful to Carl Barnes, Allen Farber, Susan Shedd, and Susan Straight for their helpful suggestions, and to Helen Kelley for her photographic skills. In addition, I am deeply indebted to Carol Bradley for her unflagging assistance in obtaining a number of the illustrations. I should also like to thank Cyril I. Nelson for his support in the preparation of this book.

ROBERT G. CALKINS

Ithaca, New York
October 1978

Introduction

The term *Middle Ages* refers to the period between the fall of Rome and the Renaissance of the fifteenth century. As so often happens when historical periods are categorized, the label is both misleading and deprecatory, applied after the fact and with biased hindsight. The concept of this historical era as one sandwiched between two other periods of enlightenment is derived from the Renaissance view of history and culture articulated by Petrarch. He branded the literature and thought of the period between the dissolution of the Roman Empire and the revival of learning in his own time (1306–1374) as ugly and barbarian manifestations of a "Dark" age: "the Age of Faith was an Age of Darkness." The idea that the period was an in-between time of stagnation was further strengthened by references to it as a *media tempestas* (1496), *media aetas* (1518), and *medium aevum* (1604), and this view was perpetuated by other Italian humanists and chroniclers in the fifteenth and sixteenth centuries, who wrote that the liberal arts of the ancients, "which were almost extinct," were revived in their own time.

The humanists of the Renaissance dismissed the contributions of the medieval period to their own era. They forgot that medieval men saw themselves as preservers of the Christian faith against the pagans and as the direct heirs of antiquity who sought, by frequently turning to classical times for inspiration, to maintain the continuity between their institutions and those of Early Christian Rome. The Renaissance historians ignored the fact that it was precisely the medieval *scriptoria* and institutions of learning, the monasteries, cathedral schools, and finally the universities that copied and preserved most of the antique texts during the period of "neglect." Neither did they realize that many of the attitudes of their own day were fully rooted in the developing traditions of the Middle Ages.

As a historical period, the Middle Ages is varied and imprecise. Generally, it can be considered to begin with the Edict of Milan in 313. Although this edict legally accorded Christianity only equal status with other religions in Rome, Constantine gave it de facto precedence through imperial patronage. Sometimes, however, an approximate date of 500 is said to be the beginning of the period, coinciding with the final dissolution of the power of the Roman Empire in the West and the emergence of a powerful Byzantine state in the East. Certainly the political, social, and economic institutions of the Early Christian period, at least through the fifth century, remain Late Roman, and the art of this era remains late antique. Yet the developments after 500 cannot be fully understood without reference to developments in the first two hundred years of transition.

At the other end of the period medieval attitudes and institutions blend into those of the Renaissance, perhaps as early as the fourteenth century and certainly by the end of the first third of the fifteenth century in Italy. In areas of northern Europe the Renaissance is not evident until the mid-fifteenth or even early sixteenth century. Between the almost imperceptible commencement and gradual denouement of the Middle Ages, we have over a millennium, in some cases up to thirteen hundred kaleidoscopic years, of changing institutions and attitudes.

The one constant factor throughout these centuries was the common center around which most of life was organized, the Christian church. As the peoples of Europe became converted to Christianity—and this process was still going on in the ninth century under the Carolingian Empire—they embraced a spiritual force that dominated every facet of their lives, an ecclesiastical hierarchy that shaped the course of political events and determined the structure of society. It is for this reason that the term *medieval* applies best to those regions of Europe and to the countries around the Mediterranean, including the Byzantine Empire, that came under the influence of Christianity.

At the same time, the climate of medieval Europe was also determined by threats from without and political disintegration from within. Waves of barbarian invasions and constant attacks from the Norsemen disrupted the fragile institutions of church and society between the fifth and ninth centuries. Within Europe, empires were created that provided periodic semblances of overall unity and political structure, but actually society became fragmented into small feudal enclaves of lords with their own local allegiances. After the seventh century the ever-present threat from Islam, which emerged as a powerful adversary, half-occupying Europe by the middle of the eighth century, still caused grave insecurity in the fifteenth. All of these forces served to mold the Christian church into the Church Militant. This militant posture culminated in the crusades of the twelfth and thirteenth centuries to free the Holy Land from the infidel.

In the process, Europeans broadened their horizons, opened new trade routes, and created an impetus for a quickening economy. Cities expanded in size and wealth, aided not only by the growth of a mercantile economy but also by an improvement in agricultural production that permitted the selling of produce in urban markets. With the growth of the cities there emerged another stratum of the populace, more or less independent of the local ecclesiastical institutions and feudal hierarchy. Thus, a complex tapestry of ecclesiastical dominion, resurgent and changing political institutions, the evolution of a feudal society, and a slow reawakening of a secular spirit provides the context for the developing forms of medieval art.

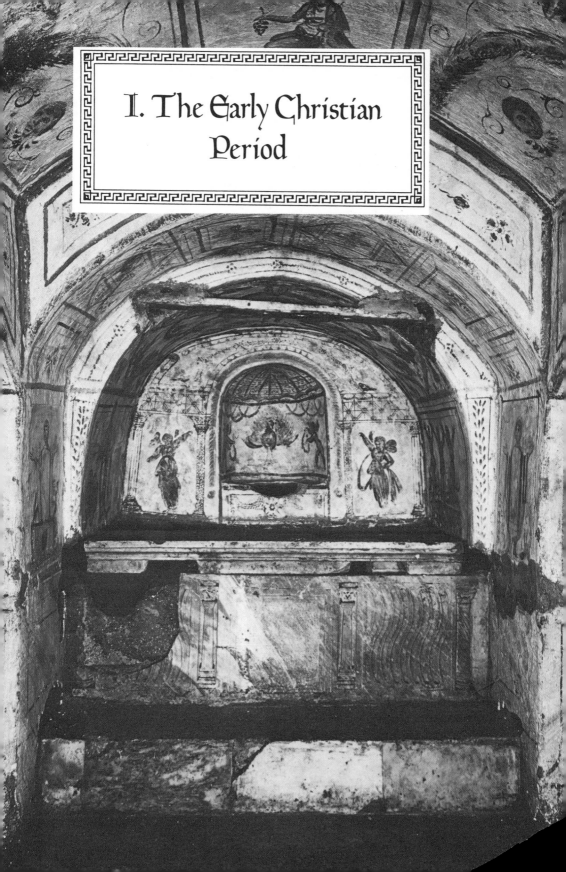

I. The Early Christian Period

1. EARLY CHRISTIANITY

n the first several centuries after Christ, Christianity was but one of several mystery cults, such as the cult of Isis or the cult of Mithras, that attracted converts from the Roman populace. All of these cults embodied a belief in life after death, but the most subversive, in the view of the Roman rulers, was Christianity because it taught complete allegiance to God rather than to Emperor and the equality of all mankind in the eyes of God. In refusing to worship the emperor as a god, and in advocating the community of goods, the liberation of slaves, and the possibility of salvation for all regardless of station in life, Christianity was believed to undermine the basis of the Roman social and economic system.

Yet Christianity was firmly based upon a mixture of traditional beliefs from a variety of cultures. It was firmly founded on the Judaic historical tradition of the Old Testament and therefore made frequent use of Old Testament incidents to bolster the authenticity of events in the New Testament. For example, the Old Testament story of Abraham instructed to sacrifice his son, Isaac, was equated with the Crucifixion in which God permitted the sacrifice of his son, Christ. This typological comparison showed that the Old Testament incident prefigured that of the New. Such a comparison also gave the New Testament additional authority because the Crucifixion was demonstrated to be part of a long-evolving divine plan for the redemption of Man, indicated by prior events in history. The incidents of the Old Testament and the Judaic tradition of the prophets became, therefore, an integral part of the Christian Bible and a basis for much Christian imagery.

Some of the precepts of Christianity are founded on a Greek heritage, particularly the Platonic view of the imperfection of things on this earth and the existence of perfection in an ideal realm. Plotinus' writings on this Platonic philosophy were adapted to Christianity, asserting that the state of perfection was something to be striven for rather than, as was the case with Plato, a lost Golden Age. The concepts of the Trinity and of the immortality of the soul were in part derived from Greek and Judaic thought. Ancient Rome also contributed doctrines to the growing faith: the stoic belief in the brotherhood of man, as well as a tradition of almost Puritan-like virtues that had prevailed in the period of the Roman Republic. Perhaps the most important Roman contribution, however, was the ability for organization, which led not only to the establishment of a rigid ecclesiastical hierarchy but also to the codification of Christian doctrine. Early Christianity, therefore, evolved in the first four centuries, A.D. from casual groups of fervent believers into a well-organized faith with a functioning administration and doctrine, yet with discernible roots in the continuing traditions around it.

3

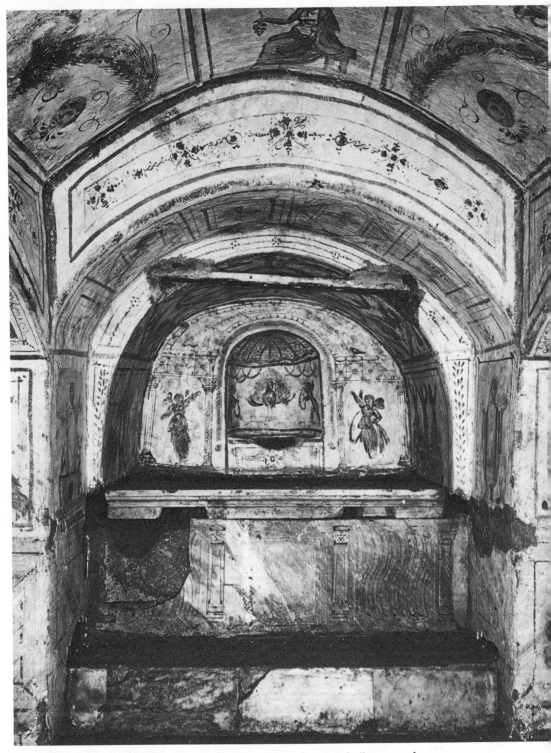

Fig. 1. Cubiculum. Catacomb of the Vita Dino Compagni, Rome. 3rd
century. (Pontificia Commissione di Archaeologia Sacra, Rome)

2. THE EARLY CHRISTIAN CATACOMBS AND THEIR DECORATION

During its first century and a half, Christianity was primarily a lower-class movement. Cult meetings were not highly organized, the practice of the Christian services was not formalized, and meeting places were usually in rooms of private dwellings, such as on the upper floors of multistory apartment houses known as *insulae.* Not until the next phase of development, between 150 and 250, do we find alterations made in rooms in private dwellings for specific Christian rites, such as the establishment of a small baptismal chamber in a villa at Dura Europas that dates from about 230. Also during this period we find an increasing number of structures that functioned as Christian community centers, buildings without, however, any specifically Christian distinguishing features. Many of these *tituli,* or first parish churches, still occurred in the context of a large private dwelling, hence they are often known as *domus ecclesiae.* The period between 250 and the Edict of Milan in 313 was marked by violent persecutions under the reigns of Decius in 250 and of Diocletian from 303 to 305. Memorial structures (*martyria*) were constructed over the graves of martyrs, and in scattered instances more elaborate buildings were erected as public meeting places.

In the period before the Edict of Milan the most numerous and remarkable examples of Early Christian art were the decorations of the subterranean graveyards known as catacombs. Numerous grave sites were needed because the Christians, believing not only in the eternal life of the soul but also in the resurrection of the dead, preferred the practice of interment, which preserved the body for that moment, and shunned cremation, which destroyed it. In Rome, where surface land was scarce and often difficult for Christians to gain possession of, vast networks of passages, stairs, and *cubicula,* or *hypogea,* were excavated underground. In the walls of the passageways horizontal niches in which to place the bodies of the deceased were dug. Wealthy Christian families had *cubicula* dug, square chambers with niches for the sarcophagi off the central space. The practice of family burial, of holding funerary banquets at the grave site, and even the tradition of painted decorations in these spaces, were derived from Etruscan and Roman funereal practices.

The walls, niches, and domical vault of the *cubiculum* (fig. 1) were usually divided into a variety of geometric fields by circular, semicircular, and rectangular painted frames. Within these frames figures were painted against the white plaster background. This form of wall painting, known as fresco painting, had been prevalent since Roman times and continued to be a major art form in Italy throughout the medieval and into the more modern periods. (See section 25 for a discussion of the techniques of fresco painting in the Gothic period.)

The themes present in the catacomb paintings were a mixture of classical and Christian elements. One of the earliest Christian symbols was that of the fish, which symbolized Christ because the letters of the Greek word for fish, *ICHTHYS*, stood for the first letters of the words in the phrase "Jesus Christ, God's Son, Savior." The fresco in the crypt of Lucina, in the Catacomb of Calixtus, shows a fish supporting a basket of bread (fig. 2). Thus, in addition to being a Christological symbol, reinforced by the frequent reference in the Scriptures to Christ as the fisherman and the apostles as fishermen of men's souls, this painting may also refer to the miraculous feeding of the five thousand, in which fishes and loaves were multiplied to feed the vast multitude. As such, this scene undoubtedly also served as a prefiguration of another miraculous meal, the Last Supper, in which Christ pronounced the bread was his body, and thereby established the rite of Holy Communion. Through the participation in this sacrament of Holy Communion the Christian could participate in this sacrificial rite: fish and bread thus became fitting, interlocking symbols for a funerary context.

Another frequent representation was that of "The Good Shepherd" (fig. 3), usually a youthful figure holding a lamb on his shoulders with a few sheep at his feet. Although this figure undoubtedly called to mind the parable of the Good Shepherd (Luke 15:4–7 or John 10:11–16) and therefore, by implication, stood for Christ as the Shepherd saving the errant member of his flock (halos were not yet used to indicate divinity), this theme had classical origins. It was a widely used bucolic motif in Greek and Roman art, and its interpretaton could have been either pagan or Christian, according to the preference of the beholder.

A remarkable example of the fusion of pagan and Christian motifs is the fresco of "Orpheus" playing his lyre in the Catacomb of Domitilla (fig. 4). The mythological story of Orpheus, whose beloved Eurydice died and was taken to Hades, is purely classical in origin. Orpheus charmed Pluto, the god of the Underworld, with his music and almost won Eurydice back. Although he failed because he looked back to see if she was following, the theme was appropriate for a pagan tomb because of its implications of salvation from Hades. But it could also be read in a Christian context, as referring to Christ's three-day descent into Purgatory between the Crucifixion and the Resurrection, and carrying with it a promise of an ascent from the dead for the blessed. The Orpheus legend served as a classical prefiguration of the Christian theme of salvation.

Other stories such as that of Daniel in the Lion's Den or of Jonah and the Whale serve as historical and Judaic precedents for salvation. The story of Jonah in the Tomb of the Via Anapo (figs. 5–7) is particularly apt, for Jonah swallowed by the whale is the equivalent of Christ's descent into Limbo, "Jonah Cast Up," to Christ's Resurrection, and "Jonah Under the Gourd Vine," to the theme of salvation and eternal bliss.

Stylistically, these paintings are similar to the traditional manner of Late Roman fresco painting. The fish and basket of bread recall illusionistic still lifes found at Pompeii, and frequently the painting of figures shows the same swarthy tonalities, modulated highlights and shadows of their Roman counterparts. In many of the catacomb paintings the contours are heavier, the proportions of the figures are stockier, and the transitions from light to shade are more arbitrary than in earlier paintings. Some of this increased stylization of form may be a reflection

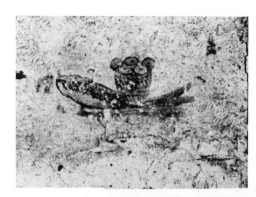

Fig. 2. "Fish and Bread" fresco. Catacomb of Calixtus, Crypt of Lucina, Rome. Early 3rd century. (Pontificia Commissione di Archaeologia Sacra)

Fig. 3. "The Good Shepherd" fresco. Catacomb of Calixtus, Crypt of Lucina, Rome. Early 3rd century. (Pontificia Commissione di Archaeologia Sacra)

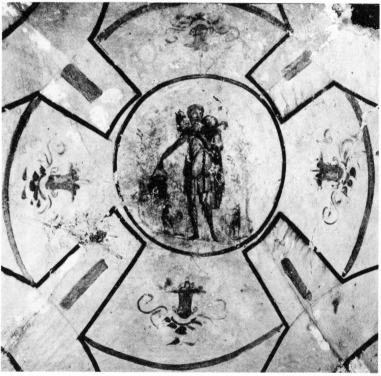

Fig. 4. "Orpheus" fresco. Catacomb of Domitilla, Rome. 3rd century. (Pontificia Commissione di Archaeologia Sacra)

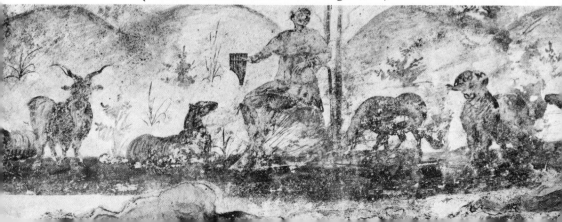

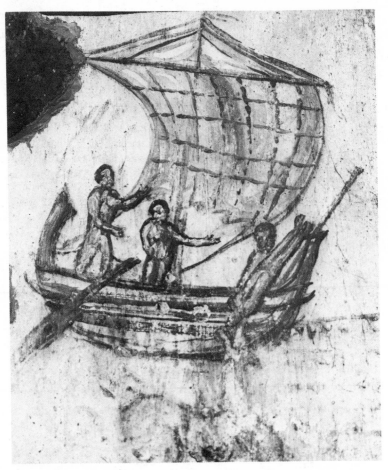

Fig. 5. "Jonah Cast Overboard" fresco. Tomb of the Via Anapo, Rome. 3rd century. (Pontificia Commissione di Archaeologia Sacra)

of the fact that many of these paintings are the equivalent of a folk art produced by lesser artisans than those who worked for wealthy patrons. Nevertheless, some of the abstraction may also have been the result of an interest in representing the symbolical significance of the scene rather than its corporeal actuality. Occasionally, however, a painting such as the presumed Head of an Apostle (pl. 1) in the Tomb of the Aurelians, although now badly damaged, is imbued with the implication of volume through vivacious, impressionistic brushstrokes. It is a close equivalent of the sensitivity to form and feeling for introspective attitudes often found in Late Roman portraiture.

In style and iconography the subjects painted in the Early Christian catacombs were often interchangeable with motifs in Late Roman painting. Frequently it requires a recognizably Christian context to differentiate between a pagan or a Christian meaning. The Early Christians drew broadly from the religious, literary, and historical traditions of the Judaic Old Testament, incorporated themes from pagan mythology, and reused traditional Roman modes of painting.

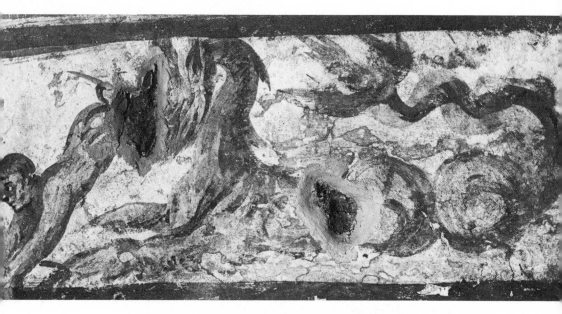

Fig. 6. "Jonah Cast Up" fresco. Tomb of the Via Anapo, Rome. 3rd century. (Pontificia Commissione di Archaeologia Sacra)

Fig. 7. "Jonah Under the Gourd Vine" fresco. Tomb of the Via Anapo, Rome. 3rd century. (Pontificia Commissione di Archaeologia Sacra)

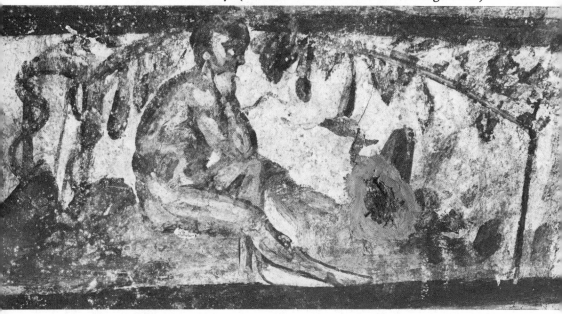

3. THE EARLY CHRISTIAN BASILICA
AND ITS DECORATION

The most dramatic advance made in Christian art occurred after Constantine had proclaimed the Edict of Milan in 313. Although the edict did not favor Christianity, Constantine threw the weight of Roman Imperial patronage behind the faith and in the process gave it visibility and de facto supremacy over the other religions.

A vast building program was initiated, which included the construction of Saint John in the Lateran (the cathedral of Rome), the churches of the Nativity in Bethlehem, the Holy Sepulcher in Jerusalem, and at the end of Constantine's reign, plans for the construction of Old Saint Peter's in Rome. These structures were each designed for different usages, but certain characteristics became consistent, and a new form of building and decoration evolved.

The new buildings in Rome, such as Saint John in the Lateran (c. 320), Saint Peter's (begun 320), and Saint Paul's Outside the Walls (begun 385), turned away from the massive engineering of the brick-and-concrete Roman baths and from the simpler, classical form of temple with colonnade surrounding a chamber or *cella*. Instead, the Early Christian basilica derived elements of its form from a long tradition of marketplaces, riding and military halls, and judiciary buildings in which an interior colonnade divided the space into aisles and a major longitudinal space. These elements were assimilated in a new way to create a religious assembly hall with an innovative ground plan and different exterior and interior effects to accommodate new functions dictated by the developing liturgy of the Christian church.

The basilica of Saint Peter's, begun around 320 (figs. 8, 9), typifies this kind of structure and planning. Because of its situation on the side of the hill, a monumental stairway led up to the entrance gate. Inside was a large colonnaded court (*atrium*), with a fountain for purification. The church itself was a five-aisled basilica, with two aisles separated by colonnades flanking the higher and wider nave. This longitudinal space led to a wide arch opening into a transverse space, the transept. Beyond the transept was an elevated sanctuary (*bema*), on which was situated the high altar in a semicircular area, or apse. The building was covered with a timber roof: sloping roofs over the aisles and a gabled roof over the nave. Sometimes, as at Saint Paul's Outside the Walls (c. 385; fig. 10), the ceiling consisted of open trusswork; sometimes, as at S. Maria Maggiore (432–440; fig. 11), an enclosed ceiling covered the higher nave. The flat wall above the nave arcade, corresponding to the area of the sloping roof over the aisles, was decorated with panels of mosaic or fresco decoration, and above them were windows in the clerestory level.

The exterior of such a building presented a series of longitudinal volumes ascending to the peaked roof over the nave, a vast, simple, unarticulated, barnlike

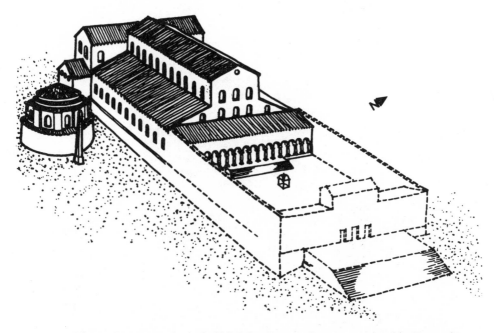

Fig. 8. Reconstruction of Old Saint Peter's, Rome. c. 400. (A. Frazer in Richard Krautheimer, *Early Christian and Byzantine Architecture*)

Fig. 9. Plan of Old Saint Peter's, Rome. c 400. (A. Frazer in Richard Krautheimer, *Early Christian and Byzantine Architecture*)

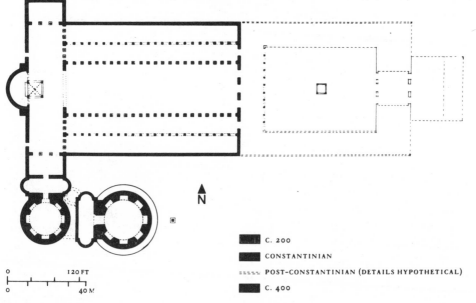

C. 200

CONSTANTINIAN

POST-CONSTANTINIAN (DETAILS HYPOTHETICAL)

C. 400

0   120 FT

0   40 M

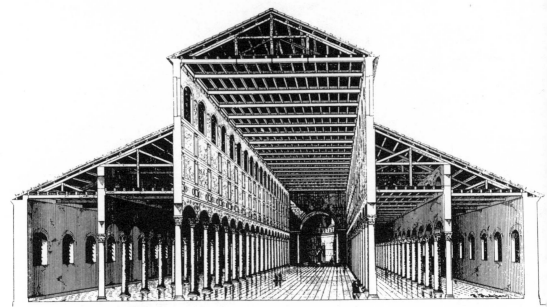

Fig. 10. Reconstruction of Saint Paul's Outside the Walls, Rome. c. 385.
(After Dehio and Bezold)

structure. The interior space of the nave of such a building, as exemplified by the
fifth-century basilica of S. Maria Maggiore, had a strong longitudinal axis, but was
broad and light. The nave elevation was punctuated by alternating horizontal bands
of clerestory windows, planar decorated surfaces, and open colonnades screening
the shadowy spaces of the aisles beyond. Sometimes, as at Saint Peter's, the nave
colonnade supported a horizontal entablature in the traditional classical manner;
sometimes, as at Saint Paul's, the columns supported an arcade. In many cases
classical columns and their elaborately carved Corinthian or Composite capitals
were reused from Roman monuments. When they were not available, they were
copied.

The decoration of the Early Christian basilicas constitutes the major artistic
achievement of the period. The vast wall surfaces above the nave colonnade, the
triumphal arch over the entrance to the sanctuary, and the half dome of the apse
provided ample area for the development of narrative themes and didactic representations. Some of these decorations were paintings in fresco, but many were
executed in mosaic. They all differed from the paintings of the catacombs in that
they were created under the patronage either of the imperial family or of the upper
hierarchy of the church. The financial resources were greater, the scale was larger,
and the major artisans of the period were employed.

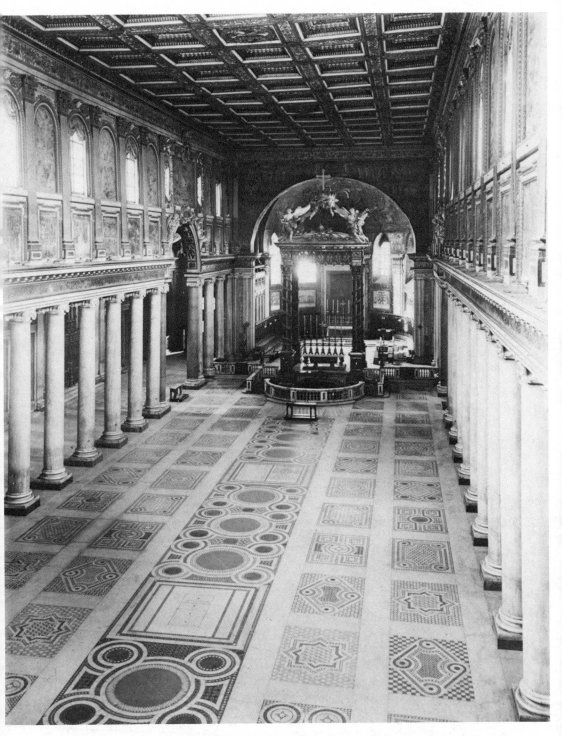

Fig. 11. Interior of nave toward apse. S. Maria Maggiore, Rome. 432–440, and 17th century. (Gabinetto Fotografico Nazionale, Rome)

Mosaics had been used extensively throughout the antique world. Made of small cubes of colored stone or glass (*tesserae*), they were usually fitted together on the floors of *atria* or the rooms of villas to create intricate designs or pictures. Although patterned silhouettes were most easily made in this medium, the Greeks and Romans became accomplished masters at achieving the same illusionistic effects as in their paintings through the subtle gradations of the colored stones to achieve modeling. One of the major achievements of the Early Christian mosaicists, although they did not invent the method, was to perfect and extensively use mosaics on the vertical walls and curved vaulted surfaces of their buildings.

The basilica of S. Maria Maggiore in Rome (432–440), although reworked in the seventeenth century, still retains many of its mosaic panels above the colonnade, mosaic decoration over the triumphal arch, and a revised mosaic of the thirteenth century in the apse. The scenes on the arch (fig. 12) executed under Pope Sixtus III (c. 432–440) represent the coming of Christ and depict incidents of Christ's birth and childhood. The arch mosaics therefore present an expansive narration of the theme of the Incarnation of the Son of God as man and the beginning of his mission on earth. At the left of the arch, the Christ Child is seated upon a bejeweled throne with four attendant angels behind him—a Christian reuse of a traditional Roman imperial representation. Actually part of a scene of the "Adoration of the Magi," the representation of Christ on a heavenly throne with celestial attendants stresses his divine nature. The Virgin, clothed in a blue cloak, is seated next to Christ's throne, and above, she is clothed in the richly embroidered and bejeweled garments of an imperial princess. This emphasis on the role of the Virgin is a visual reflection of the dogma pronounced by the Council

Fig. 12. Triumphal arch mosaics. S. Maria Maggiore, Rome. 432–440. (Anderson-Alinari)

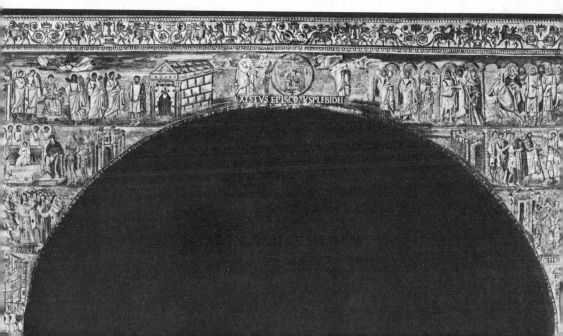

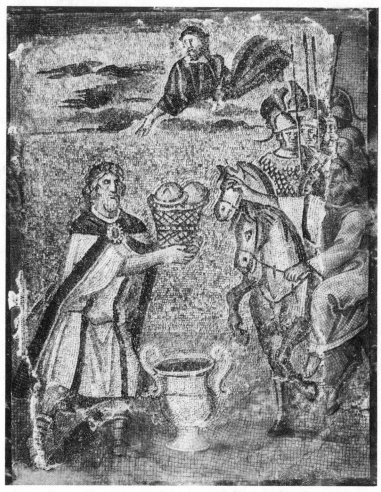

Fig. 13. "Offering of Melchizedek" mosaic. S. Maria Maggiore, Rome. 432–440. (Anderson-Alinari)

of Ephesus in 431 reaffirming the nature of the Virgin as *theotokos*, the Mother of God. At the top of the arch Saints Peter and Paul, with the four animal attributes of the Evangelists as envisioned by Saint John in the Book of Revelation, flank a medallion containing an enthroned bejeweled cross, a symbol of Christ triumphant in heaven at the moment of his Second Coming. Narrative scenes of Christ's infancy below are drawn from the popular apocryphal gospels of the Pseudo Matthew and the Protoevangelium of James. At the bottom, on the left and right, are the golden walls set with jewels of the heavenly cities of Jerusalem, the place of Christ's sacrifice, and Bethlehem, the place of his birth. Lambs, symbols of the apostles and by extension, Christ's followers, cluster before the portals. Christ's triumphal First and Second Comings serve, therefore, as appropriate themes for the triumphal entryway into the holiest space of the Christian basilica, the sanctuary with the high altar.

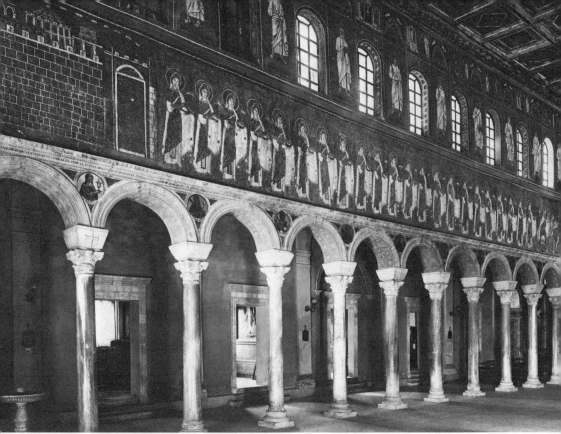

Fig. 14. "Procession of virgin martyrs" mosaic. S. Apollinare Nuovo, Ravenna. c. 550. (Alinari)

Fig. 15. "Adoration of the Magi" mosaic. S. Apollinare Nuovo, Ravenna. c. 550. (Hirmer Fotoarchiv)

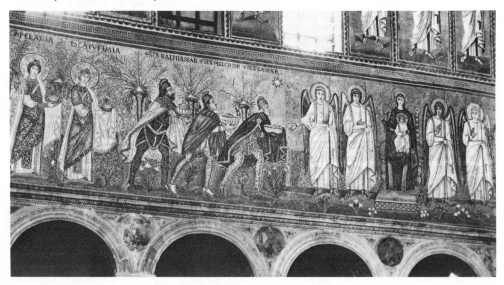

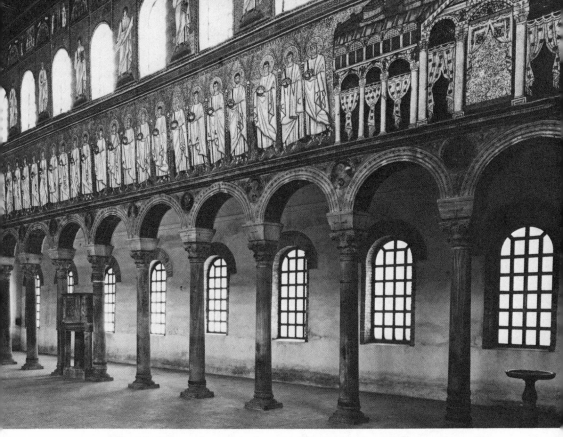

Fig. 16. "Procession of male martyrs" mosaic. S. Apollinare Nuovo, Ravenna. c. 550. (Antonello Perissinotto, Padua)

The narrative scenes along the nave contain stories drawn from the Old Testament. The stories of Abraham, Jacob, Moses, and Joshua serve as historical Judaic antecedents of the new order under the Christian church and function as prefigurations of the incidents related in the New Testament. In the scene of the "Offering of Melchizedek" (fig. 13), Abraham, the Israelite general, receiving gifts of bread and wine from the High Priest, prefigures the institution of the Eucharist and the celebration of Holy Communion in the Christian Mass. The position of these antecedent incidents in the nave, preparing for and leading up to the Christological scenes on the arch, accompanies the direction and the progress of the celebrant down the length of the nave to that place where he enters the sanctuary, heralded by the representation of the Incarnation.

This conformity of the content of the mosaic decoration and the function of the Early Christian basilica achieves its most complete statement in the church of S. Apollinare Nuovo (begun c. 490) in Ravenna after alterations made during the Byzantine occupation in the mid-sixth century. Along the unbroken expanse of wall above the arcades on each side of the nave are mosaics of stately processions, virgin martyrs on the left and male martyrs on the right. The virgins proceed from a representation of Classis, the port city of Ravenna, toward the apse (fig. 14). They are dressed in Byzantine imperial court raiment, with gold brocaded robes studded with pearls. Between them are palm trees, symbols of martyrdom, and each virgin holds a crown, also a symbol of martyrdom. Their flat, patterned forms are repetitive, creating a steady rhythm along the wall. They are led by the three Magi who kneel before the enthroned Virgin and Child at the end of the nave next to the apse (fig. 15). The Virgin, clothed in a purple robe, and flanked by four angelic attendants, is an imperial princess receiving gifts not only from the Magi but also from the entire train of virgin martyrs. The saints have given their lives for Christ in the same way that the Magi have presented their precious gifts.

On the right wall, proceeding from a representation of the imperial palace at Ravenna, the line of male martyrs dressed in white robes is led by Saint Martin of Tours (fig. 16). They approach Christ enthroned between four angels. He, too, is dressed in purple and is seated on a bejeweled throne and receives the gifts of the saints' martyrdoms. These pictorial processions, even more clearly than the narrative scenes in S. Maria Maggiore, reiterate the procession of the celebrants down the nave of the church to participate in the sacrifice of the Mass. The rhythmic progression of the forms repeats the measured cadence of the colonnade below. Architecture, decoration, and liturgical practice are fused in a statement of the processional quality of the Early Christian basilica as it came to be used in Byzantine-dominated sixth-century Ravenna.

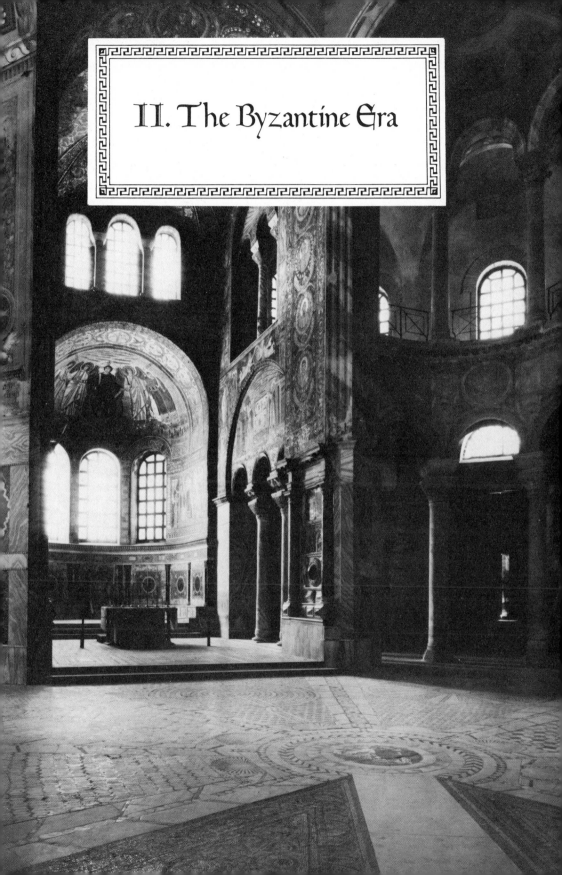

II. The Byzantine Era

4. Byzantium

n addition to the Edict of Milan and the imperial patronage of the Christian church Constantine was also responsible for an act that ultimately led to the division of the empire and church into two factions. In 330 he founded the city of Constantinople (now Istanbul) on the Bosporus in order to locate the capital of the empire closer to the eastern borders, which were constantly threatened by invading tribes. The empire was divided between East and West upon Constantine's death in 337, a division that became formalized after the unified reign of Theodosius I (emperor of the East 370–395, and of the West 392–395), when he bequeathed the Eastern empire to Arcadius (d. 408), and the Western to Honorius (d. 423). This political division eventually widened into irreconcilable religious and political differences. The Greek Orthodox Christian Church developed, closely affiliated with a powerful Eastern empire that, from the fifth century, we can identify as the Byzantine Empire. Concurrently, the Latin Roman Church in the West remained only loosely affiliated with a failing political regime that succumbed to numerous barbarian invasions in the sixth and seventh centuries.

After a brief cultural revival under Honorius and his half-sister Galla Placidia at Ravenna in the first quarter of the fifth century, the capital of the West became a Byzantine outpost, first under the Ostrogoth, Theodoric (who founded S. Apollinare Nuovo in 490), and then under the Byzantine Archbishop Maximianus. With the reign of Justinian I (527–565) the Byzantine Empire was firmly established and Byzantium became the major administrative and military power in the Mediterranean basin. The West, subjected to continuing barbarian incursions, could no longer maintain the semblance of a political entity.

The Emperor Justinian, after a brief period of populist revolts that were brutally suppressed, established a strong, authoritarian rule. Under his regime splendid new buildings were erected in Constantinople (notably Hagia Sophia) and throughout the Byzantine realm. The elaborate programs of mosaics at Ravenna mark not only the culmination of the Early Christian tradition in fusing architecture and decoration but also the first fully developed monumental expression of Byzantine court art. The Ravenna mosaics herald the development of new artistic concerns for abstraction in the representation of imperial and holy personages.

Most significant was the development of the icon as a votive image. A violent iconoclastic controversy in reaction to their use disrupted the empire between 726 and 843. A strong inbred monastic tradition supported the use of these images of divine personages in the churches; the imperial administration of Leo III, opposing idolatry, sought to forbid it. Over a century of bitter conflict was to pass before image worship was finally and permanently restored.

A return to stability was accomplished under the reign of Basil I (867–886), the founder of the Macedonian Dynasty. Under him and his successors, Byzantine troops were able to hold the frontiers against the incursions of the Bulgars and the Moslems. In this time of greater stability Byzantine art and culture flourished. Because of the influence of court ceremony and the strength of the monastic tradition, which adhered to conservative images, art took on a formal and abstract style. Occasionally, as during the so-called Macedonian Renaissance of the tenth century, striking approximations of the effects of classical art appeared. But, for the most part, under the patronage of the imperial court or the patriarchs, a surprising unity of style persisted almost unbroken until the intrusion of the West with the sacking of Constantinople in 1204, and the establishment of the momentary Latin Empire of the East (1204–1261).

Throughout this period, the Byzantine and the Roman churches grew further and further apart. In matters of dogma the schism between the Eastern and Western churches became evident at the Council of Nicaea (325): between the Arians in the East who believed that Christ was of a different substance than God, and the Athanasians in the West who believed that he was of the same substance. Although Arianism was repudiated by the East by the fifth century, the primacy of Rome and of the pope became another bitter source of contention, the iconoclastic controversy worsened relations, and the Fourth Council of Constantinople (869–870) formalized the split that was to continue for centuries.

Fig. 17. Portrait of a man. Egypt. 1st century. Tempera on linen, 17" x 7½". (Ny Carlsberg Glyptotek, Copenhagen)

Fig. 18. Portrait of a lady. Egypt. 4th century. Tempera on wood, 12¾" x 7½". Fogg Art Museum, Harvard University, Cambridge, Massachusetts. (Gift, Mrs. John D. Rockefeller. Jr.)

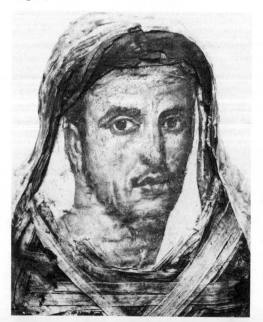

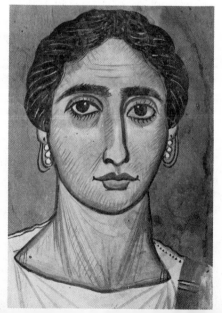

5. THE BYZANTINE ICON

An icon is any divine image, whether executed on a large scale in fresco or mosaic on the wall of a church or in some other medium as a small, portable votive image. Some were made as miniature mosaics, others as small beaten-metal or enamel medallions.

The earliest surviving painted Byzantine icons date from the sixth and seventh centuries; how many earlier ones were destroyed by the iconoclasts we shall never know. Usually, these are paintings on panels of wood representing divine personages or incidents from the Bible. Their continued use led to the development of panel painting, first in Italy and then throughout Western Europe in the later Middle Ages.

The earliest icons were painted in encaustic, a wax medium to which pigments were added, and used while still warm. The wooden panels to which this substance was applied were carefully smoothed and sometimes filled in with a plasterlike substance called *gesso*. Later, pigments were mixed with egg yolk (*tempera*), which dried quickly to give brilliant but opaque colors. If gold leaf was applied to the panel, it was rubbed over a layer of reddish clay, or *bole*. Sometimes the gold surface was punched or tooled to provide subtle light-catching patterns.

The tradition of representing revered personages can be traced back to the use of funerary portraits in Egyptian tombs, where a likeness of the deceased was painted on the mummy cover and on the sarcophagus. A similar tradition was carried on by a sect of Christians in Egypt, the Copts, who placed encaustic portraits of the deceased in their tombs. Known as Fayoum portraits from the locale in the Nile valley where many of them have been found, these paintings were commemorative and were meant to invoke the presence of the deceased. The vital, realistic portrait of a man of the first century (fig. 17), embedded in mummy wrappings, is obviously linked with the Egyptian funerary tradition, but is painted with a sensitivity to actual features and momentary expression that stems from the Roman tradition of portraiture. The later portrait of a lady (fig. 18) dating from the fourth century shows a greater sense of abstraction, a more planar treatment of the face and larger, staring eyes, all stylizations that may have been meant to invoke not the physical but the spiritual presence of the person. In this tradition of funerary portraits we have the genesis of the idea that becomes a basis for the Byzantine icon.

Another tradition also lent authority to the use of icons. It was reputed that Saint Luke had painted a portrait of the Virgin with the Christ Child seated upon her knee. It is doubtful that this painting has survived, but reflections of its basic theme were painted for centuries, and the legend sanctioned the continued use of such divine images. A sixth-century icon, showing the Virgin and Child enthroned

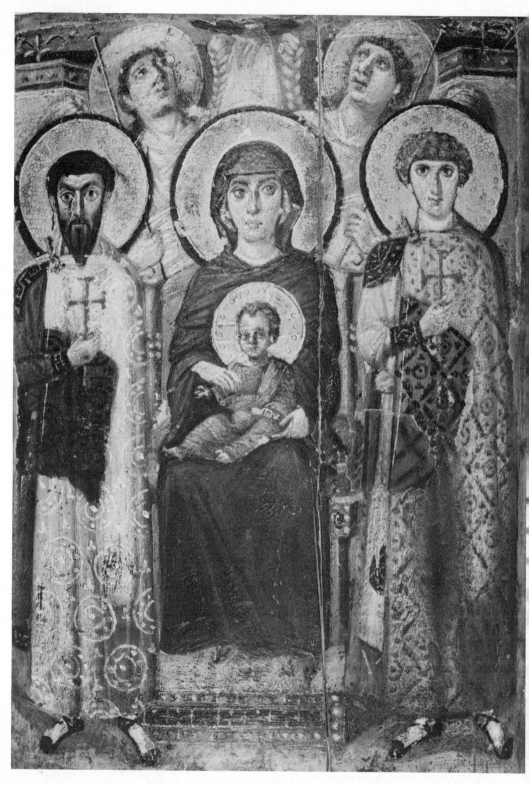

Fig. 19. Icon of Virgin and Child enthroned between angels and saints. Monastery of Saint Catherine, Mount Sinai. 6th century. Encaustic on wood, 27⅝" x 17¾". (Published by permission of the Michigan-Princeton-Alexandria Expedition to Mount Sinai)

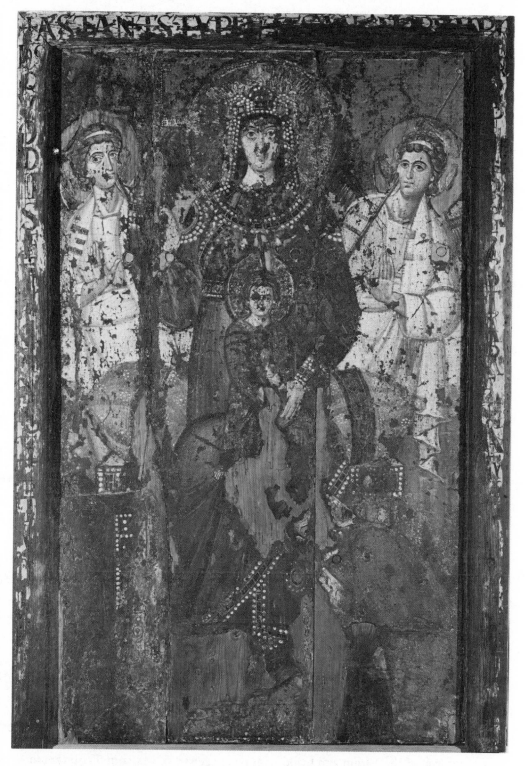

Fig. 20. Icon of Virgin and Child with two angels. S. Maria in Trastevere, Rome. 8th century. Encaustic on canvas and wood, 60″ x 41¼″. (Gabinetto Fotografico Nazionale, Rome)

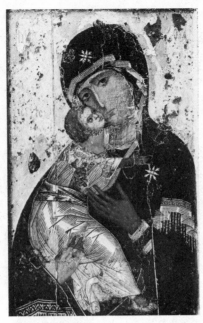

Fig. 21. Icon of Virgin of Vladimir.
Constantinople? c. 1125. Tempera on wood,
H. c. 31". Tretyakov Gallery, Moscow.

between angels and saints at Mount Sinai (fig. 19), represents this tradition. Probably intended to be a close copy of the archetype, this panel embodied the spiritual presence of the Virgin and Child. By contemplating the icon, the worshiper could enter into a mystical union with them. By the eighth century in the Greek East, a growing cult of saints led to a multiplication of images of revered personages, of sainted martyrs, bishops, ascetics, founders of monasteries, and performers of cures and miracles. So widespread was the production of icons and the worship of images that a century of iconoclasm erupted in 726, during which their use was brutally suppressed.

In the Mount Sinai icon the Virgin, wearing a purple robe, is the Mother of God enthroned in majesty between angelic attendants and Saints Theodore and George. The form of this representation has its roots in the secular, imperial tradition of official portraits of the emperors and has been adapted to Christian usage. The hands of the Virgin lead the eye to the figure of the Christ Child seated in her lap: this is a *Hodegetria* ("Indicator of the Way") icon in which the Virgin designates that Christ is the way to salvation. With the exception of the angels who look upward at the ray of divine light emanating from the hand of God above, the figures are rigidly frontal. The Virgin's halo is larger than the others, giving her added prominence. Although the forms are still modeled in a manner reminiscent of Roman painting, the large staring eyes, rigid poses, and uninterrupted patterns of the drapery reiterate the flat abstraction of the dematerialized virgins in procession in S. Apollinare Nuovo.

An icon of the Virgin and Child with two angels at S. Maria in Trastevere in Rome (fig. 20) of the eighth century reveals how closely this format was adhered

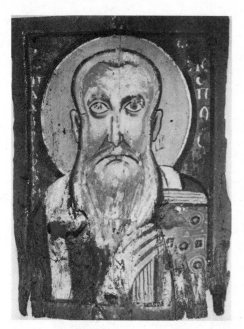 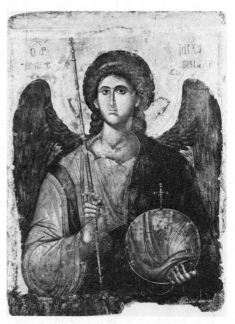

Fig. 22. Icon of Bishop Abraham. Bawit, Egypt. 6th–7th century. Tempera on wood, 14½" x 10½". Frühchristliche-byzantinische Sammlung, Staatliche Museen, Berlin.

Fig. 23. Icon of Saint Michael. Constantinople. Second half 14th century. Tempera on wood, 43⅝₆" x 32". Byzantine Museum, Athens.

to in the following centuries. She is seated on a bejeweled throne on a bolsterlike cushion, and similar angels behind her serve as attendants. The imperial connotation is explicit, for she wears the same court diadem as Theodora in the mosaics of Ravenna. She occupies the elevated status of theotokos. Her hand is lifted in benediction, and at the same time, she serves the Hodegetria function.

In contrast with these severe, hieratic representations, a new strain of emotionalism began to make itself felt in the twelfth century. In the Virgin of Vladimir icon (fig. 21), believed to have been painted around 1125 in Constantinople, a half-length representation of the Virgin is shown bending over the Christ Child and giving him an embrace. Known as the *Glykophilousa* or *Eleousa* type, or affectionate madonna, this icon emphasizes the maternal, tender relationship between mother and child rather than the role of the Virgin as Queen of Heaven and intercessor for us with Christ.

In provincial areas the impetus toward abstraction in order to heighten the spiritual impact of the icons became exaggerated to the point of caricature. An icon of Bishop Abraham (fig. 22) from the Coptic community of Bawit presents a flat, stylized diagram of a human face, an hourglass shape that accentuates the essential features. A more fully modeled, but equally abstracted formula, repeated with little variation for centuries, is manifested by an icon of Saint Michael (fig. 23) in Athens, dating from the second half of the fourteenth century. Painted with dark brown tonalities and a stylized cap of hair around the spheroid face, the figure emanates a spiritual calmness that transcends its material form. Shimmering light-catching gold striations in the wings and draperies contribute to its ethereal quality.

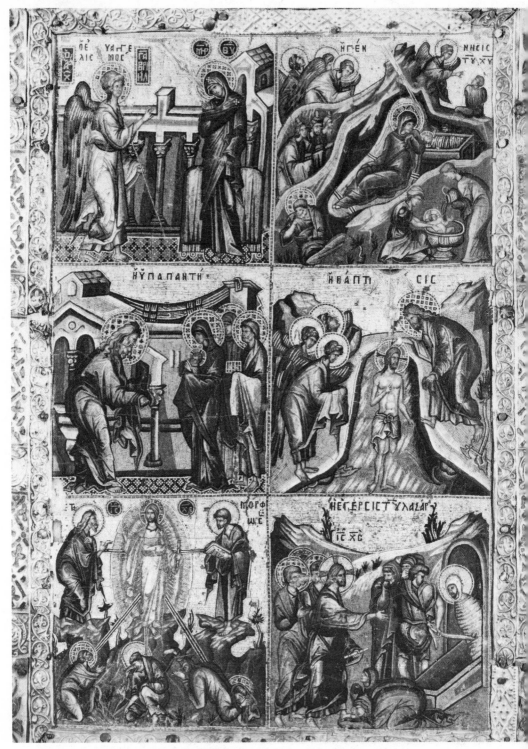

Fig. 24. Icon of the twelve liturgical feasts. Early 14th century. Mosaic, 10⅝″ x 7½″. Museo dell'Opera del Duomo, Florence. (Alinari)

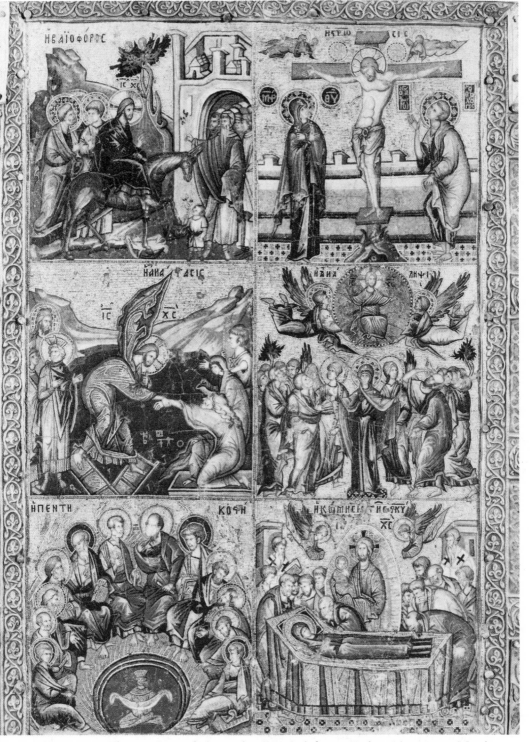

Fig. 25. Icon of the twelve liturgical feasts. Early 14th century. Mosaic, 10⅝" x 7½". Museo dell'Opera del Duomo, Florence. (Alinari)

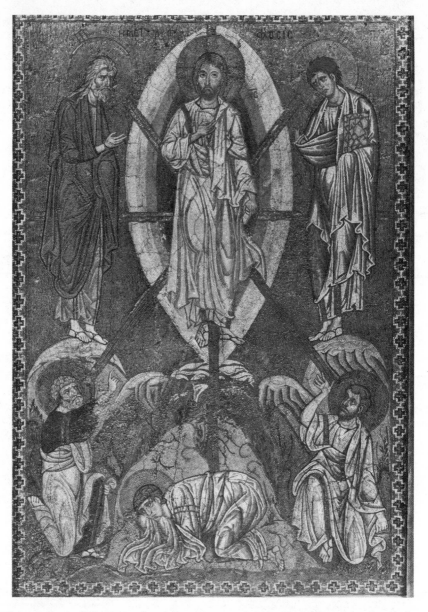

Fig. 26. Icon of the Transfiguration. Constantinople. End of 12th or beginning of 13th century. Mosaic, 20½″ x 14¼″. Musée du Louvre, Paris. (Giraudon)

In addition to representing holy personages, icons also depicted scenes from the life of Christ and the life of the Virgin. Normally these scenes comprised, as shown in two miniature mosaic panels in Florence (figs. 24, 25), the twelve principal liturgical feasts of the year: Annunciation, Nativity, Presentation at the Temple, Baptism of Christ, Transfiguration, Raising of Lazarus, Entry into Jerusalem, Crucifixion, Descent into Hell, Ascension, Pentecost, and Death, or Dormition, of the Virgin.

One of the most frequently represented incidents in Byzantine narrative icons was the scene of the Transfiguration (fig. 26). This is an event recounted in the Gospels of Saint Matthew (17:1–6) and Saint Mark (9:1–8):

And after six days Jesus taketh unto him Peter and James and John his brother, and bringeth them up into a high mountain apart: And he was transfigured before them. And his face did shine as the sun, and his garments became white as snow. And behold, there appeared to them Moses and Elias talking with him. . . . And as he was yet speaking, behold a bright cloud overshadowed them, And lo, a voice out of the cloud, saying: "This is my beloved Son, in whom I am well pleased: hear ye him." And the disciples hearing, fell upon their face, and were very much afraid.

As Christ's first manifestation of his divinity (*theophany*) before his disciples, it becomes an often repeated didactic image in which the shimmering white figure of Christ is placed at the center of radiating rays of light, the Old Testament prophets flanking him and the apostles prostrate in fear at his feet.

In the later Byzantine period, icons of saints and of the twelve liturgical feasts were placed upon a screen (*iconostasis*), separating the nave of the church from the sanctuary. These scenes play a key role in the celebration of the Mass and perform an important function in relation to the building as a whole. The celebration of the Mass in the Byzantine Church was a three-part enactment of the life of Christ. The first part, the *prothesis* or preparation of the gifts, enacts the childhood of Christ and is reflected by the scenes from the Annunciation through the Presentation at the Temple. The second part, the *synaxis* or the assembly of the gifts, covers the ministry and miracles of Christ, beginning with the Baptism and ending with the Raising of Lazarus. The final part, the *anaphora* or offering of the gifts, culminated with Holy Communion and relates to the Passion and Resurrection of Christ, beginning with the Entry into Jerusalem.

In the Greek Orthodox ritual, the priest normally enacts the Mass in the sanctuary situated behind the iconostasis, separating it from the nave and the congregation. A simple variant of an iconostasis can be seen at Hosios Lukas in Greece (pl. 5), where icons of the Virgin and of Christ shut off the sanctuary from the nave. The central door of the iconostasis, sometimes called the "royal door," is open only for seven days after Easter; during the remainder of the year it is closed, and the monks are completely segregated from the congregation. As they perform the liturgical drama, the various chants and prayers provide cues for the private devotions of the congregation who understand the unfolding drama, but rarely see it. The narrative scenes on the iconostasis are thus visual reminders of the liturgical drama that unfolds during each Orthodox service, as well as during the liturgical year.

6. THE CENTRALIZED BUILDING:
S. VITALE AND COURT CEREMONY

Although S. Vitale in Ravenna (527–548) represents another major tradition of building in the Early Christian period, that of the centralized structure, it also manifests a culmination of this tradition and a starting point for developments in later Byzantine architecture. The circular form has a long history and was most frequently used for tombs or commemorative *mausolea* in Roman times. They were adapted by the Christians for the additional function of the baptistry. The symbolic cleansing and rebirth into a new Christian life embodied in Baptism was appropriately placed in buildings reminiscent of mausolea with their implications of death. resurrection, and salvation in the hereafter.

S. Vitale, however, is a special case, for it served as the principal church of the Archbishop Maximianus, the personal representative of the Byzantine Emperor Justinian, after the Byzantine occupation of Ravenna in 540. Structurally, it followed a traditional plan (figs. 27, 28), a double-shell building in which the exterior wall forms an octagon surrounding a higher central octagonal core surmounted by a dome. On all but one side a groin-vaulted aisle or ambulatory on the ground floor and gallery above surround this central core. Semicircular niches (*exedrae*) curve outward from the central space into the aisle and gallery areas, creating an undulating effect (fig. 29). Triple arcades penetrate these exedrae on the ambulatory and gallery levels, reducing the curving walls to billowing screens. A two-story arch encloses each exedra, emphasizing the height of the building and leading the eye upward to the dome above (reworked in the seventeenth century). On the eighth side a two-story, groin-vaulted rectangular sanctuary interrupts the ambulatory and gallery, leading to the semicircular apse with its half dome. This sanctuary imposes a longitudinal emphasis on what would have otherwise been an entirely centralized building.

The exterior of S. Vitale (fig. 28) is a simple, direct statement of its basic geometric volumes and structure, a revealing statement of its wraparound exterior ambulatory, vertical central core, and penetrating sanctuary with its accumulation of three chapels. The interior (fig. 29), however, presents a varied sequence of shifting curved screens of columns in the exedrae, contrasts between dark and lighted areas, and an undulating interior core that soars to the dome above. In its original condition, with its full complement of variegated marble veneer in the lower areas, vast areas of shimmering mosaics and richly carved, painted capitals, light and color would have worked together to create a diffuse and elusory architectural space.

This building must be seen in the context of the elaborate program of mosaics that occupy the walls and vaults of the sanctuary (pl. 2). They are the most complete set of mosaics surviving from the time of the Emperor Justinian and

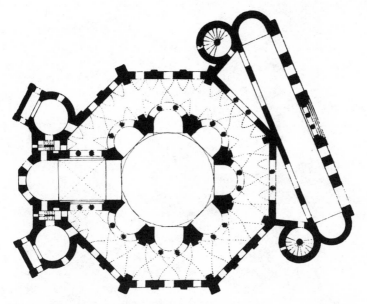

Fig. 27. Plan of S. Vitale. Ravenna. 527–548. (After Dehio and Bezold)

Fig. 28. Airview of S. Vitale. Ravenna. 527–548. (Fotocielo, Rome)

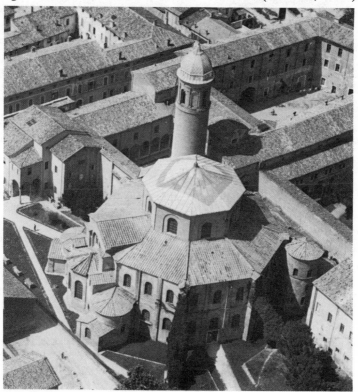

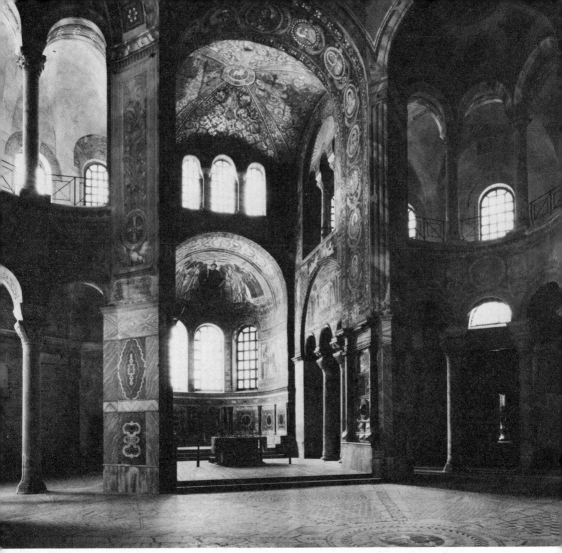

Fig. 29. Interior and sanctuary. S. Vitale, Ravenna. 548. (Hirmer Fotoarchiv)

reflect, as in the case of the almost contemporary mosaics of S. Apollinare Nuovo, a complete fusion of architecture and decoration for a higher purpose.

In the groin-vaulted canopy over the sanctuary (fig. 30) we find a medallion with the Lamb of God placed against a blue background studded with golden and white stars. Four angels hold this medallion aloft, and they are surrounded with vine scrolls inhabited by various animals and birds. This is the canopy of Heaven itself, an eternal paradise in which the sacrificial lamb, symbol of Christ, reigns triumphant. Below, on the flanking walls of the sanctuary, next to the openings into the gallery are the figures of the four Evangelists. They are receiving divine inspiration from their winged attributes above, the eagle for Saint John,

Fig. 30. South sanctuary wall and vault. S. Vitale, Ravenna. 548. (Hirmer Fotoarchiv)

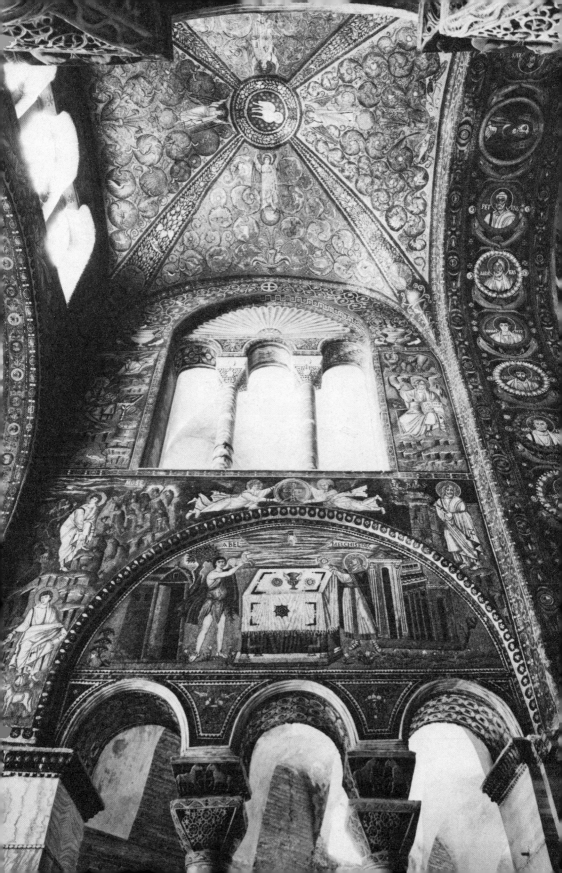

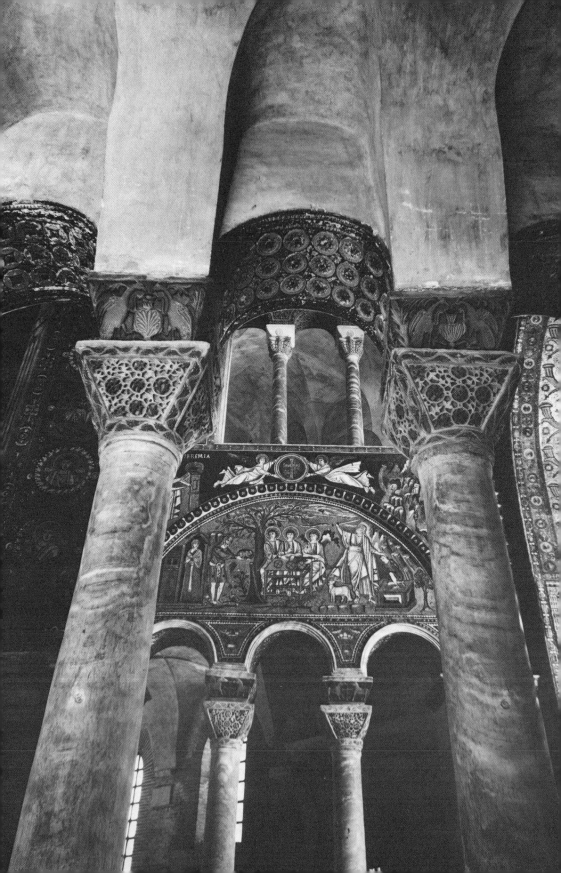

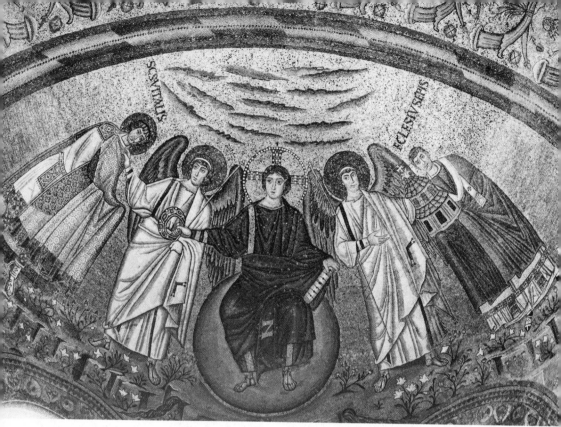

Fig. 32. Apse mosaic. S. Vitale, Ravenna. 548. (Hirmer Fotoarchiv)

the ox for Saint Luke, the lion for Saint Mark, and the man in the form of an angel for Saint Matthew. They represent the new order and the promulgation of the Christian doctrine under the church. Below them are representations of the old order under Judaic law: Moses removing his sandals before the burning bush, an incident just preceding his leading the Exodus from Egypt, and the prophet Isaiah. On the opposite wall (fig. 31) are the prophet Jeremiah, Moses receiving the Ten Commandments, and above, the Evangelists Matthew and Mark.

In the semicircular lunette between Moses and Isaiah, Abel and Melchizedek make sacrificial offerings of a lamb, and the bread and wine (fig. 30). In the opposite lunette (fig. 31), the three angels come to Abraham to tell him that his wife Sarah shall bear a son, Isaac. Abraham is about to carry out God's command that he sacrifice his son at the right of this scene, when the hand of God stays his sword, and Abraham is informed that he may sacrifice the ram caught in the thicket instead. This story is often used as a prefiguration for the Crucifixion, where God sacrifices his son so that mankind may be saved. In this context the sacrifices of Abel and Melchizedek develop this theme. Abel's sacrifice of a lamb on the opposite wall is a symbolic prefiguration of the sacrifice of Christ, who is often referred to as the Paschal Lamb, and who is thus represented in the vault above. Melchizedek's

Fig. 31. North sanctuary wall from ambulatory.
S. Vitale, Ravenna. 548. (Hirmer Fotoarchiv)

offering of bread and wine therefore also refers to this sacrifice as well as to the symbolic sacrifice of the Eucharist partaken of in the rite of Holy Communion.

In the apsidal mosaic (fig. 32), a youthful Christ, dressed in purple and seated on the globe of the cosmos, is flanked by two angels in a Christian variant of the traditional secular imperial portrait. On the right Bishop Ecclesius, the founder of the church, presents a model of the building to an angel: this is a donor portrait in which the church is given to Christ. On the left Saint Vitalis, the patron saint of the church, is presented to Christ, who in return hands the saint a crown of martyrdom. These two additional scenes of offerings or sacrifices amplify the theme stated in the lunettes.

In the transitional area where the sanctuary curves into the apse are two rectangular panels of mosaic containing imperial portraits (pls. 3, 4). On the left Justinian and his courtiers, including Archbishop Maximianus, the person under whom the mosaics at S. Vitale were completed, form a solemn procession. Justinian wears the imperial diadems of office and in his hands holds a large golden bowl. He proffers it toward the high altar, as though he were participating in the offerings depicted in the apse. On the right wall of the sanctuary we find a similar procession with the Empress Theodora and her ladies-in-waiting. She too is clothed in the imperial raiment and she offers a large chalice toward the altar. Thus, the two imperial figures also seem to be making donations of precious vessels to the church. This idea is reinforced by the representation on the hem of Theodora's robe of the Magi bearing gifts.

These mutually reinforcing themes of offerings and sacrifices work together to establish an even deeper meaning. Although the vessels held by the imperial figures appear to be empty, the chalice and the bowl refer to the vessels used to celebrate Holy Communion, the bowl to hold the wafers of the Eucharist, the chalice to hold the wine. The Mass is considered to be a sacrificial service culminating in the supreme offering, or sacrament, of Holy Communion. Throughout the program of mosaics in the canopy, sanctuary, and apse we have prefigurations and symbolic parallels to this climax of the Mass. The representative of the Byzantine Emperor, Maximianus, and the imperial court itself, present in abstracted, flattened, frontal iconic portraits, eternally participate, not only in the act of offering, which is mirrored in the other mosaics, but also in the celebration of the Mass. S. Vitale, an immaterial, richly decorated architectural space, therefore, embodies the most complete reflection of the mystical quality and splendor of early Byzantine architecture, combined with a pictorial fusion of Byzantine court ceremony and Christian liturgy.

7. THE BYZANTINE CHURCH AND ITS DECORATION

Byzantine churches exist in a wide variety of forms. Many of them consist of a Greek cross of equal sides inscribed within a square or rectangular plan, preceded by an entry porch (*narthex*) and terminating in one or three apses at the opposite end. Frequently a dome is placed over the crossing. Sometimes, as in the case of the small church of La Cattolica at Stilo (fig. 33) in southern Italy, which was built during the eleventh and twelfth centuries, this dome and four others over the corners are placed on tall, cylindrical drums articulated with decorative brickwork. Sometimes the four additional domes are placed along the main axis of the building, as in the imposing church of S. Marco in Venice (figs. 34, 35). Begun around 1063, S. Marco is believed to have been copied after the now-destroyed sixth-century Church of the Holy Apostles in Constantinople.

Fig. 33. La Cattolica. Stilo, Italy. 11th–12th century. (R. G. Calkins)

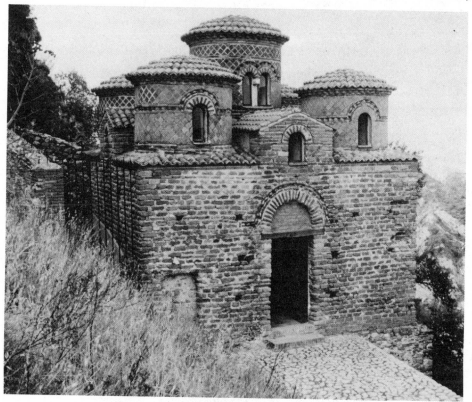

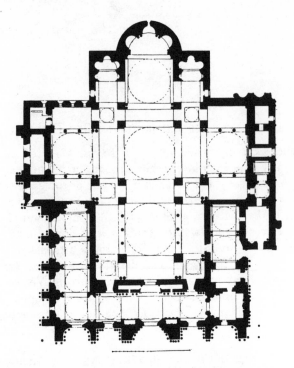

Fig. 34. Plan of S. Marco. Venice. After 1063. (After Dehio and Bezold)

Fig. 35. Airview of S. Marco. Venice. After 1063. (Fotocielo, Rome)

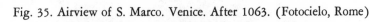

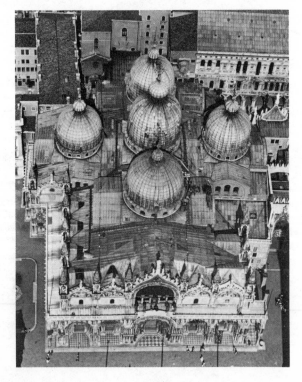

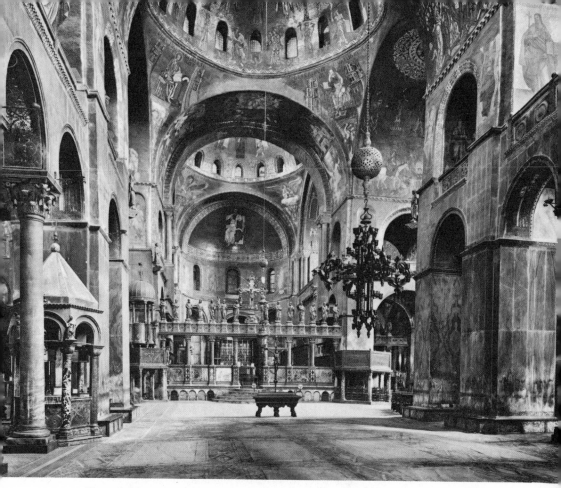

Fig. 36. Nave toward apse. S. Marco, Venice. After 1063. (Anderson-Alinari)

Although the exterior of S. Marco has been greatly transformed by restorations in the Gothic and Baroque periods, the five-domed structure accurately reflects the interior space of such a Byzantine building. The plan reveals a dome over the crossing and domes over each arm of the cross, interspersed by short barrel vaults. Massive piers, pierced by openings for the aisles support the ensemble (fig. 36). Each dome is set upon four pendentives, curved triangular areas that make the transition from the square bay to the circular rim of the dome. The main body of the building is preceded by a transverse narthex with a series of domes and barrel vaults. The narthex and the nave of S. Marco, with their sequence of domes, barrel vaults, and apsidal vault encrusted with mosaics and marble veneer, provide a glittering, resplendent interior worthy of the tradition previously stated at S. Vitale in Ravenna. But S. Marco is a Western copy of a Byzantine church, and for a complete demonstration of the relationship of Byzantine architecture to its decoration, we must turn to another building in the Greek East.

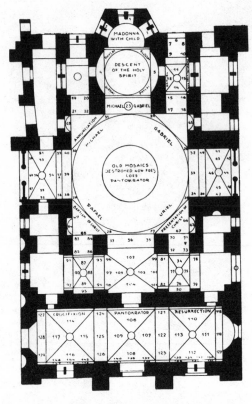

Fig. 37. Plan of Katholikon. Hosios Lukas, Greece.
1011 or 1022. (After Diez-Demus: courtesy of
the American School of Classical Studies at Athens)

Fig. 38. South flank of Katholikon. Hosios Lukas, Greece. 1011 or 1022. (R.G.Calkins)

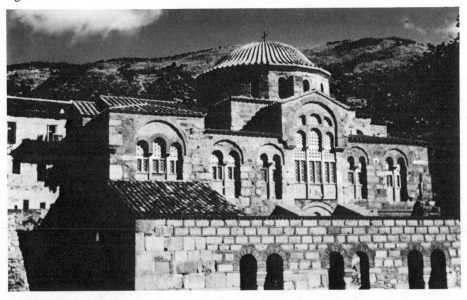

The Katholikon of Hosios Lukas in Phocis, near Delphi, Greece, built in either 1011 or 1022, consists of the standard plan of a Greek cross set within a square, prolonged by transverse narthex and three-faceted apse (figs. 37, 38). The single dome, set on a short drum, rests upon four squinches, diagonal arches across the corners of the crossing bay. Although the plan is self-contained within the basic rectangle, in elevation the short arms of the transepts manifest themselves as gabled volumes abutting the drum of the dome. Over the sanctuary is a smaller dome and in the apse a half dome.

Although some of the decoration of Hosios Lukas has been damaged, lost, or replaced, this building originally contained mosaic decorations on every wall surface, vault, and dome (pls. 5, 6). Mosaics in the preparatory area or narthex depict scenes of Christ's Death and Resurrection, making explicit Christ's humility in washing the feet of the apostles, his death on the cross, the implied salvation of mankind through the rescuing of Adam and Eve from Hell, and the proof of his triumph over death in the doubting of Thomas. In the *naos,* or main hall of the church, the dome originally contained a representation of Christ Pantocrator, Omnipotent Ruler, and below were the four archangels, now replaced by a fresco. In the squinches below were four scenes from the Infancy of Christ; only three, the "Nativity," "Presentation," and "Baptism," remain. In the small dome above the sanctuary (pl. 6) we see the "Pentecost," or "Descent of the Holy Spirit," the miraculous event in which the apostles were given the gift of many tongues and were instructed to spread the message of Christianity to the four corners of the world. Here, rays of light with dancing flames descend from a medallion containing the enthroned dove of the Holy Ghost. Then, in the half dome of the apse, Mary, the Mother of God and Protectress of the Church, sits enthroned in a Hodegetria pose with the Christ Child on her lap making a gesture of benediction.

Throughout the rest of the building are representations of a multitude of saints, a virtual pantheon of over 140 of them who were revered in the course of the Byzantine liturgical year. Their arrangement follows a preordained scheme, lesser saints and martyrs in the lower areas of the church reflecting the terrestrial world, and prophets, apostles, archangels, the Virgin, and Christ himself in ascending order in the upper vaults and domes, reflecting the celestial Kingdom of Heaven. Thus, this Byzantine church, as Otto Demus has pointed out, is a veritable iconostasis in space. The presence of all of the saints is invoked by their portraits, and nine of the principal liturgical feasts serve as visual reminders of the progress of the service and cycle of the liturgical year. This elaborate program of mosaics at Hosios Lukas represents a more or less standard format for decoration in the major churches of the Byzantine world.

Reflections of this scheme, adapted to the different architectural properties of some Western churches, appear in Italy. At the basilican church of S. Maria Assunta at Torcello, in the lagoon near Venice, the apse contains an elongated, standing Virgin and Child above the twelve apostles (fig. 39). She is an ethereal vision of the Mother of God and Queen of Heaven, visible down the entire length of the church that is dedicated to her. She is isolated against a surface of glittering gold tesserae set at slightly varying angles into the half dome to catch the light, so

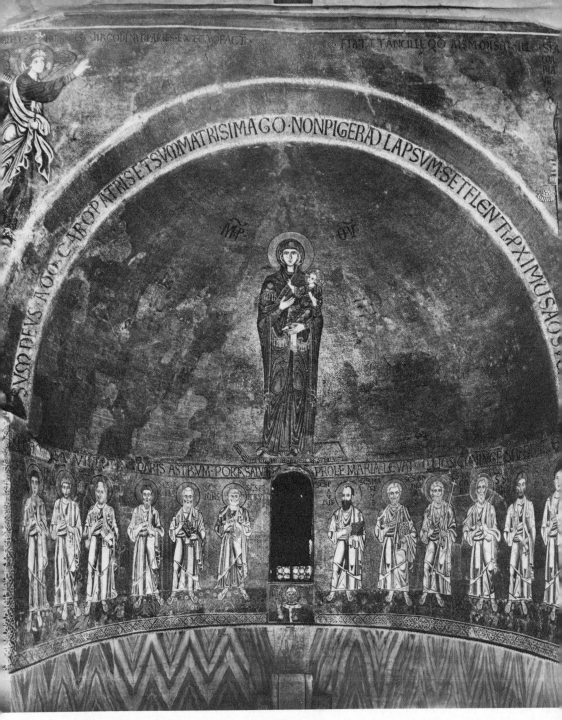

Fig. 39. Apsidal mosaic. S. Maria Assunta, Torcello, Italy.
12th century. (Anderson-Alinari)

Fig. 40. Apsidal mosaic. Cathedral, Cefalù, Sicily.
Mid-12th century. (Anderson-Alinari)

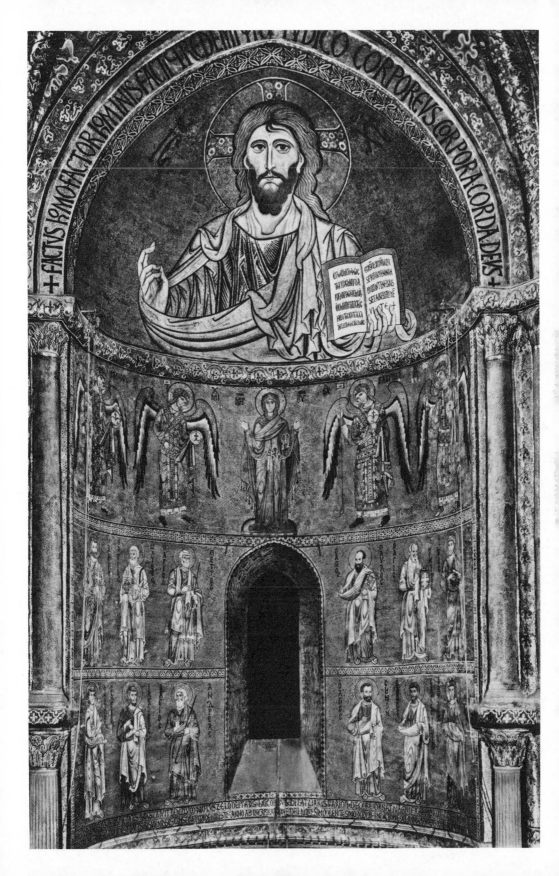

that she ascends in a space that is dematerialized by light. Her divinity is further accentuated by her larger size (hieratic scaling) than that of the apostles below. The apostles are arranged in static, frontal poses, yet because of their position in the curved apse, the outermost figures face each other and form a semicircle around the high altar. This apsidal mosaic thus becomes an icon in space, bringing the high altar into the midst of its divine presences.

The theme of the Christ as Pantocrator was one of the most dominant in the Byzantine church. At Hosios Lukas, Christ as Omnipotent Ruler not only occupied the highest point in the main crossing dome, but also a lunette over the central door leading into the naos from the narthex and another lunette below the apsidal mosaic of the Virgin Theotokos. He gestures to a book with an inscription in Greek: "I am the light of the world; he that followeth me shall not walk in darkness but shall have the light of life" (John 8:12). As the narthex is dimly lit, this message takes on added significance, for one enters from the shadowy narthex through the portal under this inscription to the main body of the church, which is well lit and shimmering with golden mosaics.

One of the most effective fusions of the use of an apsidal mosaic as an icon in space with the theme of the Pantocrator occurs in the cathedral at Cefalù in Sicily (fig. 40). Built by the Norman conquerors of that island in the mid-twelfth century, it is a basilican structure with an appended, vaulted and half-domed sanctuary. The apsidal mosaics depict an ascending hierarchy: in the lowest registers are the twelve apostles, above them the Virgin in an *orans* position (hands upraised in prayer), flanked by the four archangels, and in the half dome the figure of Christ as Pantocrator. These scenes have been combined here because no crossing dome was provided, and the apse therefore became the place of principal focus. Christ holds a book with inscriptions in Greek and Latin, a reflection of the mixed Byzantine and Western cultures in Sicily; the text is the same as at Hosios Lukas, "I am the light . . ." The right hand is raised in a gesture of benediction. The bust of Christ is positioned in the half dome so that the head curves over and the arms follow the curve around the spectator as though embracing him and protecting him. Although the facial features are stylized in rhythmic, curving lines, the eyes have a sad and compassionate cast. This figure of Christ is receptive, welcoming the believer to seek the true light. The shimmering golden tesserae around the figures immerse them in light. Christ is dematerialized by the accentuated bands of golden striations across his robe. Thus, the material of the mosaic, its placement on the curved surface of the apse and half dome, the statement in the inscription, the rendering of Christ's face, and his gestures all work together to create a concert of architectural space and decoration in a transcending, spiritualizing experience.

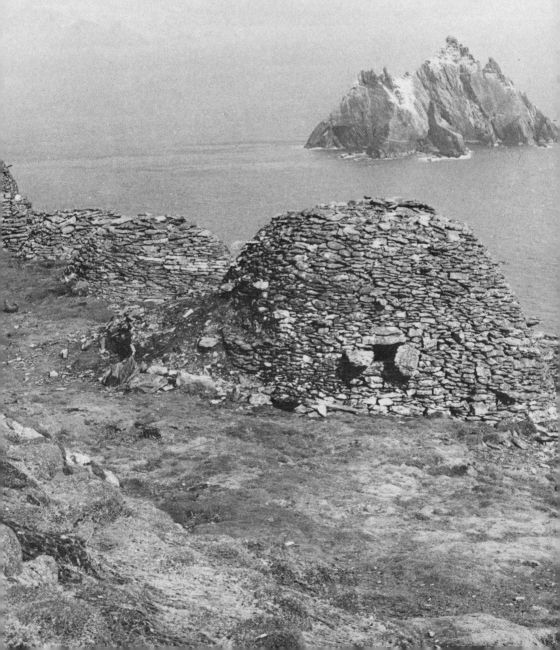

III. The Period of the Barbarian Invasions

8. THE MIGRATIONS

hroughout the Early Christian period the borders of the Roman Empire had been threatened by the barbarian tribes living to the north and east of the civilized world. In the fifth century particularly serious invasions of the Roman homeland were made by the Visigoths, the Ostrogoths, and finally by the Huns themselves, whose pressure on the peoples of the Eastern empire had been felt since the mid-fourth century. These wandering tribes followed circuitous routes across Europe, jostling each other and other groups of indigenous peoples such as the Celts, Franks, and Burgundians. As the formal institutions of the Roman Empire disintegrated in the provinces, small kingdoms were set up, soon to be displaced by others. The Ostrogoths established themselves in northern Italy, and the Visigoths in southern France and Spain by the early fifth century. The Alans and Vandals migrated from the western shores of the Caspian Sea around 400, and after winding throughout Western Europe and the Iberian peninsula, occupied the north coast of Africa around Carthage by the middle of the century. At about the same time the Angles and Saxons, who may have already mingled in their native areas of southern Denmark and northern Germany, invaded England and displaced the remnants of the Romano-Briton civilization. The Franks moved westward from the Rhineland, occupying the lands of the Gallo-Romans in France, and under the Frankish King Childeric, the son of Merowech, established the Merovingian dynasty. And then, in the seventh and eighth centuries, Islam took hold in the Mediterranean area, and the Moslems occupied Spain and invaded France. Only with their defeat by Charles Martel at Tours in 732, the subsequent strengthening of the Frankish kingdom, and the establishment of the Carolingian Empire in 800 was a semblance of political stability restored to Western Europe and the period of the migrations ended. Yet even at this moment, a new scourge appeared from the North. Vikings from Norway, Sweden, and Denmark invaded England and harassed the European coastline well into the eleventh century.

During this period of uncertainty and tumult remarkably sophisticated forms of art prevailed, but in a different medium and on a smaller scale than in the Late Roman period. It is true that a residual impact of Roman architecture and art and an increasing presence of Christianity were strongly manifested in the Rhineland and Gaul, and that elsewhere, where Roman monuments were decaying, being torn down, and artifacts were being lost and forgotten, Roman motifs and themes were being copied and transformed by local craftsmen. But these poor

49

emulations of the Mediterranean, anthropocentric tradition were overshadowed by the indigenous tribal traditions of decorative metalwork, with subtle and intricate geometric and animal designs. These traditions existed among the Sarmatians and Scythians who thrived between the Black and Caspian seas from 700 to 300 B.C., and also among the Celts of Continental northern Europe, who had their roots in the Hallstatt culture of around 700 to 400 B.C. and who flourished during the La Tène period from around 500 B.C. until the end of the first century B.C. when they were assimilated by the Romans. The migrating tribes from the East brought with them similar forms of decorative metalwork. As Europe was in a state of nomadic flux, most of the objects that have survived were small, portable artifacts: weapons, armor, and objects of personal adornment. Many of these were found in grave sites and in hidden treasure hoards, which were subsequently forgotten.

At the same time that tribes of warring barbarians were invading one part of Europe after another, and partly because of the instability created by their incursions, religious monasteries were founded by the Christians and rules for their functioning were codified. The monastic community became one of the most significant medieval institutions and the one responsible for the preservation of culture and learning, as well as providing a center of social and economic stability in these troubled times.

Fig. 41. Reconstruction of a terra-cotta brooch mold. Helgö, Uppland. 5th–7th century. L. 5″. Statens Historiska Museum, Stockholm. (R. G. Calkins)

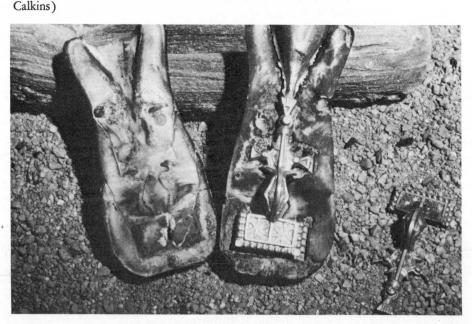

9. BARBARIAN METALWORK AND GRAVE GOODS

The techniques of barbarian metalwork were extremely varied. Brooches (*fibulae*) and buckles were frequently cast in bronze and then gilded or coated with a layer of gold or silver. From fragments of terra-cotta brooch molds found in the metalwork shops at Helgö in Uppland, Sweden, it has been possible to reconstruct the types of molds used during the migration period (fig. 41). The casting process was usually the lost-wax method, wherein a wax model was made of the object and a terra-cotta mold was then shaped around it, leaving openings for pouring in the molten metal and vents for the escaping gases. When the terra-cotta mold was fired to harden it, the wax model within melted and flowed out. After casting, the mold was opened, the unwanted cones of metal from the vents were broken off, and the rough edges were filed or chased. If the surface of the object was smooth, it might be incised with lines to create geometric patterns and stippled or punched to create areas or designs of dots. Then the object was gilded. Frequently the surfaces of brooches were modeled to create a series of interlocking patterns in relief and the rim was punctuated with knobs.

A prevalent decorative device was the use of chip carving. A gilt harness mount (fig. 42) from a Viking grave at Vendel in Uppland contains curving lines of V-shaped indentations with V-shaped ridges in between. These were carved in a wax plaque before casting by the method discussed above. These

Fig. 42. Harness mount. Vendel, Uppland. 7th century. Bronze gilt with enamel, L. 2⅞". Statens Historiska Museum, Riksantikvarieämbetet, Stockholm. (Antikvarisk-Topografiska Arkivet, Stockholm)

Fig. 43. Strickland Brooch. Anglo-Saxon. 9th century. Silver and niello, Diam. c. 4½". The British Museum, London.

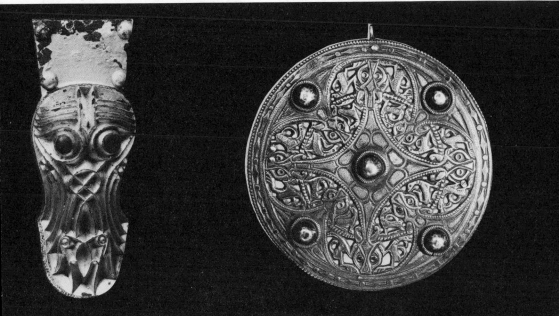

designs were either curvilinear or rectilinear, depending upon the shape of the object and the predilections of the craftsman. The ridges on the Vendel harness mount are symmetrically arranged to create the impression of an animal head with flaring nostrils, bulging eyes filled with glass paste, and ridged brows.

The circular Strickland Brooch (fig. 43) in The British Museum was molded and cast in bronze, incised and gilded with silver, and then the incisions were filled with a black sulfurous substance called *niello*. The contrast of the blackened design against the gold or silver heightens the effect of the pattern and accentuates the animals clambering about in the four-lobed foliate design.

More elaborate effects were achieved by setting semiprecious stones and colored enamel into mounts brazed onto the surface of the object. One of the most resplendent objects of this "polychromed style" is the Wittislingen Fibula (pl. 7) of the seventh century, signed by its makers, Wigerig and Uffla, on the back, and found in a royal grave in southern Germany in the nineteenth century. Because of the pronounced curve between the semicircular headplate and the tapering footplate, this is called a bow fibula. Actually a huge, decorative safety pin, it would have been worn at the shoulder, footplate up, to fasten the corners of a garment together. The headplate is "digitated" with ten protruding knobs. The terminal of the footplate contains the stylized implication of an animal head, and two carved silver beaks appear just below. Thus, zoomorphic ornament, which appears in more recognizable forms in other barbarian ornament, is here fully abstracted. The surface of the brooch contains composite decoration, a combination of gold filigree, niello, and enamelwork. In some of the compartments gold threads have been braided or beaded and arranged in continuous knotlike interlacing patterns. Contrasting with the freely moving lines of the filigree decoration, are the tight little compartments colored with garnet inlay. These compartments (*cloisons*) are made of golden wires placed on edge, into which, sometimes, powdered glass was fused: the resultant enamelwork is called *cloisonné* enamel. In the Wittislingen Fibula, bands and areas of the cloisonné garnets create rhythmic repetitions of step-shaped, chevron-shaped, and semicircular patterns of red and gold, framed with silver and niello bands.

Another form of glasswork, known as *millefiori,* originated in the antique period but was continued in some barbarian artifacts. Multicolored rods of glass, fused together by heat and then sliced, were set together to form patterns. Millefiori glass was used in the central medallion and surrounding frame of a circular escutcheon on one of the great hanging bowls found at Sutton Hoo in East Suffolk (fig. 44). The surrounding area is filled with running golden spirals and cloisonné enamel.

Many of the resplendent artifacts from the period of the barbarian migrations were found in graves. Burial practices varied widely. A common method of disposing of the deceased was cremation, after which the ashes were buried in urns along with a few personal objects. Less frequent was the practice of inhumation, in which the body was placed in a coffin and buried. For important chieftains and kings, elaborate artifacts, a full complement of weapons and armor, and food were placed with the coffin, and mounds (*tumuli*) were frequently created

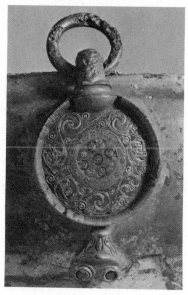

Fig. 44. Millefiori glass and enamel escutcheon, hanging bowl. Sutton Hoo treasure. First half 7th century. Diam. 2½". The British Museum, London.

over the graves. In northern countries royal persons might be buried in a ship beneath a *tumulus,* buried in an area marked out with stones in the shape of a ship, or set adrift in a ship equipped with grave goods, eventually to founder in the gales of the North Sea. The funeral of Scyld, described in the epic poem *Beowulf,* was of the latter sort:

> . . . and then they laid their dear lord,
> the giver of rings, deep within the ship
> by the mast in majesty; many treasures
> and adornments from far and wide were gathered there.
> I have never heard of a ship equipped
> more handsomely with weapons and war-gear,
> swords and corslets; on his breast
> lay countless treasures that were to travel far
> with him into the waves' domain. (ll. 34–42)

In *Beowulf* we also find the description of Beowulf's own burial in a tumulus after cremation:

> Then the Geats built a barrow on the headland—
> it was high and broad, visible from far
> to all seafarers; in ten days they built the beacon
> for that courageous man; and they constructed
> as noble an enclosure as wise men
> could devise, to enshrine the ashes.
> They buried rings and brooches in the barrow,
> all those adornments that brave men
> had brought out from the hoard after Beowulf died.
> They bequeathed the gleaming gold, treasure of men,
> to the earth, and there it still remains
> as useless to men as it was before. (ll. 3156–3168)

One of the most spectacular treasures was found in a combination ship-and-mound burial at Sutton Hoo just before the outbreak of World War II. Numerous objects of personal adornment, weapons, insignia, and utensils were discovered in a burial chamber located amidships. Among the objects were ten silver bowls, a silver plate with the imperial stamp of the Byzantine Emperor Anastasius I (491–518) and two silver spoons inscribed *Saul* and *Paulus*. These appear to have Christian significance and were undoubtedly considered by the time of their burial, sometime in the seventh century, to be part of the kingly treasure trove. A scepter-like object and a tall standard surmounted by a stag strongly suggest that this was indeed the grave of an Anglo-Saxon king. A purse contained thirty-seven gold Merovingian coins, three unstruck blanks, and two small gold ingots. There were therefore enough coins to serve as symbolic payment for the forty oarsmen that the Sutton Hoo ship could accommodate, and the two ingots would have served as payment for the steersman for the funereal nautical voyage. The dating of the coins appears to be around 625 to 630 at the latest.

This evidence, together with the fact that no body or certain evidence of cremation has yet been found at Sutton Hoo, led some scholars to suggest that this ship burial was a cenotaph or memorial to King Rædwald of East Anglia (d. 624/25). He was converted to Christianity at King Æthelbert's court, but retained strong pagan leanings. Thus, the mixture of pagan and Christian objects in the burial site could be explained. His body may have been buried in holy ground, but since he was still half-pagan at his death, his memorial was situated in an area where fourteen other tumuli were located, possibly an ancestral burial ground similar to grave sites in Scandinavia. Renewed excavations from 1967 through 1969 and sophisticated analysis of the objects revealed, however, that there may have been a body after all. Although the cenotaph theory is now discredited, the identity of the deceased remains conjectural.

Several buckles, strap ends, and a pair of hinged shoulder clasps (fig. 45) contain regular geometric step patterns of cloisonné garnets and mosaic glass or millefiori. In the pair of shoulder clasps the garnets have been applied over a background of crossed golden wires creating a gridlike texture beneath the garnets. Around the rectangular fields of step patterns are designs of elongated quadrupeds and snakelike creatures biting themselves. These animals, called *lacertines*, form a zoomorphic interlace. At the top and bottom of the clasps are a pair of interlocking razorback boars facing in opposite directions. Millefiori glass forms the upper portions of the forelegs. Even between the boars' hind legs we find snakes executed in gold filigree. The relatively accurately represented boars, although composed of decorative patterns, are made to interweave with each other in the same way that the lacertines form interlace patterns and the step-shaped cloisons interlock.

The combination of animal and geometric forms also appears in the enamel plaques on a purse lid (fig. 46) found at Sutton Hoo. Framed by a golden band set with cloisonné enamel and millefiori, it contains two hexagonal plaques of geometric cloisons. A double plaque in between contains two pairs of interlocking lacertines whose legs and snouts form an interlace pattern. Below are a pair of

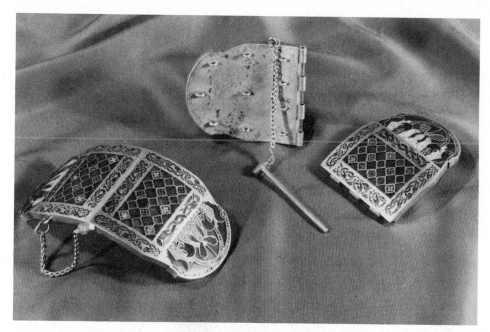

Fig. 45. Hinged shoulder clasps. Sutton Hoo treasure. First half 7th century. Cloisonné enamel and filigree, L. 5″. The British Museum, London.

Fig. 46. Purse lid with cloisonné-enamel plaques. Sutton Hoo treasure. First half 7th century. L. 7½″. The British Museum, London.

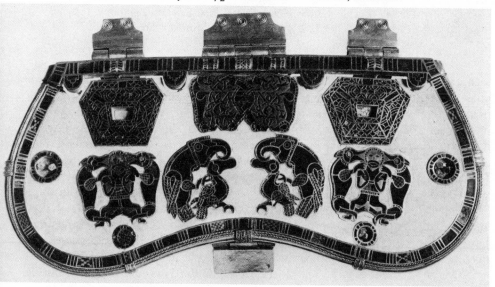

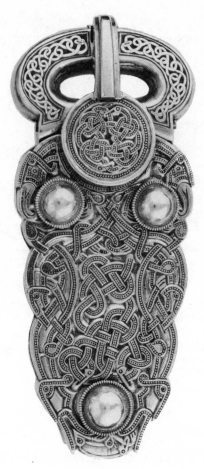

Fig. 47. Buckle. Sutton Hoo treasure. First half 7th century.
Gold and niello, L. 5¼". The British Museum, London.

identical plaques of eagles attacking ducks. Beneath the geometric plaques are two
other identical plaques showing a man between two rearing animals. The meaning
of these figures is not altogether clear; although they look like a heraldic variant
of the theme of Daniel in the Lion's Den, a motif that does appear in Continental
barbarian ornament, they may simply represent men attacked by wild beasts. This
theme would certainly be consistent with recurrent motifs of fighting animals
found in much of barbarian art. Mankind threatened by the wild forces of nature
would also have been an appropriate motif, as suggested by similar designs in some
Scandinavian artifacts. This meaning appears to be reinforced by the birds of prey
attacking the helpless ducklings on the same purse lid. Such an interpretation,
however, can only be conjectural, for we may never learn the exact context or
magical significance of many such motifs from the pagan, preliterate world.

One of the most magnificent objects in the Sutton Hoo find is a large buckle
(fig. 47) covered with a mass of writhing, interlacing snakes, interwoven in an
intricate but orderly manner. The snakelike forms and the beaked, birdlike heads

are reinforced by niello lines and dots. Serpents were evil, loathsome creatures even to the migrating tribes of the barbarian invasions. The fearsome quality of snakes is expressed in *Beowulf*, in the passage in which Beowulf and his troops approach the boiling waters of the pool where Grendel's mother lived:

> . . . The brave men all sat down;
> then they saw many serpents in the water,
> strange sea-dragons swimming in the lake,
> and also water-demons, lying on cliff-ledges,
> monsters and serpents of the same kind
> as often, in the morning, molest ships
> on the sail-road. They plunged to the lake bottom,
> bitter and resentful, rather than listen
> to the song of the horn. The leader of the Geats
> picked off one with his bow and arrow,
> ended its life; the metal tip
> stuck in its vitals; it swam more sluggishly
> after that, as the life-blood ebbed from its body;
> in no time this strange sea-dragon,
> bristled with barbed boar-spears, was subdued
> and drawn up onto the cliff; men examined
> that disgusting enemy. (ll. 1424–1440)

The meaning of these reptiles on the Sutton Hoo buckle is problematical. Perhaps the fact that they are arranged in symmetrical fashion forming the irregular but balanced shape of the buckle, and therefore *contained* by it in a recognizable order, provides a clue. If the serpents are to be construed as symbols of evil, of the dark forces of nature, they are nevertheless controlled and contained within the object. Moreover, the snakes are intertwined in knotlike configurations and plaitwork appears on the loop of the buckle. Knots and plaitwork, from the context of their frequent usage in Celtic ornament, were apparently believed to possess magical powers. Perhaps the buckle was therefore a symbol of prowess over these dark forces, and the wearer, like Beowulf who triumphed first over Grendel and then over Grendel's mother, became a person of heroic stature and power.

Perhaps a confirmation of these conjectural interpretations of the Sutton Hoo objects can be found in the back cover of the Lindau Gospels (pl. 17) of around 800. This gold metalwork plaque contains a field of writhing, biting snakes similar to those of the Sutton Hoo belt buckle. But a large cross, adorned with four representations of Christ in cloisonné enamel and containing foliate rather than zoomorphic ornament, has been superimposed on the writhing mass. As this cover was probably intended to be used on a copy of the gospels, we can surmise that this combination of motifs symbolizes the order of the Christian church imposed upon the chaos of nature and the evil of the world. Here, the techniques and motifs of barbarian metalwork are fused with Christian symbols to impart a new and higher meaning of this theme.

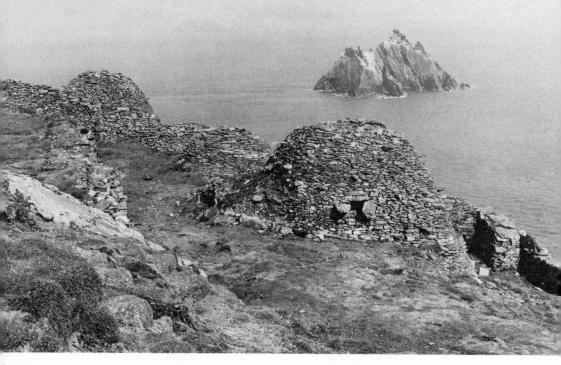

Fig. 48. Skellig Michael. County Kerry, Ireland. 9th century. (Commissioners of Public Works in Ireland, Dublin)

10. The Medieval Monastery

As Western Europe was being overrun by tribes of migrating barbarians, Christian monks gathered together and founded monastic communities throughout the countryside. These enclaves served, in part, to provide a locus of stability and security for the neighboring area. The monastic tradition has its origins in the Early Christian period when men of the church sought to remove themselves from the worldly temptations of daily life and seek a life of meditation and solitude in deserted areas. Saint Jerome and Saint Anthony were two such persons who, for a time, lived a hermitlike existence in order to meditate on their individual salvation. This form of eremitic monasticism, which was extremely austere and difficult, was especially prevalent in the eastern Mediterranean. To make life a little easier and to regularize worship, some of the hermit monks banded together in the fourth century to form communities (*cenobia*) headed by an abbot. They continued their ascetic life, but worshiped together and were loosely connected by a few rules (*regulae*). Eventually this cenobitic monasticism spread to Coptic Egypt, westward into southern Europe, was imported to Ireland by Saint Patrick in 440, and became the basis of Irish monasticism.

The monastic site of Skellig Michael (fig. 48) on an island off the western coast of Ireland exemplifies the inhospitable situation and harsh existence the early

Irish monks chose. Although rebuilt after the Viking raids of the early ninth century, the architecture is primitive. Crude, beehive-shaped cells constructed of flat, unworked fieldstones served as shelters for the monks and were clustered about a small oratory of similar construction. When not at their devotions, the monks eked out a meager existence from the rocky soil and the sea.

In the tradition of Saint Patrick, however, the Irish became zealous missionaries, and under personages such as Saint Columban (c. 521–597) founded numerous important monastic communities in northern England at Lindisfarne, and on the Continent at Luxeuil in France, Saint-Gall in Switzerland, and Bobbio in Italy.

A second form of monasticism, which was to gain ascendancy throughout Europe, was established by Saint Benedict of Nursia (c. 480–543). Around 529 he founded a monastery at Monte Cassino (fig. 49) in Italy, and formulated a *regula,* or Benedictine Rule, which specified how the community was to be organized and how it was to function. The monks were to take vows of poverty, chastity, obedience and *stabilitas loci,* that is, they were to promise not to leave the monastery. This last rule was especially important, for it guaranteed that they would stay within the community and share in the manual work that was necessary for the monastery to be self-sufficient. As Saint Benedict stipulated, "the monastery ought, if possible, to be so constructed as to contain within it all necessities . . . so that there be no occasion for monks to wander abroad, since this is in no wise expedient for their souls."

Fig. 49. Reconstruction drawing of Monte Cassino, Italy. As of 1075. (Kenneth J. Conant)

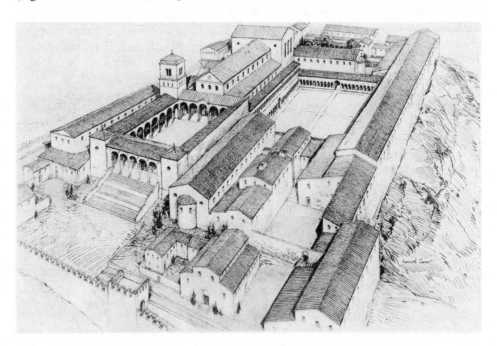

The architectural plans of medieval monasteries, from an early moment, reflected Saint Benedict's stipulation. In the early ninth century Abbot Gozbert of Saint-Gall began rebuilding his monastery from a plan (fig. 50) that had been drawn up around 820 by Abbot Heito of Reichenau. It was an ideal scheme that laid out the positions of the various buildings, and labeled their dimensions and their uses. Monte Cassino itself evolved along similar lines. The church at Saint-Gall was a long, three-aisled basilican structure with an apse at each end (fig. 51). Two tall cylindrical turrets flanked its entrance. In the immediate vicinity of the church were buildings for the housing and feeding of the monks, such as the dormitory next to the transept of the church, the refectory or eating hall, the kitchen, and the scriptorium where manuscripts were copied. These were grouped around a square courtyard or cloister, usually along the south flank of the church in order to be protected from the weather and to catch the sun, and served as a quiet oasis where the monks could meditate. A covered walk around the four sides looked out into the cloister through arcades and functioned as a sheltered walkway between essential buildings. According to the Saint-Gall plan, to the right of the church were various barns for livestock, workshops, a mill, a wine press, and storage areas. Beyond a barn with a threshing floor an orchard was planted in a cemetery. Behind the church were an infirmary and a "novitiate" where young boys were trained to be monks, and both of these buildings were linked to a two-part chapel where the sick and the novitiates could participate in the services without mingling with the rest of the community. To the left of the church the abbot had his private quarters and in front of that was a guesthouse for illustrious visitors and a hostel to accommodate travelers and pilgrims.

It is believed that the walls of the church were constructed of masonry and stone rubble with a timber roof; the remainder of the structures were built of rubble filling between upright and slanted beams and had steep wooden roofs, as shown in a model reconstruction of what the Saint-Gall monastery might have looked like in the ninth century. The "half-timbered" architecture used in the farm buildings was an indigenous mode of construction that persisted throughout Europe in the Middle Ages and may still be seen in some old European towns today.

Shortly after the year 1000 a large number of churches and monasteries were constructed all over Europe. Raoul Glaber (c. 986–1046), a Cluniac monk and chronicler, wrote,

> Therefore, after the above mentioned year of the millennium which is now about three years past, there occurred throughout the world, especially in Italy and Gaul, a rebuilding of church basilicas. Notwithstanding the greater number were already well established and not in the least need, nevertheless each Christian people strove against the others to erect nobler ones. It was as if the whole earth, having cast off the old by shaking itself, were clothing itself everywhere in the white robe of the Church. Then, at last, all the faithful altered completely most of the episcopal seats for the better, and likewise, the monasteries of the various saints, as well as the lesser places of prayer in the towns. . . .

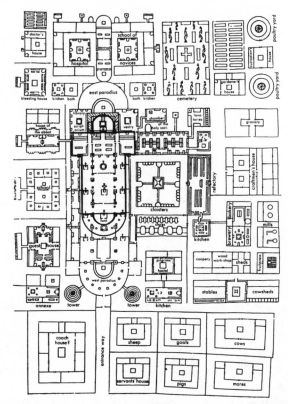

Fig. 50. Redrawn plan of Saint-Gall Monastery. Switzerland. c. 820. (After Pevsner, *Outline of European Architecture*; reproduced by permission of Penguin Books Ltd.)

Fig. 51. Reconstruction model of Saint-Gall Monastery by Walter Horn. (Wim Cox, Cologne)

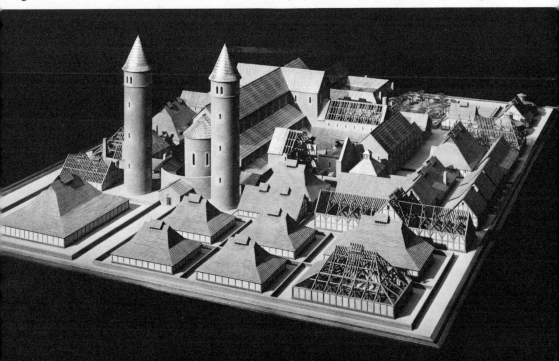

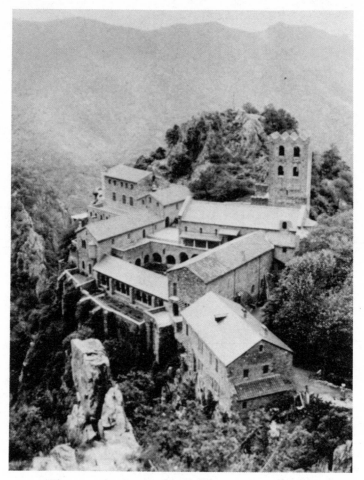

Fig. 52. Saint-Martin-du-Canigou. Southern France.
1001–1026. (R. G. Calkins)

    This spurt of building activity, Glaber implies, was occasioned by thanksgiving for being spared the anticipated end of the world and Last Judgment, which had been expected in the year 1000. The terror over this imagined event, however, may have been exaggerated in retrospect, and we can probably credit the vast building campaigns not so much to gratitude for deliverance as to a heightened religious fervor and especially to a resurgence of economic means and technical ability to accomplish large-scale projects.

    Some of the monasteries erected during this period were small and isolated, such as the diminutive Saint-Martin-du-Canigou (fig. 52) situated on a pinnacle of rock in the Pyrenees of southern France and accessible only by a steep, tortuous path. Built between 1001 and 1026, and restored in the twentieth century, this monastery consisted of only a few buildings, with a garden situated within the cloister.

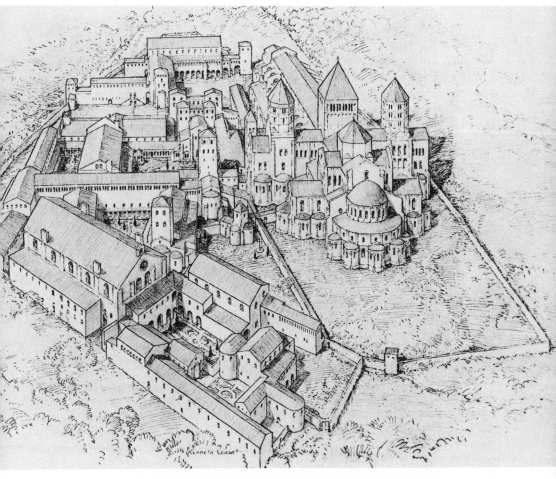

Fig. 53. Reconstruction drawing of Cluny III and monastery.
As of 1157. (Kenneth J. Conant)

In contrast, the vast Benedictine monastery of Cluny III (fig. 53), begun on
the site of two previous churches by Abbot Hugh in 1088 and finished around
1130, became the largest religious structure in Western Europe until the construction of the Renaissance church of Saint Peter's in Rome. In the *Life of Saint Hugh,*
it is recorded that

> It took twenty years to build and was so spacious that thousands of monks
> could assemble there; so magnificent that an emperor could have built nothing
> finer, and [it] surpassed all known churches in construction and beauty.

Not only was the scale and number of supporting buildings vastly multiplied but
the abbey became the motherhouse of a vast network of 1,500 member houses of
the Cluniac order in the twelfth century.

Whether large or small, the medieval monastery was built according to a plan that soon became standardized and that provided all of the necessities for a self-sufficient community. As such, it became a nucleus of economic activity in the countryside, a haven for the sick and the infirm, a refuge for the traveler, and a place of veneration for the pilgrim. In this context the description of a monastic complex by Hildebert of Le Mans in the late eleventh or early twelfth century becomes a universal appraisal:

> The house presents a four-square shape; the cloister-court is adorned with four open walks, which, enclosed by three buildings required for bodily needs and a fourth, which is the church, provide the monks with exercise, food and repose, so that here the sheep are kept as in a fold. The first of these buildings stores their bread and meat, and the second, counting next, feeds them therewith. The third provides rest for their limbs wearied by the day's labour, and the fourth forever rings with the praises of God.

The physical activity of running the establishment and the spiritual activity of the religious services and meditation were performed side by side: a balance was achieved between the *vita activa* and the *vita contemplativa*. Moreover, the establishment of sister houses, and eventually of an entire network of monasteries, as in the case of the Cluniac order, provided elements of political unity across national lines at a time when Western Europe was being fractionalized by feudalism. Perhaps most important, the establishment of schools for novices required libraries and means of producing books: *scriptoria* were established that copied not only Christian books but also ancient texts and thereby preserved them for posterity. Thus, the monastery became a principal center of learning before the establishment of cathedral schools and universities in the urban centers that developed later.

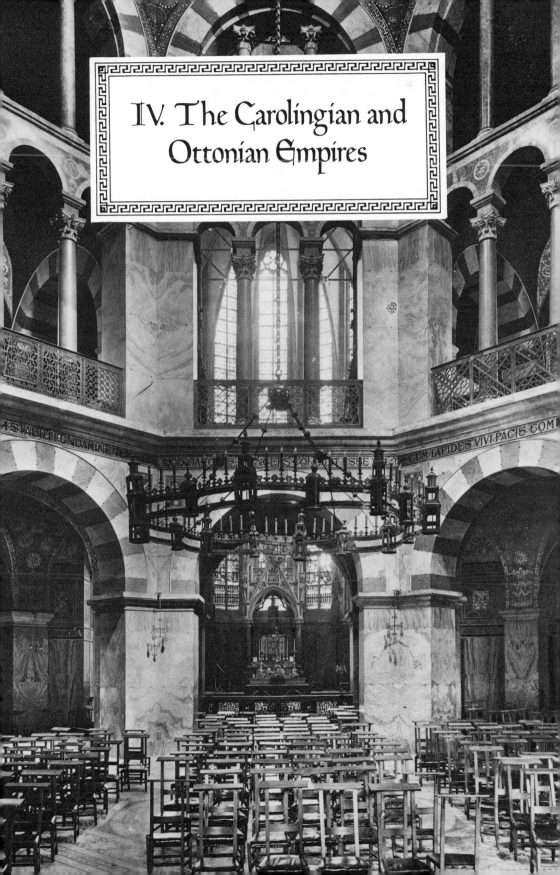

IV. The Carolingian and Ottonian Empires

11. THE RENEWAL OF THE CHRISTIAN ROMAN EMPIRE

uring the time when most of Western Europe was enduring the chaos born of the disintegration of Roman political institutions and the ravages of migrating tribes, two dynasties were founded that were to lead to a new political entity. In the mid-fifth century the Franks, a Germanic tribe occupying the area of present-day Belgium, were formed into a kingdom under Childeric I (c. 436–481), the son of Merowech. Under Clovis (466–511), the most able of the "Merovingian" kings, the territory of the Franks expanded into Gaul, a capital was established at Paris, and, after his conversion to Christianity, the Frankish kingdom was designated a consulate by the Emperor Anastasius. The movement toward centralization and stability was reversed, however, after his death, for the kingdom was split into three parts, and subsequent divisions of political and administrative responsibility resulted in feudal disintegration by the end of the rule of Dagobert (629–639).

One of the able administrators in the eastern territory of the Franks, Austrasia, was Pepin I (d. 639), who founded the succeeding dynasty. His grandson Charles Martel (714–741) stopped the Moslem invasion of Europe at Tours in 732, and his son Pepin the Short (c. 715–768) eventually forced the Moslems back over the Pyrenees into Spain in 759. Pepin the Short also consolidated the Frankish kingdom and strengthened a new sense of political and religious unity. It was under his son Charlemagne, however, that Western Europe was restored to being the most effective administrative entity since the decline of the Roman Empire.

Charlemagne (742–814) became King of the Franks in 771. He immediately set about strengthening the boundaries of the Frankish lands along the Pyrenees against the incursions of the Arabs in Spain, and defeated the Lombards in northern Italy who were threatening the existence of the papacy in Rome. Charlemagne saw himself, therefore, as the unifier of Europe and as the temporal head of a new and expanded Frankish kingdom. Seeking to renew the splendor of ancient Rome, he had himself crowned Holy Roman Emperor in Saint Peter's in Rome on Christmas Day, 800, and he ruled in this capacity until his death in 814.

In his effort to re-create what he believed to be authentic manifestations of the Christian Roman Empire under Constantine, Charlemagne surrounded himself with such able advisors as Alcuin of York, John Scotus, and Einhard, who wrote a life of Charlemagne in the manner of the Roman historian, Suetonius. Not only was Charlemagne's court patterned after a Roman model, his realm was filled

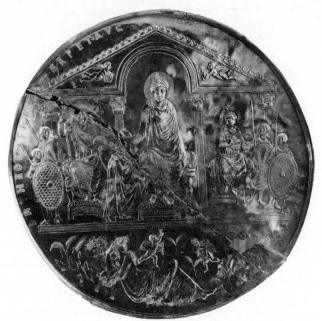

Fig. 54. Missorium of Theodosius. 388. Silver gilt, Diam. 29⅛". Real Academia de la Historia, Madrid. (Photograph: P. Witte; copyright Deutsches Archäoligisches Institut, Madrid)

with visual evocations of the Roman Christian heritage of the Carolingian Empire. In his desire to re-create an authentic continuation of the pre-Byzantine Christian church, Charlemagne sought to rival the splendor of the eastern Byzantine Empire.

When Charlemagne died, his son, Louis the Pious (778–840), was unable to maintain either the military integrity or the political administration of the empire. Quarrels among his successors resulted in a settlement in the Treaty of Verdun (843) in which the empire was divided among Louis the German (d. 876), who became King of the East Franks in Austrasia, Lothair (d. 855), who was given the kingdom of Italy and the empty title of emperor, and Charles the Bald (d. 877), who was made King of the West Franks in present-day France. The latter, in turn, became emperor from 875 until his death in 877, briefly causing a magnificent revival and development of Carolingian imperial forms of art. Charles's successor, Charles the Fat, son of Louis the German, ruled as emperor and King of the Franks for only three years, from 884 to 887, when his ineptitude caused him to be deposed. From that point on, the frequent invasions of Scandinavians along the European coast and the increasing fragmentation of the Frankish kingdoms resulted in the virtual disappearance of an imperial entity in Europe.

As the Frankish kingdoms were disintegrating, a new locus of political and military power was forming in the area of northern Germany ruled by the House of Saxony. Henry I, the Fowler, established a new dynasty and was elected Holy Roman Emperor in 919. Then followed three emperors with the name Otto, lending their collective name to the new realm that is now referred to as the Ottonian Empire. Otto I, crowned King of Germany at Aachen in 936, established a rigorous control over the Germanic lands and was crowned Holy Roman Emperor in Rome in 962. Otto II (973–983) undertook to elevate the status of the Western

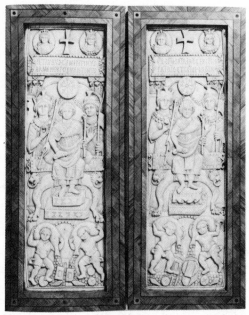

Fig. 55. Consular diptych of Clementinus. Constantinople. 513. Ivory, each panel 15⅛″ x 4⅞″. (Merseyside County Museums, Liverpool)

empire to make it comparable to that of the Byzantine Empire. He sent an emissary to Constantinople to negotiate for the hand of a Byzantine princess, and after being rebuffed once, brought back Theophanu. She proved to be a brilliant woman who ruled capably as regent from 983 to 991, while her son, Otto III, was a minor. As a result of the desire to emulate the splendor of the Eastern empire, and because of Theophanu's presence, and perhaps the presence of the Byzantine artisans she may have brought with her, a strong Byzantine influence pervaded court art. In addition, the Ottonians also derived inspiration from the art and architecture of the Carolingian period, further enriching the associations implicit in imperial representations. Unfortunately, Otto III died young, in 1002, and as he left no heir, the dynasty passed to his cousin, Henry II. For more than a century after Henry's succession, Germany remained the seat of the Holy Roman Empire in the West, and the imperial art of the period blended into and became the German manifestation of Romanesque art.

Elsewhere in Europe at the time of the consolidation of the Ottonian Empire in Germany important regional centers of art were being formed. In Anglo-Saxon England after the Viking invasions, a new kingdom centered itself at Winchester, and monastic communities flourished at Winchester and Canterbury. The scriptoria of these monasteries produced distinctive schools of English manuscript illumination.

In Spain, where the Moslems occupied three-fourths of the Iberian peninsula, a Christian enclave in the Kingdom of Asturias was able to flourish in the ninth century because it was protected in part by a formidable range of mountains. The mixing of Christian and Moslem elements of art and architecture elsewhere throughout Spain produced a blend of forms, called *Mozarabic,* which contributed greatly to the evolution of the Spanish Romanesque style by the twelfth century.

12. THE IMPERIAL IMAGE

During the Late Roman Empire, the image of the Christian emperor became standardized. The huge cult image of Constantine enthroned and placed in a monumental apsidal niche in the basilica of Constantine may have reflected imperial audiences in which the emperor sat enthroned in such an architectural framework. This context was repeated in numerous stone reliefs depicting emperors presiding over races or games from an imperial box framed by columns and topped by an entablature, arch, or pediment.

The large silver Missorium of Theodosius (fig. 54) illustrates the imperial formula around 390. The Emperor Theodosius sits enthroned beneath the central arch of an imperial *ædicula,* or *loggia,* flanked by bodyguards, his sons, Valentinian II and Arcadius, and attendants. Beneath, the allegorical figure of Tellus, the Earth, with *amorini* bringing bounty of wheat and gold, reflects not only the homage of the empire, but also its well-being under Theodosius's administration. Still imbued with a sense of classical articulation, the figures are well modeled in shallow relief, and the varied positions impart movement and vitality to the scene.

In later representations, however, the imperial image becomes abstracted and stylized. In the consular diptych of Clementinus of 513 (fig. 55), a pair of ivory tablets that were pictorial delegations of authority from the emperor to the consuls who ruled over parts of the Eastern empire, the figure of the consul has been placed within a reduced imperial arcade. Clementinus is rigidly frontal, his form is flattened and dominated by the pattern of roundels on his robe. Two armed attendants are squeezed behind the consul and in front of the columns of the architectural frame. Beneath the lion-footed throne amorini display the wealth of the empire by emptying bags of gold and grain. The image has ceased to be purely representational: it has become largely symbolic, an icon of the imperial presence embodied in the figure of the consul. In a more elaborate manner the mosaics of Justinian and Theodora, amplified with the full court retinue and the personal representative of Justinian, Maximianus, serve as similar imperial icons in the sanctuary of S. Vitale.

In carrying out Charlemagne's renewal of the Roman Empire, every attempt was made to provide authentic visual links with the Roman Christian Empire. On his way back from Rome after being crowned Holy Roman Emperor in 800, Charlemagne had an equestrian statue of Theodoric removed from Ravenna and brought to his palace complex at Aachen. The bronze statuette in the Louvre Museum (fig. 56), whether of Charlemagne or of the later Carolingian emperor, Charles the Bald, may reflect the presence of this statue at Aachen. The bronze statuette embodies the tradition of the imperial equestrian portrait, for the statue of Theodoric, and a lost one of Justinian in Constantinople, emulated the sur-

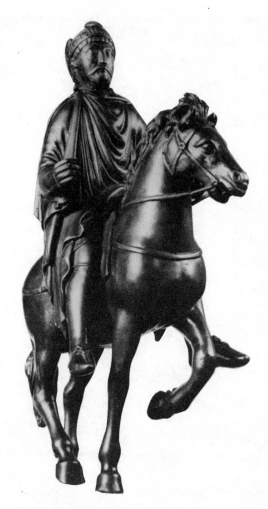

Fig. 56. Bronze equestrian statuette of Charlemagne or Charles the Bald. 9th century. H. 9¼". Louvre, Paris. (Cliché des musées nationaux, Paris)

viving Roman statue of Marcus Aurelius that was situated next to the Lateran Palace in Rome. During the Middle Ages this statue was believed to represent Constantine, the first Christian emperor. Moreover, Charlemagne's palatine chapel of the late eighth century at Aachen (fig. 57) was patterned in its basic form, although not in its details, after the most resplendent and explicitly imperial building Charlemagne had seen, S. Vitale at Ravenna (see fig. 29, p. 34). Charlemagne's chapel was connected with a large, single-apse audience hall, patterned after Constantine's Aula Palatina at Trier nearby. In addition, the entire complex of buildings was called the Lateran after the Bishop of Rome's palace, and the verbal designation was made more explicit by the presence outside of the borrowed statue of Theodoric, an earlier Christian emperor of the West.

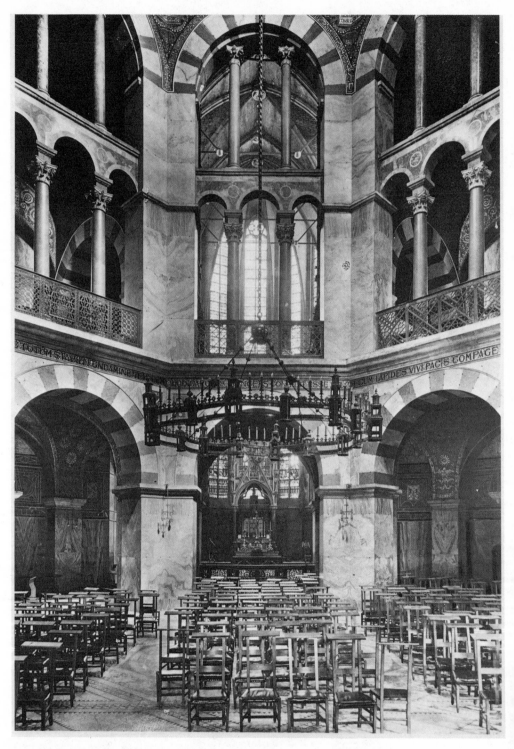

Fig. 57. Interior of palatine chapel. Aachen. Late 8th century. (Marburg)

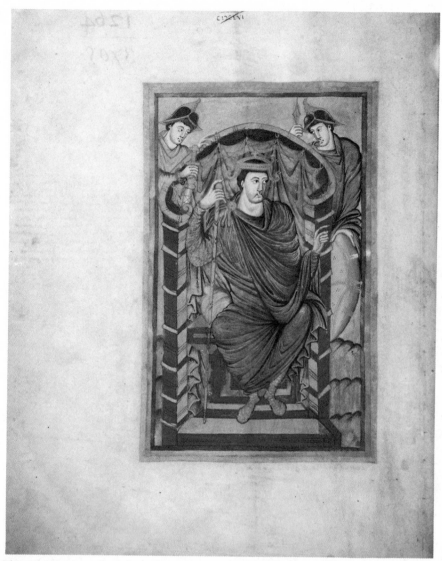

Fig. 58. "Emperor Lothair I Enthroned" from the Lothair Gospels. Tours. 849–851. 12⅝" x 9¾". Bibliothèque Nationale (MS lat. 266, fol. 1v), Paris.

Among the followers of Charlemagne, the visual imagery of the imperial tradition was kept alive and further developed. Lothair I (799–855), King of Italy and Holy Roman Emperor to 855, is shown in a portrait in his Gospels (fig. 58). He is enveloped by a large throne that almost doubles as the imperial aedicula and is flanked by two armed bodyguards in the manner of earlier consular diptychs. This manuscript was presented to Lothair between 849 and 851 by his half-brother Charles the Bald as a conciliatory gesture after settling their continuing feuds.

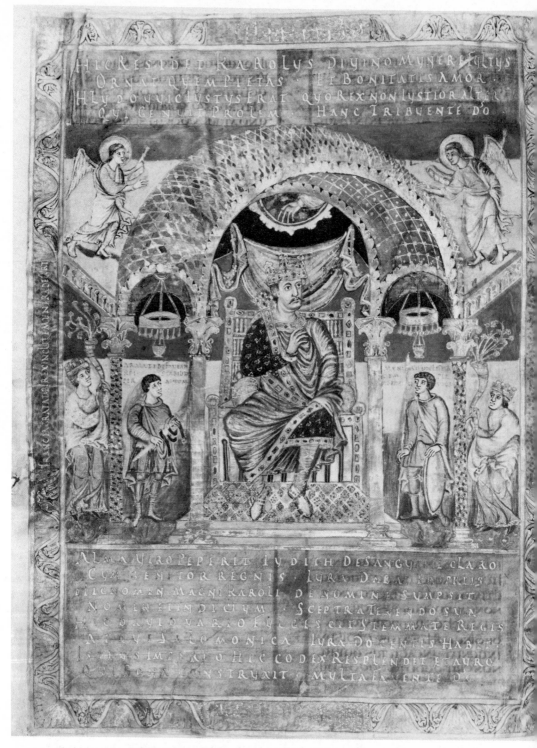

Fig. 59. "Charles the Bald Enthroned" from the Codex Aureus (Golden
Gospels) of Saint Emmeram. c. 870. 15¾" x 11¾". Bayerische Staatsbibliothek (Clm. 14000, fol. 5v), Munich.

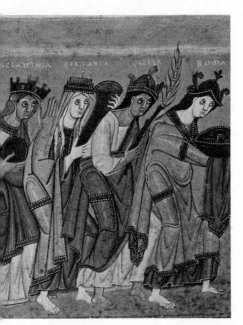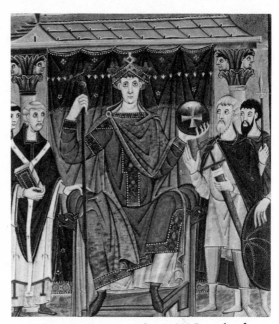

Fig. 60. "The Provinces of the Empire Bowing Before the Emperor" from the Gospels of Otto III. 997–1000. 13" x 9⅜". Bayerische Staatsbibliothek (Clm. 4453, fol. 23v), Munich.

Fig. 61. "Emperor Otto III Enthroned" from the Gospels of Otto III. 997–1000. 13" x 9⅜". Bayerische Staatsbibliothek (Clm. 4453, fol. 24r), Munich.

Charles the Bald himself was represented enthroned beneath an elaborate golden canopy (fig. 59) in his most lavish manuscript, the Golden Gospels of Saint Emmeram. Above the emperor, the hand of God, flanked by two angels, explicitly signifies the divine investiture of his authority. Standing next to the imperial baldacchino are the usual armed bodyguards and two personifications of the provinces of the empire holding cornucopias, a variation of the theme of the bounty of the empire depicted in the consular diptych of Clementinus. The remainder of the page is dyed purple, the imperial color, and the script is written in gold letters, all attesting to the power and magnificence of the imperial office. In these two Carolingian imperial representations classical and Byzantine models have been followed and elaborated, but in keeping with the continuing *renovatio,* we find a greater sense of actuality in the modeling of the figures, in the articulation of architectural space, and in the vitality of gestures and positions.

In Ottonian representations of the emperor, however, a more emphatic abstraction of forms reappears. In the Gospels of Otto III (997–1000) a two-page frontispiece (figs. 60, 61) represents the youthful emperor enthroned before the imperial loggia, which is hung with a cloth of honor. Flanking him are ecclesiastical and military members of his court. On the opposite page, four female personifications of the provinces of the Ottonian Empire—Sclavinia, Germania, Gallia, and Roma—approach bowing and proffering bounty to the emperor. These images have become flattened and stylized; in particular, the emperor is depicted in a rigid frontal position, staring straight ahead. The hieratic effect and ponderous ceremonial impact of the miniatures mark a return to the iconlike quality of the Byzantine consular diptychs of the sixth century. This may have been intentional, for the Ottonian emperors sought to emulate the court ceremony and splendor of the Eastern empire. The presence of Theophanu, wife of Otto II, regent of the empire from 983 to 991, and mother of Otto III, ensured the continuing influence of the Byzantine traditions.

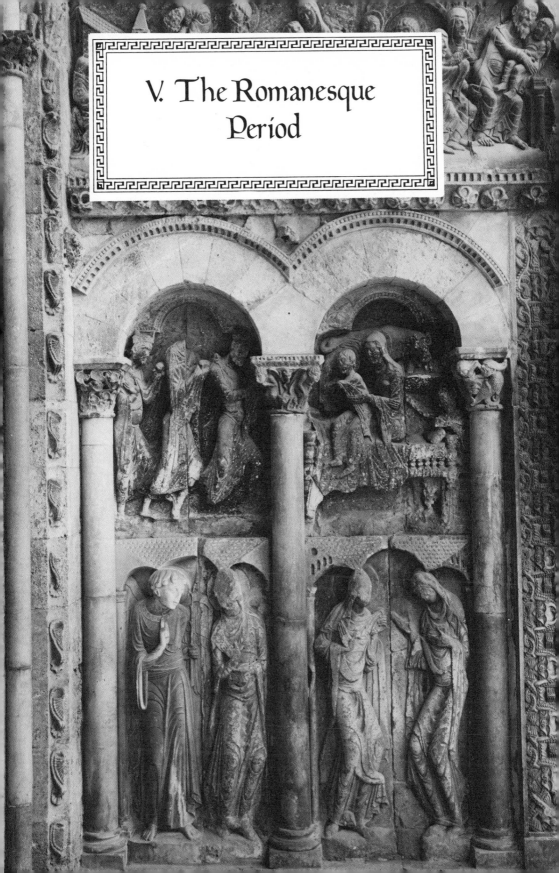

V. The Romanesque Period

13. The Resurgence

uring the eleventh and twelfth centuries, in a period that is usually called *Romanesque* because of the resurgence of the monumental architecture and sculpture considered to be "in the Roman manner," we are confronted with a diversity of regional styles and a variety of momentous changes. This time span overlaps and includes other periods and national designations, for instance, the period of the Ottonian Empire that lasted from the early tenth into the thirteenth century. In Anglo-Saxon England the way of life and its accompanying art forms were abruptly changed by the Norman invasion of 1066 and the appointment of Continental prelates to the important bishoprics. In northern Italy, France, and Spain a new form of vaulted architecture, which was soon adorned by expanded programs of monumental sculpture, began developing in the late tenth century, and these traditions, particularly in outlying areas, persisted into the thirteenth century. Yet at the very time that the Romanesque style in architecture was maturing, there appeared at the Abbey of Saint-Denis, just north of Paris, a choir constructed between 1140 and 1144 that provided the basis for the development of a new architectural style later to be called *Gothic*. Many of the new urban cathedrals built after this date developed the new transitional Gothic style and cannot be classified as Romanesque. The pervasive characteristics of sculpture and painting, however, changed more gradually and did not manifest an entirely new idiom until the thirteenth century.

Accompanying the development of more monumental architectural and sculptural ensembles, and indeed largely responsible for them, was an economic and technological resurgence throughout Western Europe. Commerce within Europe and, after the First Crusade, throughout the Mediterranean basin and the Near East pumped new vitality into the economic base of society. Better agricultural tools were made of metal, and harvesting methods were made more efficient by new technological advances. Techniques for making better building tools, such as the stone saw, were perfected and as a result, better construction materials, carefully cut ashlar masonry rather than aggregate rubble, were used to construct bigger and more lasting structures. At the same time the monastic orders grew in political importance and economic power and were able to finance new, immense, and lavishly decorated buildings. The strength of the church was enhanced by the preaching of the First Crusade at Clermont-Ferrand in 1095 by Pope Urban II, giving Christianity a powerful military and missionary focus that was bent upon expelling Islam from the Holy Land. The resulting booty from the East brought a variety of Near Eastern influences into the artistic repertoire of the West.

Also, with the growth of the monasteries and the foundation of numerous affiliated houses across Europe, it became easier for pilgrims to journey from England, Germany, or northern France south to either Rome and Monte Gargano in Italy or Santiago de Compostela in Spain, stopping at monasteries and hostelries conveniently spaced about a day's journey by foot or horseback along the way. An increased devotion to relics of saints both caused and was further encouraged by these pilgrimages, which became important sources of economic interchange. Likewise, styles of art and architecture were easily transmitted to widely separated regions and produced certain characteristics of homogeneity that some scholars have suggested are evidence of an "international" quality of the Romanesque style.

On the other hand, with the exception of the Ottonian Empire, which exerted less and less of a centralizing influence outside Germany, Europe was broken up into a myriad of small feudal principalities, for the most part centered around the castles of local lords and to whom the surrounding peasantry owed allegiance. Out of the complex networks of loyalties, codes of ethics, and standards of military comportment there evolved the chivalric code. To a large extent, the ecclesiastical and secular hierarchies paralleled each other: as the vassal promised fealty and service to his lord, so the Christian maintained his loyalty to God and the monk served his abbot. And, as the chivalric code was essentially rooted in the tradition of knighthood and military conduct, so Christianity became, with the advent of the crusades and the eruptions of local heresies that had to be suppressed, the Church Militant.

Because of the need to combat heresies in the twelfth century, Romanesque art frequently manifested strong dogmatic, even propagandistic qualities. Precepts of the faith were codified and represented in a diagrammatic manner, or were embodied in the stern, abstracted, and didactic images of Christ in a Last Judgment with all of the iconic severity of the Byzantine Pantocrator. But the Romanesque art of this period was not merely imitative of previous forms; it built upon them and added a new complexity, vitality, and intensity of message, which pervaded all of its manifestations.

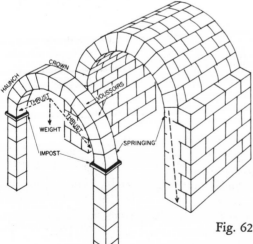

Fig. 62. Arch and barrel vault. (R. G. Calkins)

14. THE ROMANESQUE PILGRIMAGE CHURCH

The builders of Early Christian basilicas renounced the massive vaulted forms of Roman architecture and returned to the post-and-lintel system or arcaded colonnades for the interior walls and timber trusswork for the roofs. The width of the nave was limited, however, by the availability of suitable timbers, and wooden roofs greatly increased the danger of total destruction of the building by fire. As a result, efforts were made by the tenth century to return to all-masonry vaulted structures, as in the earlier Roman buildings, and to evolve new vaulting systems appropriate for longitudinal structures. In the intervening period half domes continued to be used for covering apsidal areas, and crude, intersecting barrel vaults, called groin vaults, were used for small, low crypts, aisles, and galleries.

An early solution to the vaulting problem was the development of the barrel vault. This was a semicircular vault, actually a projection of an arch in depth (fig. 62). Arches had been used since Roman times and embodied a different set of tectonic principles from the post-and-lintel system, consisting of two uprights with a horizontal member placed between them. The forces exerted in the post-and-lintel system were all vertical. An arch, however, comprises a series of bricks or stones, usually slightly wedge-shaped, set along the radii of the semicircular arch, and usually locked into place by a central keystone at the crown of the arch. The weight of these stones (*voussoirs*) is vertical, and, because they cannot move that way, they exert thrusts at an angle. As long as the average of these diagonal forces falls within the middle third of the supporting wall, the arch will stand; if it falls outside that area, the walls will collapse outward. There must also be an equilibrium of weight over the curved shoulders, or haunches, as well as over the crown of the arch to keep it from popping open or caving inward. To build an arch required a timber scaffolding or centering with a curved ramp along which the voussoirs were laid. Once the mortar had set, the centering could be removed and used again on another arch. The structural properties of the barrel vault are the same as those of the arch, but the diagonal forces generated by the length of the vault require massive wall construction along the entire length in order to stabilize it satisfactorily.

For this reason, a variety of other modes of buttressing the barrel vault were developed that allowed for aisles and more ample interiors. In the church of Saint-Martin-du-Canigou (figs. 63, 64) in the French Pyrenees, constructed from 1001 to 1026, the central nave is barrel-vaulted and is flanked by two lower barrel vaults over the aisles. The forces exerted by the nave vault are thus diverted downward onto the nave arches and the spindly nave columns. Occasionally a massive square pier and a corresponding transverse arch under the vault divide it into smaller sections that were easier to erect, one at a time. Although this church was restored in the twentieth century, we can still see that it was built of courses of rough fieldstone; only the capitals and the columns were carefully carved.

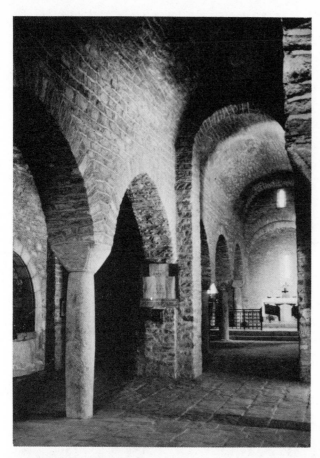

Fig. 63. Nave toward apse.
Saint-Martin-du-Canigou,
southern France. 1001–1026.
(R. G. Calkins)

Fig. 64. Nave and aisle vaults.
Saint-Martin-du-Canigou,
southern France. 1001–1026.
(R. G. Calkins)

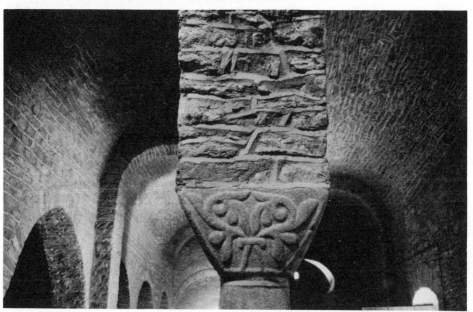

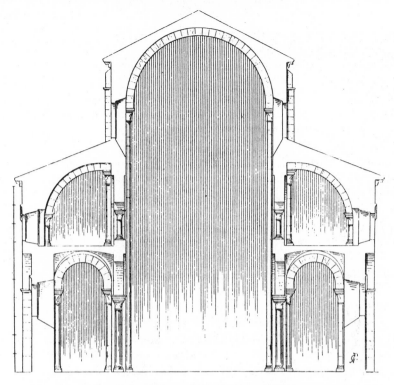

Fig. 65. Section. Saint-Étienne, Nevers, Burgundy. 1083–1097.
(After Dehio and Bezold)

A second system of buttressing the nave vault was evolved that made use of half barrel vaults, or quadrant vaults (fig. 65). These curved up and inward from the exterior wall to abut the nave vault at its springing point. In some early Romanesque churches these quadrant vaults were employed directly over the aisles; in the mature pilgrimage churches the quadrant vaults were used over a gallery situated above the aisles. These vaults abut the nave vault, diverting some forces downward and transmitting some outward. Because the exterior walls support a smaller vault, they, in turn, need not be so thick.

Yet another vaulting system, with important implications for the evolution of Gothic vaults, was used, sometimes on a large scale, sometimes on a minor scale, since its invention in Roman times. This was the groin vault (see fig. 116, p. 138) formed by the intersection of two barrel vaults at right angles. It formed a canopy resting on four points or piers with sharp angles (groins) at its lower extremities blending into a domical surface at the crown of the vault. It had the advantage of concentrating the thrusts exerted by the weight of the intersecting barrel vaults upon four supports, and allowing for an open flow of space through all four sides. In some Romanesque churches the groin vault was used in the bays of the aisles to buttress the barrel vault of the nave, providing a rigid intermediary structure between it and the exterior walls. Occasionally, as at Vézelay and Anzy-le-Duc, large groin vaults, separated by heavy transverse arches, were used over the nave (see fig. 117, p. 139).

Numerous French Romanesque churches could serve as the example of the mature formulation of Romanesque structure and plan. The church of Saint-Étienne at Nevers (figs. 66, 67) in Burgundy may be one of the earliest fully developed examples. Probably constructed between 1083 and 1097, it is in plan a three-aisled basilica with a projecting transept, a curved aisle around the apse called an ambulatory, and chapels radiating off of it. The ambulatory and aisles are divided into bays by transverse arches, and each bay is groin-vaulted. The nave is barrel-vaulted with transverse arches between corresponding semicircular shafts at each pier articulating the walls on either side. Over the crossing is an octagonal dome set on squinches. On the plan, massive walls at the facade indicate the bases of the two western towers.

The section (fig. 65) of the building clearly reveals the barrel-vaulted nave flanked by aisles and quadrant-vaulted galleries above them, with the curve of the gallery vaults performing a buttressing function at the point where the forces generated by the nave vault "emerge" from the wall.

An interior view of Saint-Étienne (fig. 67) shows a massive, dark, longitudinal space periodically punctuated by tall unbroken nave shafts and transverse arches. In contrast with Saint-Martin-du-Canigou, the building is constructed of finely cut and shaped quarried stones, ashlar masonry, indicating a greater sophistication in tools and stone-cutting techniques. In elevation, the nave has three stories: the nave arcade, the pair of gallery arcades within a single enclosing arch, and, unusual for a Romanesque church of such an early date, small clerestory windows set at the springing of the vault. These windows give evidence of a growing awareness that one could use small arched openings with a barrel vault without greatly weakening the structure. The rugged, sculptural effect of the nave wall is enhanced by the massive compound piers, composed of a square core and half-cylindrical columns engaged on each face, two corresponding to the nave arcades, one corresponding to the transverse arch of the aisle, and one consisting of the nave shaft that rises through the gallery level and terminates in a capital supporting the transverse arch of the nave. These shafts read as sculptural members set against the wall and, together with the layering of the nave and gallery arcades, emphasize its massive thickness.

Such a stone-vaulted interior was well adapted to processions and to the singing of plainchant during the celebration of the Mass. Plainchant, or Gregorian chant, is choral music that evolved in the tenth century from the tradition of singing the psalms. Smoothly flowing, unpunctuated melodies rose and fell as the words were sung, but lacked the interweaving melodic lines of later polyphonic music. The resultant strong, pure, sonorous music not only filled the vessel of the church but was amplified by the stone vault as though by a megaphone.

The sanctuary of Nevers is no longer an enclosed semicircular apse surmounted by a half dome. Instead, an arcade follows the semicircular curve of the apse beneath the wall with a blind arcade and the half dome, and beyond this arcade curves the ambulatory with three radiating chapels. This radial chevet plan was an ingenious solution to the problem of throngs of pilgrims circulating through the building and worshiping at various altars dedicated to, and sometimes

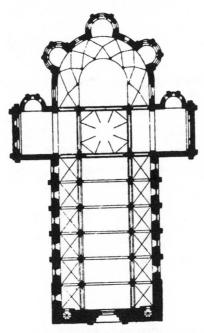

Fig. 66. Plan of Saint-Étienne, Nevers, Burgundy. 1083–1097.
(After Dehio and Bezold)

Fig. 67. Nave toward apse. Saint-Étienne, Nevers, Burgundy. 1083–1097.
(R. G. Calkins)

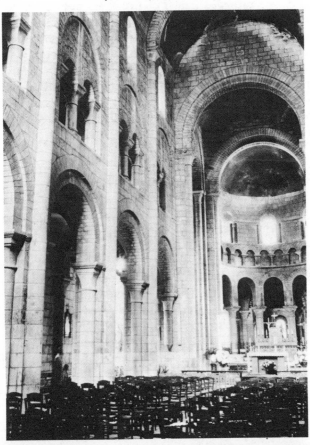

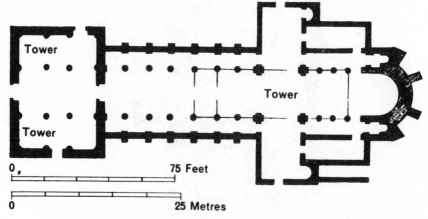

Fig. 68. Plan of Cluny II. 981. (After Kenneth J. Conant)

supporting, the relics of saints. Earlier plans to provide subsidiary chapels for additional altars had resulted, as at Cluny II (fig. 68), in an *en échelon* plan with chapels arranged in a parallel sequence behind the apse. But the entrances to the chapels were bottlenecks, and no passageway for circulation was provided. At Nevers, the three radial chapels and two additional chapels on the eastern flank of the transepts (fig. 69) provided a total of five altars in addition to the main altar for the celebration of the Mass. The chapels provided seclusion for devotions, but their openings were wide, allowing easy access, and the ambulatory permitted easy circulation. The extreme development of this plan was created at the third church at Cluny (fig. 70), erected between 1088 and about 1130. Here, a massive, five-aisled basilican structure was given two transepts, each with crossing towers and towers over the ends of the main transept. The eastern walls of the transepts were lined with chapels, and the radial chapels around the ambulatory were multiplied so that a total of fifteen individual altars were provided in addition to the main altar.

The exterior effect of the Romanesque church was partially a consequence of this radial apsidal plan. Seen from the apse, Nevers and Cluny III are an accumulation of geometric volumes, an amassing of the cylindrical forms and conical roofs of the chapels against the larger cylinder of the ambulatory, building upward to the conical roof over the apsidal dome, ultimately leading to the clifflike rectangular volume of the transept and the octagonal tower crowning the crossing (now partially destroyed at Nevers). This harmonious accumulation of volumes into a massive pyramid over the sanctuary of the building would have been partially balanced by two facade towers (also destroyed at Nevers). Originally, an irregular, picturesque silhouette would have resulted from this grouping of towers. At Cluny III, the powerfully juxtaposed volumes and the resolute accumulation of forms were multiplied, the mounting cadence of volumes building up to a crescendo of transept and crossing towers.

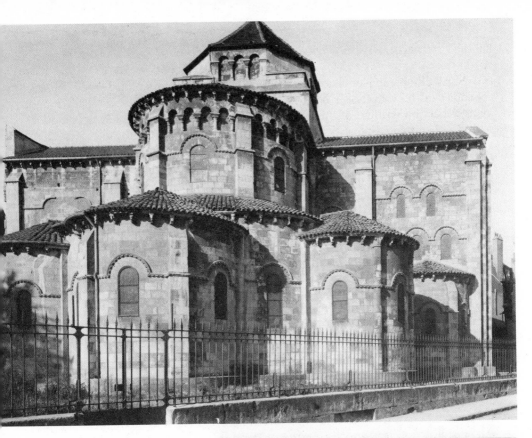

Fig. 69. View of apse. Saint-Étienne, Nevers, Burgundy. 1083–1097. (Marburg)

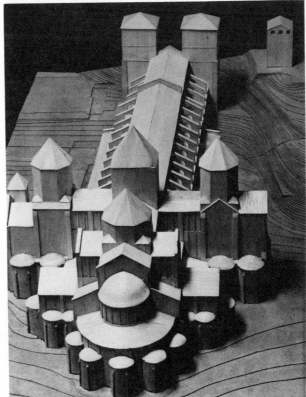

Fig. 70. Model of Cluny III. c. 1088–1130. (J. Combier, Mâcon)

Small Romanesque churches with triple apses or simplified radial plans abounded in the countryside of eleventh- and twelfth-century Europe. Larger and more elaborate variations of this plan, such as Cluny III or Saint-Sernin at Toulouse, served either major monastic houses or urban centers along major routes from France into Spain. As many of the larger and more developed churches of this type, such as Saint-Martin at Tours, Sainte-Foy at Conques, or Santiago de Compostela, were sites of important pilgrimages, they are frequently referred to as "Romanesque pilgrimage churches."

Indeed, the invention and elaboration of the radial apsidal plan was rooted in the growing cult of relics, a veneration of the remains of saints that had been steadily increasing since the ninth century. In addition, the discovery of the remains of the apostle Saint James the Major in Galicia in northwestern Spain attracted local pilgrimages in the mid-ninth century and increasing numbers of pilgrims from all over Europe from the middle of the tenth century. Santiago de Compostela, where the relics were housed, became, along with Rome and Monte Gargano in Italy, one of the principal pilgrimage centers of Europe. Monastic houses situated along the several conventional routes through France and Spain to Galicia not only served as hospices for the weary travelers but also attracted pilgrims to worship at the altars of their local saints.

So considerable was the traffic along the routes to Spain that a manuscript of the life of Saint James, the *Libri Sancti Jacobi*, written perhaps between 1150 and 1173, devotes its fifth book to a guide detailing the perils and highlights along the way. For instance, it warns the pilgrim of the terrible flies that abound in the pine-wooded area of Landes in southwestern France. It cautions the traveler about the people who live in Navarre,

> . . . a barbarous people, different from all the other people by their costumes and their race, full of wickedness, swarthy of color, ugly of visage, debauched, perverse, perfidious, disloyal, corrupt, voluptuous, drunk, and expert in all kinds of violence.

In a chapter titled "Good and Bad Rivers Which One Encounters on the Route of St. James," one learns,

> . . . in a place called Lorca, towards the east of Puenta la Reina flows a river called the Salty Brook; there, beware of drinking or of allowing your horse to drink, for this river causes death. On its banks . . . we find two Navarrais seated, sharpening their knives; they have the custom of skinning the mounts of the pilgrims who drink this water and die.

On the other hand, we learn that the River Ebro gives good water and is full of fishes, and that at Estella the "bread is good, the wine excellent, meat and fish abundant."

Seen in the context of the cult of relics and the arduous pilgrimages which it occasioned, the Romanesque church became a monumental symbol of the church *as* reliquary for the remains of the saints housed within it. Looming above the other structures of the monastery, village, or town, and perhaps seen from afar in the landscape, as at Saint-Nectaire (see fig. 102, p. 117), Vézelay, or Conques (see fig. 222, p. 260), the Romanesque church would have served as a beacon of refuge for the weary traveler and as the focus of devotion for the devout pilgrim. Fine ashlar masonry, and sometimes even military details such as crenelations, lent the building a militant stance commensurate both with the need of the monks to defend themselves from the incursions of marauding Vikings and Hungarians in the eleventh century and with the avowed militant purpose of the church to wrest the Holy Land from the infidel with the crusades of the twelfth century. To this must also be added the recurrent belief that the church was an earthly reflection of the heavenly city of Jerusalem, as explicitly stated in an invocation found in the ninth-century church at Corvey: "Protect this, O Lord, thy Heavenly City of Jerusalem." The measured accumulation of volumes and the multitowered silhouette transformed the church into a vision of the citadel of Heaven.

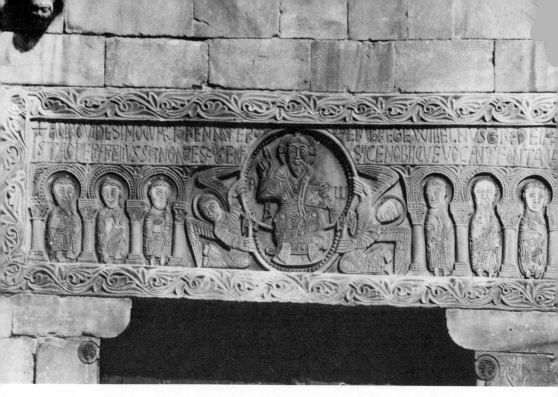

Fig. 71. Lintel over doorway. Saint-Genis-des-Fontaines, southern France. 1020–1021. (Archives photographiques, Paris, S.P.A.D.E.M.)

15. THE ROMANESQUE PORTAL

With the revived interest in constructing large, vaulted buildings came renewed attention to architectural decoration. Throughout the Merovingian period in France slabs of foliate or geometric relief decoration had been used as framing elements for doors and windows, and attempts had been made to emulate the architectural detail or decorative masonry work of the Gallo-Romans. Forms of this ornament persisted, sometimes accurately, sometimes misunderstood, throughout the Carolingian period. In the eleventh and twelfth centuries, however, we find a return to the application of monumental figurative sculpture to the fabric of buildings. Their use and placement vary according to region and date, but in general we can see an increasing elaboration of sculpted forms and a growing complexity of iconographical programs.

An early figurative portal sculpture at Saint-Genis-des-Fontaines (fig. 71) on the French side of the Pyrenees can be dated to 1020–1021 by an inscription that states that it was carved during the twenty-fourth year of the reign of King Robert. It is a simple rectangular block of stone reused now as a lintel over a doorway to a twelfth-century church. In the center, Christ in Majesty presides, enthroned in a double-curved mandorla, symbolizing that Christ is Lord of Heaven and Earth. He is flanked by three figures standing on each side within arcades, while two angels kneel and support the mandorla. Carved in the background on either side of Christ are the Greek letters *alpha* and *omega,* a reference to the Book of Revelation of Saint John in which Christ appears and pronounces, "I am Alpha and Omega, the First and the Last, the Beginning and the End" (Rev. 21:6). Thus Christ is Lord of the universe from the Creation to the Last Judgment, from the First Coming to the Second Coming, and he manifests his divinity to the witnesses, the assembled apostles. The impact of this revelation of divinity (*theophany*) is enhanced by the larger size (hieratic scaling) of Christ, who looms twice as large as the other figures. This commanding presence may also embody the eschatological prophecy of Saint Matthew (25:31) ". . . the Son of Man shall come in his glory, and all the holy angels with him, then shall he sit upon the throne of his glory" and the apocalyptic vision of Saint John in the Book of Revelation when Christ returns in triumph at the Second Coming to perform the Last Judgment.

The forms of Christ and the apostles are abstracted and reduced to flattened relief. The surfaces, however, are broken by zigzag lines of drapery carved in V-shaped incisions approximating the metalwork technique of chip carving. The figures of the apostles reiterate the shape of the arcades in which they are standing, the horseshoe arch surrounding the head, the sloping shoulders paralleling the capitals, the straight body echoing the columns, and the indentation for the feet followed by the broadening bases. This conformity of human figure to architectural frame, often called the *homme-arcade* motif, is derived from antique sources in which three-dimensional figures stood freely in architectural settings, particularly on sarcophagi and ivories. In the Saint-Genis lintel, however, constraints are imposed upon the figures by the echoing proximity of the arcades and their compression into flat images. These constraints introduce tensions that are further heightened by the simplification of features and contours and the enlivening activity of the incised angular drapery folds. The figures are thereby removed from a human context and placed in an abstract realm not unlike the process that occurs in Byzantine icons, where abstraction heightens the impact of the spiritual presence. At Saint-Genis these devices intensify the visionary role of the apostles as witnesses to Christ's theophany. For the pilgrim who beheld this lintel as he passed through the portal beneath, the sculpture served as a statement of dogma, a reaffirmation of the divinity of Christ and a reminder of the impending Last Judgment.

The sculpture of the Porte Miégeville (fig. 72) on the south side of the nave of the large pilgrimage church of Saint-Sernin at Toulouse presents a more complex accumulation of sculpted elements and a fusion of different iconographical themes. Dating from around 1115, almost 100 years after Saint-Genis-des-Fontaines, this portal consists of a massive rectangular frame projecting from the flank of the building. Into this block is recessed a large semicircular arch. Above the arch a heavy cornice is supported by carved corbels. This "corbel table" provides an upper frame to the ensemble, although a pediment with projecting columns and two circular windows rises above it. Beneath the corbel table and

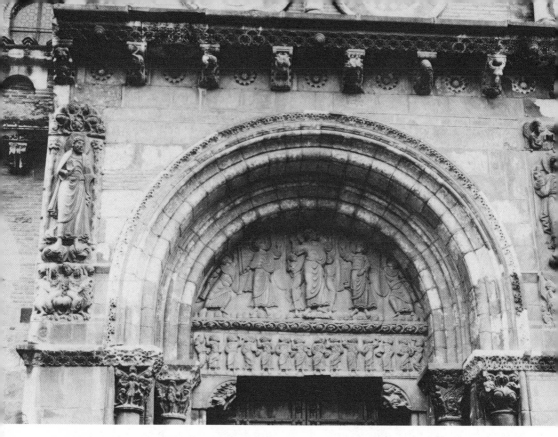

Fig. 72. Porte Miégeville. Saint-Sernin, Toulouse. c. 1115. (R. G. Calkins)

flanking the arch are two large figures in relief, Saint Peter on the right and Saint James the Major on the left. Appropriately, they are placed so that they represent the goals of two major pilgrimages in the twelfth century, to Santiago de Compostela in Spain to the West, and to Saint Peter's in Rome to the East. Carved from massive slabs of marble, they possess a rounder, more three-dimensional quality than the figures at Saint-Genis, and the drapery pulled taut over their thighs reveals recognizable human forms beneath. In terms of the composition of the overall portal, however, they are merely inserts serving as vertical accents on either side of the arch. Later such figures will be made a more coherent part of the sculptural and architectural composition.

Within the deeply recessed arch of the portal is a semicircular field (*tympanum*) and below it, a horizontal lintel. The tympanum contains a representation of the Ascension of Christ, while the apostles in the lintel below witness the event. This theme must be seen in the context of the Incarnation in which the Son of God was made flesh, for in this event Christ, as man, is returned to a spiritual state, the Son is reunited with the Father. The Ascension also serves as an antecedent for the Second Coming and as a reminder of the inevitability of the Last Judgment.

The tympanum and lintel work together to state the theme of Ascension effectively. The shape of the tympanum lends itself to the representation of upward movement, for Christ in the center is taller than the accompanying angels, and the angels in the outer corners stride and lean inward with arms upraised, not only conforming to the curve of arch but also contributing to the upward motion. Although the movement is less violent in the figure of Christ, the contortion of the angels hoisting him upward and the accentuated rhythm of upward-curving folds in his garment impart the effect of levitation. In the lintel the apostles throw back their heads, straining to observe the scene above, and the upward-curving folds of their draperies reinforce their actions. For the pilgrim who beheld this portal, the activity of the apostles in the terrestrial realm of the lintel renders more credible the visionary Ascension in the celestial tympanum above.

Still other architectural elements around the Romanesque church door were sculpted into coherent iconographical programs. At the twelfth-century church of Saint-Pierre-de-la-Tour in Aulnay, the *archivolts* (fig. 73)—the stones that make up the layers of arches as the doorway penetrates the fabric of the building —were carved into a meaningful sequence of representations. In the central portal of the west facade, carved between 1130 and 1160, figures were carved along the circumference of the four archivolts. The outermost arch contains the signs of the zodiac, a reference to the calendar, the passage of time, and a reflection of the workings of the cosmic realm. In the next register inward we find ten female figures, the five Wise and the five Foolish Virgins flanking Christ in the center. This is a reference (Matt. 25:1–13) to those in the terrestrial world who are prepared for the Last Judgment and those who are not. The third archivolt contains female figures holding shields and standing on deformed hybrid creatures. These are the personifications of the Virtues triumphing over the Vices. This theme was derived from the poem, the *Psychomachia* ("Battle of the Soul"), written by Prudentius around 400, and embodies the perennial struggle of the forces of good over evil. On the innermost archivolt a series of angels hold, at the apex of the arch, a medallion displaying the Paschal Lamb. This is the heavenly realm. Reading this series of archivolts as a processional sequence, the pilgrim entering the church is made aware of the passage of time in the cosmos, the need to be prepared for the moment of the Second Coming, the need to triumph over the vices in order to attain the Kingdom of Heaven. And the heavenly kingdom on this earth is God's church into which the beholder then proceeds.

In contrast, on the portal of the south transept at Aulnay (fig. 74), figures in the archivolts were placed along the radii of the semicircular arch. Reading from the exterior inward, these arches contained an imaginary bestiary with a variety of real and mythical animals, the elders of the Apocalypse holding their viols—witnesses to the Second Coming—and an assemblage of apostles, and saints. The final arch contains six griffins (a cross between an eagle and a lion) within an elaborately entwined vine. Perhaps here the sequence reads from the wild, untamed beasts of the earth to those who foresaw the coming of Christ and were therefore accepted into the Kingdom of Heaven, to those who witnessed and embraced Christ, to the beast that sometimes symbolized the Savior himself.

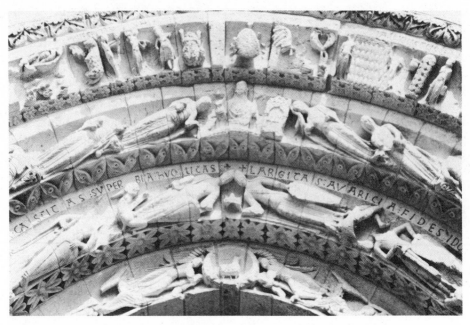

Fig. 73. Detail of archivolts, west-central portal. Saint-Pierre-de-la-Tour, Aulnay. 1130–1160. (R. G. Calkins)

Fig. 74. Detail of archivolts, south transept portal. Saint-Pierre-de-la-Tour, Aulnay. 1130–1160. (R. G. Calkins)

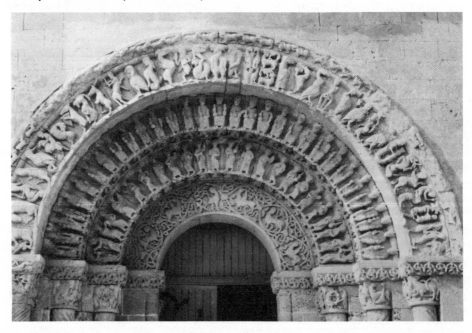

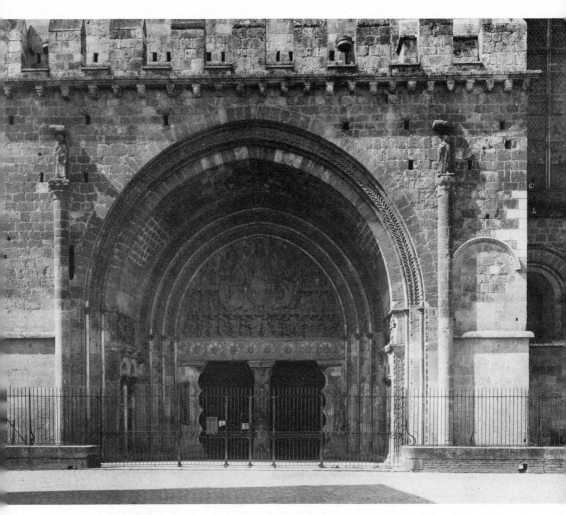

Fig. 75. South porch and portal. Saint-Pierre, Moissac. 1120–1130. (Marburg)

One of the most complex and fully developed Romanesque portals was created at Saint-Pierre at Moissac (fig. 75) between 1120 and 1130. It is situated on the south side of a massive bell tower, facing the village square. Deeply set into the porch, it consists of carved reliefs on the side walls of the embrasure, decorative archivolts and a lintel surrounding a carved tympanum, scalloped doorjambs with inset relief plaques of figures, and an elaborately carved doorpost (*trumeau*) supporting the midpoint of the lintel.

On the exterior of the porch, set on top of tall engaged columns flanking the arched entrance, are reliefs representing Abbot Roger (1115–1131), under whose direction the portal was carved, and Saint Benedict, the founder of the Benedictine Order of which Moissac was part. They watch over the entrance to their church.

On the right wall of the porch (fig. 76) as one enters are a series of reliefs set within a double arcade. Reading from the left to right in the lowest level, we find the Annunciation and the Visitation, the meeting of the Virgin and Saint Elizabeth, the mother of John the Baptist, while they are both with child. This relief prefigures the later meeting of Christ and John the Baptist. In the relief above, continuing across both panels of the arcade, is the Adoration of the Magi. In the frieze above the arcade are the Presentation of Christ at the Temple and the Circumcision combined and the fall of the pagan idols as the Holy Family enters Heliopolis on the Flight into Egypt. Although Joseph is participating in the Presentation scene, he turns to listen to the angel whispering in his ear the warning that they must flee, and thereby serves as a link with the Flight at the left. Considered together, these lively scenes of the Nativity and Infancy of Christ stand for the larger theme of the Incarnation, the moment when Christ is made flesh.

Fig. 76. Right embrasure reliefs. Saint-Pierre, Moissac. 1120–1130. (Marburg)

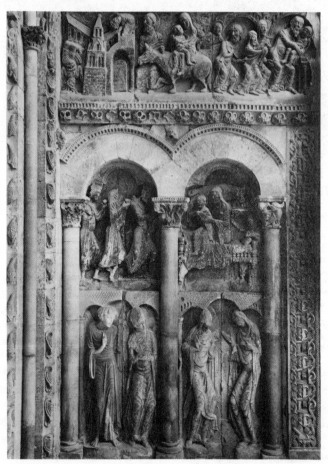

In contrast, on the left wall (fig. 77) of the embrasure we find parables and moralizing scenes. In the top frieze, we see the beginning of the parable of the rich man Dives and the poor beggar Lazarus (Luke 16:19–31). Dives is seated at his banquet table ignoring Lazarus, who lies on the ground at the left with dogs licking his sores. Dives refused to give the beggar the crumbs from his table. When Lazarus died, he was received in the bosom of Abraham, depicted to the left. As the rich man was dying, however, he beheld Lazarus in Heaven, shown above, while he was tormented by demons who stole his money. One devil grabs the soul of Dives as it leaves his mouth at the moment of death. The lowest reliefs, divided into two scenes, as were the Annunciation and Visitation opposite, contain personifications of Avarice and Luxuria as old hags, each accompanied by demons. The theme of these reliefs concerns the salvation of the poor and the damnation of the avaricious.

Fig. 77. Left embrasure reliefs. Saint-Pierre, Moissac. 1120–1130. (Marburg)

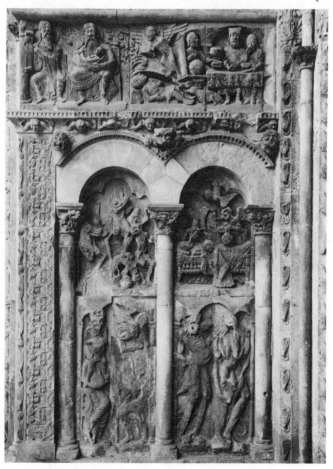

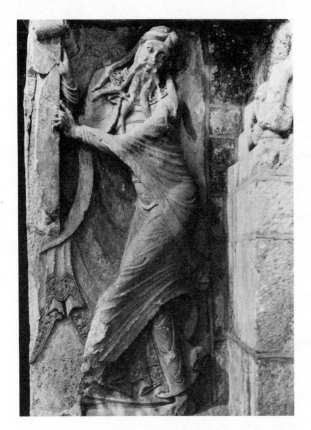

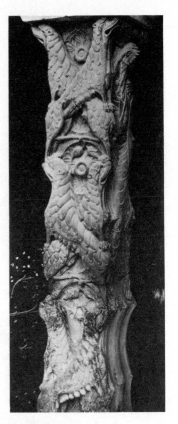

Fig. 78. Relief of Isaiah. Souillac. c. 1130. (Archives photographiques, Paris, S.P.A.D.E.M.)

Fig. 79. Front of trumeau. Saint-Pierre, Moissac. 1120–1130. (Marburg)

Set into the walls of the scalloped doorjambs flanking the entrance are reliefs of Saint Peter and Isaiah. Although they are independent plaques, similar to those in the spandrels of the Porte Miégeville, these figures bend in harmony with the curves and projections of the adjacent jambs. Saint Peter, holding his attribute, the Key to the Kingdom of Heaven, is placed next to the Lazarus and Dives reliefs, thereby implying the theme of Christian salvation through just and charitable acts. The figure of Isaiah on the right jamb is appropriately placed next to the reliefs of the Incarnation, for Isaiah foretold of the Virgin Birth.

Both of these jamb figures, in their elongated proportions and bent, moving postures, reflect the style and effect of one of the supreme examples of Romanesque sculpture, the relief figure of Isaiah at nearby Souillac (fig. 78). In the Souillac relief the figure is compressed, its volume contained as though behind an invisible plane. Yet the prophet is contorted in a crossed-leg, dancelike posture with bent torso and twisted head. The garment is pulled tautly over the body, revealing some of the volumes and contributing, through the rhythm of the concentric folds, to the movement of the body. The oppositions of movement and constraint, of volumes and containment behind rhythmic surface articulation, heighten the ecstasy of

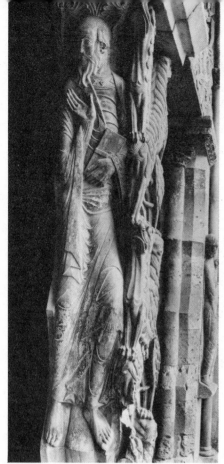

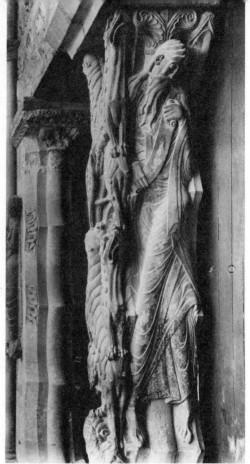

Fig. 80. Saint Paul(?), trumeau.
Saint-Pierre, Moissac.
1120–1130. (Marburg)

Fig. 81. Jeremiah, trumeau.
Saint-Pierre, Moissac.
1120–1130. (Marburg)

Isaiah's vision as he points to the scroll and pronounces his prophecy of the Incarnation. The jamb figures at Moissac are more elongated, but similar tensions result in a similar ecstatic effect.

The scalloped shape of the trumeau (fig. 79) echoes the undulating edge of the doorjambs and also coincides with the placement of three pairs of crossed male and female lions on its outer face. Although a wide variety of real and imaginary animals were depicted in Romanesque sculpture, as we have seen at Aulnay, these lions may carry the connotation, often found in medieval bestiaries, that they are the watchdogs of the church, for they were believed to sleep with their eyes open.

The sides of the trumeau contain figures compressed between the scalloped edges. On the left side (fig. 80), facing the jamb figure of Saint Peter, is possibly Saint Paul, the cofounder of the Christian church. Elongated, legs bent, hand gesticulating, and crowded in his narrow niche, Saint Paul appears to be propounding the law of the church with considerable energy. On the right side of the trumeau (fig. 81) the prophet Jeremiah, who foretold the Last Judgment, faces his fellow prophet Isaiah. The cross-legged posture creates an uncertain-

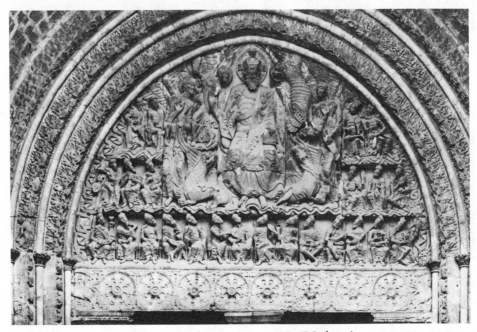

Fig. 82. Tympanum. Saint-Pierre, Moissac. 1120–1130. (Marburg)

equipoise, the surface is activated by sweeping hemlines and rippling folds, and the downcast head imposes a trancelike, meditative mood. Seen in its entirety, the trumeau is an architectural member utterly transformed into a sculptural ensemble. At the same time the figures and the lions have been made to conform to the architectural purpose of the doorpost. The tensions of their vital organic forms are increased by their imprisonment in its arbitrary shape.

Above the trumeau the tympanum (fig. 82) contains the fruition of the symbolic program of the portal. Christ in Majesty is enthroned, surrounded by the *tetramorph* (the four attributes of the Evangelists), and surrounded by three rows of bearded figures holding viols. This is the apocalyptic vision of the Second Coming of Christ as recounted in the Book of Revelation (4:4, 7–8), in which he appeared with the four and twenty elders "clothed in white raiment and they had on their heads crowns of gold," and prophesied by Isaiah (6:1), ". . . I saw also the Lord sitting upon a throne, high and lifted up, and his train filled the temple." It is also an elaborate theophany, Christ revealing himself as the embodiment of the Word in the midst of the attributes of the four Evangelists and witnessed by the twenty-four elders who symbolized the books of the Old Testament. This is not actually the Last Judgment, but the moment before. It is the Second Coming prepared for by the Incarnation on the right wall of the doorway and prophesied by the prophets below. It is the moment of reckoning implied by the parable of salvation and damnation on the left wall and the promise of salvation through the church administered by Saints Peter and Paul.

The impact of the tympanum is ecstatic, stern, and foreboding. The huge figure of Christ (fig. 83) is flattened, bound tightly by the concentric bands of drapery across his torso and charged with frenetic energy by the profusion of compressed angular hemlines. The activity of the surface movement and swirling folds of Christ's garments is picked up and carried throughout the contorted postures of the Evangelists' attributes, the attitudes of the twenty-four elders, and even the undulating clouds separating the rows of figures. The richness of detail and energy of movement transform the tympanum into an ecstatic vision. Although Christ is making a gesture of benediction, his head is a solid, blocklike form and his staring eyes sternly transfix the beholder. Christ as depicted in this image will be a harsh judge. The entering pilgrim would have understood the various ingredients of this portal and would have comprehended the awesome message of the entire ensemble.

Although the theme of the Last Judgment was only implicit in the portal at Moissac, it was frequently made explicit in the portals of other Romanesque churches. At Saint-Lazare in Autun in Burgundy, a "Last Judgment" (fig. 84) was carved in the tympanum over the main doorway of the facade, which made its message emphatically clear. The large figure of Christ entirely fills the middle portion of the tympanum, dwarfing even the attendant angels. His symmetrical

Fig. 83. Detail of Christ, tympanum. Saint-Pierre, Moissac.
1120–1130. (Marburg)

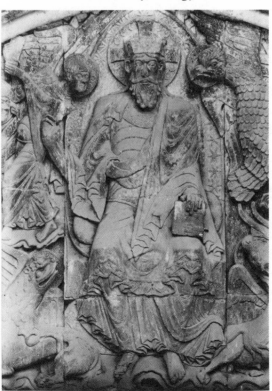

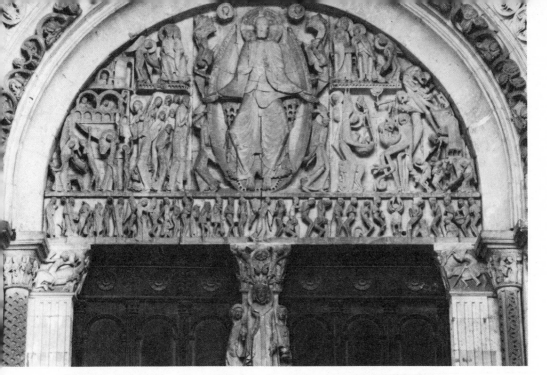

Fig. 84. Gislebertus: "Last Judgment," tympanum. Saint-Lazare, Autun. c. 1125–1135. (Archives photographiques, Paris, S.P.A.D.E.M.)

form is entirely flattened and filled with a myriad of concentric lines that create a rhythmic, echoing movement across the surface. On the left side of the tympanum rise the towers of the heavenly kingdom into which the blessed placidly proceed. On the right, however, various misshapen demons dispatch souls into Hell, and an angel and a devil weigh souls on a large balance. The lintel below is filled with small rectangular sarcophagi from which the naked souls of the dead arise as angels blow the trumpets of the Last Judgment. One of these is being plucked from his tomb by great talons as he grimaces with despair. Beneath the feet of God, as though commending himself, along with the adjacent souls of the dead, to God's mercy, the sculptor signed his work in bold letters: "GISLEBERTUS HOC FECIT." Around the tympanum the archivolt contains roundels with the signs of the zodiac and scenes of the labors of the months, signifying the passage of the calendar year and, more important, the passage of time between the First and Second Comings.

The calmness of the entry into the Kingdom of Heaven, the tormented activity of demons clutching at souls in the Hell scene, and the impassive and stern, abstracted image of Christ in the center would have served as ample warning to those who entered through the portal below to live the Christian life. Thus, Romanesque portals, whether simply decorated with the theophany, or developed into elaborate symbolic programs, were often vehicles for preaching, for exhorting the congregation to follow in Christ's footsteps, and sometimes for reaffirmations of dogma and condemnations of heresies. Their messages were always strong, clear, and didactic.

16. THE BRONZE DOOR

Another means of displaying visual narrative at the entrances of medieval churches was the sculpted door. As early as the fifth century carved doors of cypress wood were provided for the Early Christian basilica of S. Sabina in Rome, and for S. Ambrogio in Milan. Bronze doors were cast in Constantinople and some were imported to the West, as were the doors of Amalfi Cathedral, installed around 1060. These gave rise to a tradition of bronze doors throughout Italy at Verona, Benevento, Monreale, and Pisa during the eleventh and twelfth centuries.

A monumental pair of bronze doors (fig. 85), constituting one of the major pieces of Ottonian sculpture, was cast for Archbishop Bernward of Hildesheim (993–1022) for the Abbey Church of Saint Michael in 1015. These doors were possibly inspired by the doors of S. Sabina or S. Ambrogio seen on one of Bernward's trips to Rome. He may have seen them in 1001, when, as tutor of Otto III and chaplain at the imperial court, he lived in Otto's palace near S. Sabina. Bernward's doors are remarkable because each door is cast in a solid piece with high reliefs of narrative scenes. Previous bronze doors, of which those at Amalfi are representative, had been cast in plaques, or in flat sheets with attached emblematic designs, monograms, crosses, or incised representations, which were then placed over a wooden core. The Hildesheim doors were cast as a unit in the lost-wax process. The upper third of the figures (fig. 86) project at an angle from the background, inspired, perhaps, by the style of detached heads evident on such Roman monuments as the Column of Trajan. Undoubtedly the individual scenes were patterned after miniatures in Carolingian Bibles and in the Ottonian manuscripts derivative from them (see fig. 185, p. 224).

The Hildesheim doors follow a closely organized symbolic program. On the left door the eight panels read downward with scenes from Genesis: "Creation of Eve," "Introduction of Eve to Adam," "Temptation," "God Accusing Adam and Eve," "Expulsion from the Garden of Eden," "Adam Tilling the Soil and Eve Nursing Her Children," "Offerings of Cain and Abel," and "Murder of Abel by Cain." On the right door, the eight panels read upward with scenes from the life of Christ: "Annunciation," "Nativity," "Adoration of the Magi," "Presentation at the Temple," "Christ Brought Before Pilate," "Crucifixion," "Three Marys at the Tomb," and "Noli me tangere," a scene in which the Magdalene sees Christ walking in the garden after his Resurrection and reaches out to touch him, and he responds, "Touch me not, for I am not yet ascended to my father . . ." (John 20:17).

These narrative panels of Old and New Testament incidents are linked horizontally by symbolic implications. For instance, God removing the rib from Adam to create Eve is equated with Christ made whole again, the spirit made flesh after his Resurrection. God introducing Eve to Adam parallels the angelic message

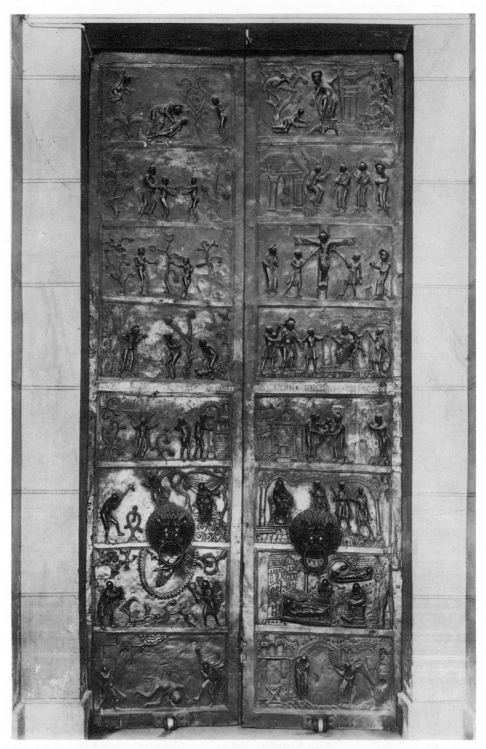

Fig. 85. Bronze doors of Bishop Bernward for Abbey Church of Saint
Michael. 1015. H. 16′ 6″. Cathedral, Hildesheim. (Marburg)

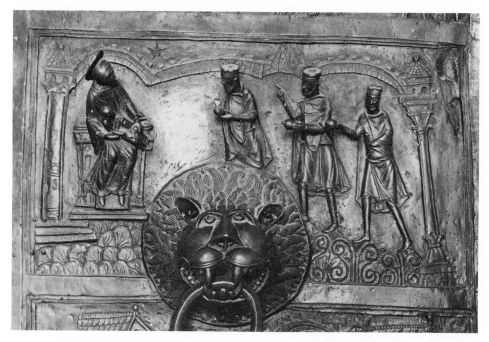

Fig. 86. Detail of "Adoration of the Magi." Bronze doors of Bishop Bernward for Abbey Church of Saint Michael. 1015. Cathedral, Hildesheim. (Marburg)

Fig. 87. Detail of "God Accusing Adam and Eve." Bronze doors of Bishop Bernward for Abbey Church of Saint Michael. 1015. Cathedral, Hildesheim. (Marburg)

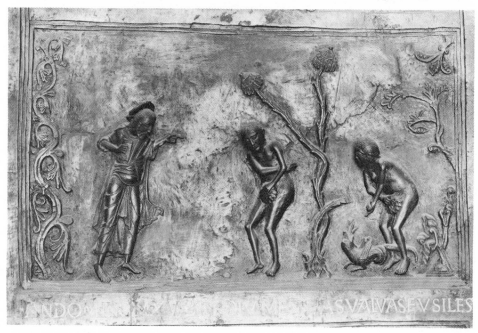

that Christ is risen. In a frequently used parallel, the Temptation is equated with the Crucifixion: the Fall of Man, the first sin, is the reason for the necessity of Christ's sacrifice on the Cross, to redeem man from his fall from grace. God's accusation of Adam and Eve is opposed by mankind's, Pilate's, condemnation of Christ. The expulsion from the Garden of Eden, man's fall from grace, is the opposite of Christ's reception into the Temple, the first step of his ministry. Thus, Old Testament scenes are placed so that they provide visual prefigurations, oppositions, or parallels to the New Testament scenes on the other door.

Individual panels are executed with sensitivity to narrative impact, composition, and psychological insight. In "God Accusing Adam and Eve" (fig. 87), God, leaning forward, rises up on tiptoe in wrath, his finger pointed forcefully at Adam. God's left arm is pulled back, adding additional horizontal force to his gesture, which is echoed by the fluttering hemline below. Adam, crouching in his newfound shame, points under his arm to Eve, saying that it was she who tempted him to disobey God's command. The branches of the tree echo his position and gesture, and the lower branch also points to Eve. She crouches even lower and points to the serpent at her feet. The tree behind Eve emphasizes her stoop, and the curved branches reiterate the position of the serpent to whom, in a very human way, final blame has been transmitted.

In the twelfth century similar narrative doors were made in both northern Europe and Italy, but the Hildesheim doors were the beginning of a new monumental tradition, exercised particularly in regions where it was not customary to adorn the facades or portals with carved stone sculpture.

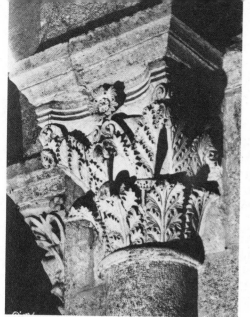

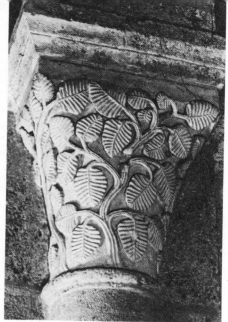

Fig. 88. Corinthian capital. Saint-Andoche, Saulieu, Burgundy. c. 1120. (J. Combier, Mâcon)

Fig. 89. Foliate capital. Saint-Andoche, Saulieu, Burgundy. c. 1120. (R. G. Calkins)

17. THE ROMANESQUE CAPITAL

In a simple system of post-and-lintel architecture the shaft of the vertical support abuts the horizontal member without any visual transition. In order to broaden the area where the load is supported upon a relatively thin column, and to provide a transition from cylindrical support to rectangular or square load as well as from vertical to horizontal, capitals were developed. These take on different forms in various periods of architectural history. The most familiar ones to us today are those that were used in the period of classical antiquity. The flaring, cushionlike Doric capital of archaic Greece makes an empathetic statement of upward thrust of the column and downward load of the supported member. The curled volutes of the Ionic capital above the egg-and-dart decorated band of the *collerette* also give this empathetic effect, although with a more refined and delicate design. The third classical solution was the Corinthian capital, made up of rings of veined, ragged acanthus leaves around a flaring basketlike form. Usually curved tendrils rise up from the mass of foliage to the corners of the flat square block or abacus above, and circular rosettes appear in the middle of each side. This foliate decoration makes a transition from the cylinder of the column to the square abacus beneath the load, and the rising volutes make a supporting statement. Frequently in late antique architecture the Ionic and Corinthian forms were combined in a Composite form.

In the construction of medieval churches, classical ruins were often pillaged, and columns and capitals were frequently reused. Partially as a result of this practice, and partially because so many examples were available to serve as models, some medieval sculptors copied the Roman forms with a fair degree of accuracy. In the church of Saint-Andoche at Saulieu in Burgundy, two tiers of stiff, jagged acanthus leaves make up a Corinthian capital (fig. 88) of Romanesque vintage, lacking only the vitality of a Roman original. Often foliate capitals in Romanesque churches did not follow classical models. Another capital (fig. 89) at Saulieu contains a freely meandering vine of strongly ribbed leaves closely adhering to the surface of its flaring basketlike form.

An innovation in the design of the capital (fig. 90) was made in Archbishop Bernward's Abbey Church of Saint Michael at Hildesheim in the early years of the eleventh century. A half sphere, corresponding with the cylindrical shaft below, was cut to form a cube above, relating to the square abacus, impost block, and archivolt on top. This simple fusion of sphere and cube, known as a *cushion capital*, stated with abstract, crystalline clarity the geometric transition from cylin-

Fig. 90. Cushion capital. Abbey Church of Saint Michael, Hildesheim. 1010–1033. (Marburg)

Fig. 91. Hartmanus: inhabited capital, trumeau. Domkapelle, Goslar. c. 1150. (R. G. Calkins)

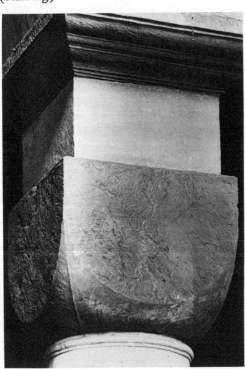

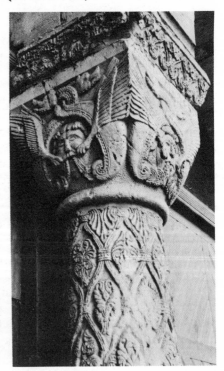

der to rectangular volume. In Ottonian churches this pure geometric form of the cushion capital was frequently used unadorned. But it also provided fields for sculptural relief, as evidenced by a capital carved by Hartmanus (fig. 91) on the trumeau of the portal to the Domkapelle of around 1150 at Goslar, West Germany. Here, the upraised wings of interlocked dragons meet at the upper corners and act visually to enhance the supporting function. In a similar capital of around 1120 in the crypt of Canterbury Cathedral (fig. 92) the composition is freer. A dogheaded, dragonlike creature prances to the left across the face of the capital, turning back to spear the dog leaping to the right. The sweeping movement and countermovement of these animals echo the curving shape of the capital without being constrained by it as at Goslar. In contrast to the foliate capitals at Saulieu, these are *inhabited capitals,* peopled with human figures or animals, sometimes entwined within plant forms, but not depicting any particular incident.

In the Romanesque period in particular the capital assumes a new and important function as a vehicle for narrative sculpture. Frequently on the columns running down the length of the nave and the aisles as well as on those separating

Fig. 92. Inhabited capital, crypt. Canterbury Cathedral. c. 1120. (R. G. Calkins)

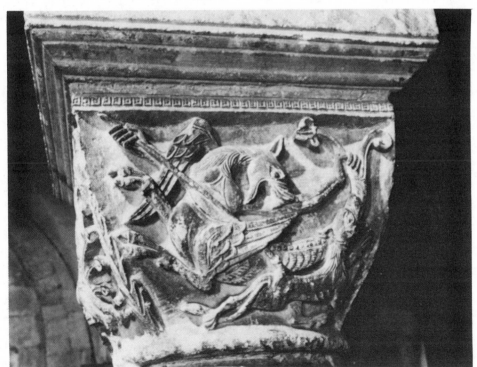

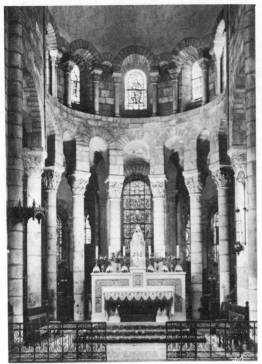 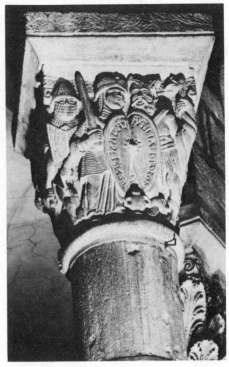

Fig. 93. Master Robert of Clermont: ambulatory capitals. Notre-Dame-du-Port, Clermont-Ferrand. c.1150.(S.P.A.D.E.M.)

Fig. 94. Master Robert of Clermont: "Battle of the Virtue of Charity Against the Vice of Avarice." Notre-Dame-du-Port, Clermont-Ferrand. c. 1150. (R. G. Calkins)

the sanctuary from the ambulatory, the capitals were carved with scenes of biblical incidents, allegories, or personifications. In the ambulatory of the church of Notre-Dame-du-Port at Clermont-Ferrand (fig. 93) capitals carved around 1130 by Master Robert of Clermont consist of foliate examples interspersed by *historiated* ones. On the face of one of these (fig. 94) we find a female clad in chain mail with a shield confronting a half-nude bearded man. As the inscriptions on their shields make clear, this is the "Battle of the Virtue of Charity Against the Vice of Avarice" from the *Psychomachia* by Prudentius. The placement of such a representation within the Romanesque church serves the same function as those on the archivolts at Saint-Pierre at Aulnay, a reminder to the beholder of the ever constant battle of the virtues against the vices.

An ideal placement for the historiated capital recounting the incidents of the Bible was on the columns engaged against the nave piers of the Romanesque church. As the pilgrims proceeded down either the nave or the aisles, they would see a multitude of scenes that amplified the narrative content of the portal sculpture they had just passed. Every Romanesque church is different in its choice of theme for the portal or arrangement of the capitals within, yet the stories are told simply and directly.

The capitals at Saulieu, which may date around 1120, may have been influenced in part by capitals in the nearby cathedral of Saint-Lazare at Autun, which were carved by Gislebertus, the sculptor who had also carved the Autun tympanum. A "Flight into Egypt" at Saulieu (fig. 95) shows the Virgin and Child riding a donkey on the principal face of the capital while Joseph, tucked around the left corner, carries a sack over his shoulder and leads the animal with a rope. This composition is similar to a capital by Gislebertus at Autun. The figures are placed before an elaborate and deeply carved vine scroll that virtually dissolves the basic shape of the capital.

An effective use of the shape of the capital for narrative purposes may be seen in another capital at Saulieu, that of "Balaam and the Ass" (fig. 96). Balaam was a false prophet in the Old Testament who disobeyed God's commandment to cease preaching untruths. One day when Balaam set out to a neighboring city to make prophecies, the Lord sent down an angel who barred the way. The ass Balaam was riding saw the angel and stopped, but because Balaam did not see him, he beat his animal to make him go forward. Finally the ass turned to Balaam and told him that his path was blocked by the angel of the Lord, whereupon Balaam saw the angel and repented of his ways. In the capital the angel is situated

Fig. 95. "Flight into Egypt," capital. Saint-Andoche, Saulieu, Burgundy. c. 1120. (R. G. Calkins)

Fig. 96. "Balaam and the Ass," capital. Saint-Andoche, Saulieu, Burgundy. c. 1120. (R. G. Calkins)

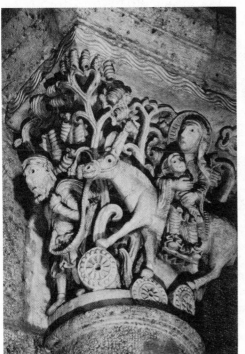

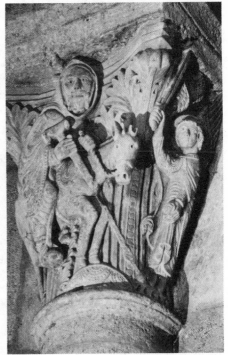

around the corner from Balaam, out of his sight, and only the ass, whose head projects beyond the corner, can see him. Balaam's blank-eyed stare and the staff he holds emphasize that he is blind to God's messenger. The doleful expression of the donkey emphasizes his plight as he turns to inform his master of the situation. The physical properties of the capital were used to heighten the impact of the story. In addition to its moralizing content the capital may have had another message as well: it may be directed against the many heresies that were abundant in France in the twelfth century, thus warning the beholder not to believe in the current false preachings.

The historiated capitals were deliberate and careful extensions of the narrative scheme and must be considered in the same context as the carved portals. Seen as a whole, the church became a vehicle for the visual narrative of biblical incidents and Christian moralizations for the benefit of a congregation that could not read. But the populace would recognize the scenes from the readings of the lessons and the sermons of the clergy and they would be reminded of their content and meaning. And even if the congregation could not see all of the historiated capitals, for some of them were high up under the springing of dimly lit vaults, they and the monks tending the church would know that they were there and that God's house was embellished with the appropriate decoration.

Frequently, however, foliate capitals, such as the Corinthian example at Saulieu, were richly carved, and most of the inhabited capitals became so fanciful that any biblical content seems impossible. At Saulieu one capital contains a gilded centaur with a bow and arrow (fig. 97), a motif ultimately derived from Greek mythology and usually having lascivious connotations, but here probably having the connotation of the sign of the zodiac, Sagittarius. Elsewhere, centaurs appearing on capitals served to remind the congregation of man's base, animal instincts, which must be subdued. The clawing lions on a capital (fig. 98) at Saint-Michel-de-Cuxa in the Pyrenees of southern France may also reflect the brute forces of nature or the daemonic forces of evil, but as they are contained by the shape of the capital and are physically forced to support the fabric of the church, they are symbolically subdued by it.

Although the "Centaur" capital was repainted in the nineteenth century, it serves as an indication of what much of Romanesque sculpture may have looked like, for capitals and portal sculpture were often polychromed. Instead of the pleasing aesthetic of raw stone and subtle plays of light and shadow we see now, many of the sculptures would have been brightly, even garishly colored. Capitals at Issoire and vestiges of polychrome on the tympanum at Conques suggest that this practice may have been widespread.

The centaur may have been an explicit symbol of evil, but many of the other hybrid animals and monsters became marvels of ferocity and contortion. They not only abounded in the churches, but also on the capitals of the cloisters of monasteries. In an example in the cloister at Cuxa (fig. 99) heads of lions biting a pair of detached legs appear beneath the corner volutes while a half-nude figure stands between them. In another capital at Cuxa (fig. 98) we find a procession of lions clawing the backs of the ones in front. The prevalence of these inhabited

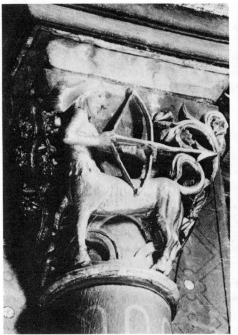

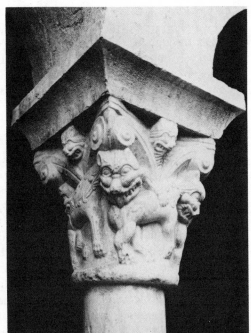

Fig. 97. "Centaur (Sagittarius)," capital. Saint-Andoche, Saulieu, Burgundy. c. 1120. (R. G. Calkins)

Fig. 98. Inhabited capital. Saint-Michel-de-Cuxa, cloister, southern France. 12th century. (R. G. Calkins)

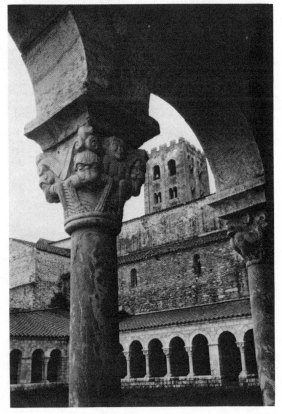

Fig. 99. Inhabited capital and cloister. Saint-Michel-de-Cuxa, southern France. 12th century. (R. G. Calkins)

capitals throughout the monasteries of Western Europe in the twelfth century led to a severe and violent reaction. Saint Bernard of Clairvaux, one of the early members of the Cistercian movement, which broke away from the Cluniac order, wrote a famous letter in which he castigated the monks for allowing such representations in their midst:

> But in the cloister, under the eyes of the Brethren who read there, what profit is there in those ridiculous monsters, in that marvelous and deformed comeliness, that comely deformity? To what purpose are those unclean apes, those fierce lions, those monstrous centaurs, those half-men, those striped tigers, those fighting knights, those hunters winding their horns? Many bodies are there seen under one head, or again many heads to a single body. Here is a four-footed beast with a serpent's tail; there, a fish with a beast's head. Here again the forepart of a horse trails half a goat behind it, or a horned beast bears the hindquarters of a horse. In short, so many and so marvelous are the varieties of divers shapes on every hand, that we are more tempted to read in the marble than in our books, and to spend the whole day in wondering at these things rather than in meditating the law of God. For God's sake if men are not ashamed of these follies, why at least do they not shrink from the expense?

It is evident from the quality of language that Saint Bernard used that he, too, was susceptible to the attractions of such sculpture, for his phrasing captures the essence of form and counterform, of fugal convolution and inversion, found in the interlocked members of the sculpted monsters.

As a result, the Cistercians renounced the elaborate figurative, foliate, and historiated capitals of the Cluniac order and resorted to simple, pristine, unarticulated foliate decorations. It is this more austere trend that, although it does not supplant the richly carved Romanesque capital, provides the genesis for a new, simple foliate capital that will be used in the Gothic period.

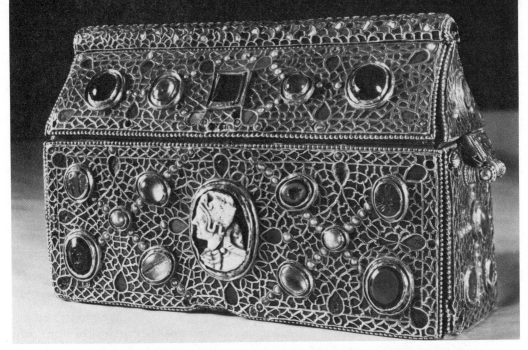

Fig. 100. Undiho and Ello: Shrine of Saint Maurice made for Theuderich. 7th century. Abbaye de Saint-Maurice-d'Agaune, Switzerland. Cloisonné enamel and semiprecious stones. H. 5″, L. 7⅜″, W. 2⅝″.

18. METALWORK OF THE CHURCH TREASURIES

Many of the decorative motifs and techniques found in objects of Romanesque metalwork are a continuation of motifs and techniques used in the fabrication of artifacts found in barbarian graves. At the same time we find the development of new techniques, a new repertoire of objects for devotional and liturgical use, and a reuse of familiar motifs in a new way

The reuse of artifacts from a previous period may be seen in the Cross of Lothair II (pl. 8) in the Cathedral Treasury in Aachen. Made around 1000, possibly for Otto III, this cross consists of sheets of gold over a wooden core inset with semiprecious stones, gold filigree work, a Carolingian seal from the reign of Lothair II (855–869), and a magnificent Roman sardonyx cameo of the Emperor Augustus crowned with a laurel wreath and holding an eagle scepter. Both the seal and the cameo lend legitimacy to this imperial Ottonian object, establishing the direct line of succession back through the Carolingian to the Roman Empire. In spite of the fact that the cameo was a pagan and secular object, its inclusion on the cross was undoubtedly meant to signify that the emperor was the earthly representative of the divine power of God above.

In the reliquary casket made for Theuderich (fig. 100) at the Abbaye de Saint-Maurice-d'Agaune in Switzerland we find a profusion of antique seals set in the surface along with semiprecious stones. Both were meant to enhance the beauty of this rectangular box with a gabled roof that contained relics of Saint Maurice. The cameo in the center is a seventh-century copy of an antique cameo in which the features of the human face are crudely executed. Nevertheless, it too must have been regarded as a valuable object worthy of being placed upon the container for venerated relics. The metal plaques covering a wooden core are divided into little cells containing cloisonné enamel, a technique that was used with great profusion on the artifacts from Sutton Hoo. This casket is remarkable not only for its early date and its continuation of the cloisonné-enamel technique but also because it was signed by its makers, Undiho and Ello, and by its donor: "Theuderich the priest had this made in honor of St. Maurice."

The shape of the reliquary casket, a rectangular box with a gabled roof, was undoubtedly derived from the similar form of sarcophagi. As they usually held a relic of a saint, a member, a bone, or an organ, they performed, on a smaller scale, a similar function. But their main purpose was to house the relic in a place where it could be venerated, usually on an altar of one of the chapels of a Romanesque church. By the eleventh and twelfth centuries the cult of relics had grown to such proportions that it was responsible for the evolution of the radial plan in church architecture. Pilgrims on their way to Rome or Santiago de Compostela made it a point to visit renowned relics in the churches along the way, with resultant economic benefit to those monasteries where they stopped. Sometimes in their zeal to advance the reputation of their monastery, monks stole relics from neighboring churches, as in the case of the relics of Sainte Foy, which the monks of Conques stole from Agen in the ninth century.

The shape of the reliquary casket was also similar to that of a building, particularly the shape of a church. This connection is made explicit in a German reliquary of around 1190 (fig. 101) in the Victoria and Albert Museum in London. But as the reliquary can be thought of as a miniature church, so the Romanesque pilgrimage church can be thought of as a monumental reliquary (fig. 102), containing not one, but many relics within its radial chapels. This connotation must be equated with the role of the church as a beacon and refuge in the landscape for the traveling pilgrim, as a proud and militant force with the inception of the crusades, and as a vehicle for living dogma in its decoration.

A variety of new techniques of metalwork and types of objects were developed in the Romanesque period. A reliquary casket in The Metropolitan Museum of Art (pl. 9) contains, on its front side, Christ on the Cross flanked by the Virgin and Saint John and four apostles standing beneath an arcade. On the sloping roof, in the celestial realm, Christ is enthroned in a mandorla surrounded by the four attributes of the Evangelists, again flanked by apostles within arcades. The gilt-copper background was tooled to create foliate designs called *vermiculé*. The figures, however, are executed in enamel that has been placed in a shallow basin hollowed out of the plaque. The name of this technique, *champlevé* enamel, or "raised field," refers to the area that is not enameled or "in reserve." Occasional gold striations across the body of Christ to indicate drapery folds have the appearance of cloisonné enamel but are actually in reserve.

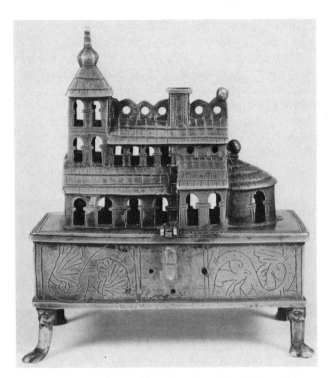

Fig. 101. Reliquary in the shape of a church. Germany. c. 1190. H. 6¾″. Victoria and Albert Museum, London. (Crown Copyright)

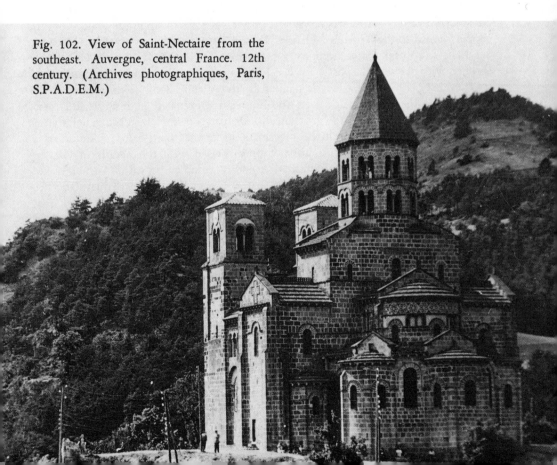

Fig. 102. View of Saint-Nectaire from the southeast. Auvergne, central France. 12th century. (Archives photographiques, Paris, S.P.A.D.E.M.)

On a reliquary casket in the Musée de Cluny (pl. 10) depicting the martyrdom of Thomas à Becket, the background is enameled in blue and the figures are left in reserve. They were incised to indicate drapery folds, features, and decorative bands, and then gilt. The heads of the figures are in relief. Sometimes these were cast separately and riveted to the plaques. The tricolored patterns were formed by placing dark blue, light blue, and white enamel together and then firing them. In contrast with the cloisonné enamel and with the plaques with gilt, incised backgrounds and enameled figures, the simplified technique of executing figures in reserve with broader, more uniform areas of background color allowed for virtual mass production of these objects during the thirteenth century. Since many of the champlevé-enamel artifacts were made in the region of Limoges, they are frequently referred to by the generic name "Limoges" enamels, although some of them may have been made elsewhere, particularly in Spain.

The reliquary casket depicting the martyrdom of Thomas à Becket (pl. 10) retains the simplified churchlike shape set on four legs. On the lower side two assailants attack Archbishop Thomas à Becket at a transept altar in Canterbury Cathedral. This event took place on December 29, 1170, and Becket's subsequent canonization in 1173 raised this heinous crime to the status of martyrdom and provided the inspiration for frequent representations of this event. The cult of Saint Thomas quickly spread across Europe after the exhumation of his remains in 1220. On the sloping roof two acolytes place the archbishop in his sarcophagus.

In contrast to the Saint Thomas casket, a reliquary made in honor of Sainte Fauste (pl. 11) contains figures on the principal side in appliqué reliefs of gilt copper riveted to the enameled plaque. The casket thus becomes a vehicle for more emphatic sculptural representations. On the roof Christ in Majesty is depicted enthroned with six seated apostles in a celestial realm, while beneath, on the terrestrial level, Christ on the Cross is flanked by the Virgin, Saint John, and six other apostles. On the reverse, however, the figures are executed in reserve and relate the tortures of Sainte Fauste's martyrdom. On the principal face the relief figures retain the frontality and even the placement in arcades of the Romanesque style, although the cylindrical forms are not only incised with the details of drapery folds but also modulated to indicate the bodily volumes beneath. Although executed well into Gothic period, possibly in the 1240s, this casket displays the prevailing conservatism that persisted in many of the Limoges enamels.

In addition to reliquary caskets, a variety of other metalwork objects were manufactured for Christian usage. One class of artifacts made for use in the Mass are called eucharistic vessels because they served a function in the celebration of Holy Communion. Chalices were made to hold and serve the wine; plates or patens held the unleavened bread; altar cruets or ewers held wine and water, which were mixed in the chalice; round boxes or pyxes (*ciboria*) and sometimes hollow doves suspended above the altar served to store the Host when not in use.

The enameled eucharistic dove (fig. 103), a symbol of the Holy Ghost, was a particularly fitting object for housing the Host. Usually it was suspended above the altar, sometimes beneath a small votive crown. A wing or the back might be hinged so that the Host could be placed within its hollow interior. The smoothly

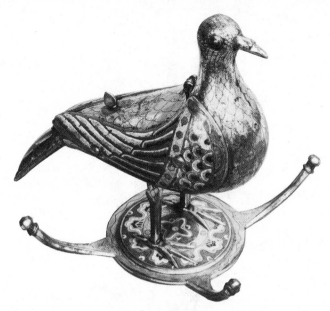

Fig. 103. Eucharistic dove. France. 13th century. Gilt bronze with champlevé enamel, 7″ x 9″. Albright-Knox Art Gallery, Buffalo, New York.

shaped form of a eucharistic dove in the Albright-Knox Art Gallery, Buffalo, is gilded and incised with an overlapping scalelike pattern to suggest feathers on the body, while champlevé-enamel roundels and stripes indicate the feathers on the wings. Sensitively and engagingly executed, Limoges enamel doves were most popular in the late twelfth and thirteenth centuries.

A variety of other liturgical objects also served important roles. Liturgical combs and ewers were used in the ceremonial cleansing and preparation before the Mass. Processional crosses, such as the Cross of Lothair, and crosiers, crooked staffs carried by bishops as symbols of their role as the shepherds of their flock, were carried triumphantly in processionals and recessionals.

Candlesticks, often made of gilded bronze, were usually placed upon the high altar. One of the most elaborate surviving examples is the Gloucester candlestick (fig. 104) in the Victoria and Albert Museum, London, one of a pair made between 1104 and 1113 for the church of Saint Peter's at Gloucester. Approximately twenty-three inches high, it consists of an intricate design of inhabited vine scrolls rising from three dragon-headed feet through a pyramidal base, up a vertical shaft with a knob to the grease pan, which is supported by three more dragons. Cast in the lost-wax process, it depicts a variety of humans and animals seemingly enmeshed in the tentaclelike tendrils, much like the ones found in inhabited Romanesque capitals. The knob on the shaft, however, contains the representations of the four attributes of the Evangelists, and just above, a figure climbs through the vine toward the grease pan, which contains the inscription "The debt of Life is the practice of Virtue." The figure of mankind caught in the chaos of the world, striving toward the "true light," which would have been physically present in the form of a lighted candle, recalls the message of the Romanesque portals: man must break away from the enmeshing vices of the world and continually strive toward virtue and thereby toward the life everlasting.

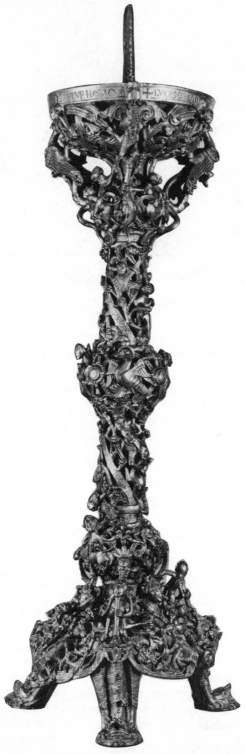

Fig. 104. Gloucester candlestick. England. 1104–1113. Gilt bronze, H. 23″.
Victoria and Albert Museum, London. (Crown Copyright)

Bookcovers set with precious stones and covered in gold plaques with figures in low *repoussé* relief constitute some of the most splendid objects of medieval metalwork. A Carolingian bookcover made for a gospel book of Charles the Bald (pl. 26), now in Munich, contains Christ in Majesty surrounded by scenes of his ministry. Many of the jewels are placed in settings that have an architectural form, miniature arcades topped by the domelike surface of the stones. These settings constitute miniature visions of the heavenly city of Jerusalem, and the substances of the stones themselves take on symbolic meaning: red rubies are equated with the blood of the martyrs, and white pearls or transparent crystal with the purity of the Virgin.

Such resplendent objects of expensive materials and exquisite workmanship in monastic treasuries incurred the stern admonition of Saint Bernard of Clairvaux:

> But I say, as a monk, ask of my brother monks. . . . "Tell me, ye poor men . . . (if indeed ye be poor), what doeth this gold in *your* sanctuary?" And indeed the bishops have an excuse which monks have not; for we know that they, being debtors to both the wise and the unwise, and unable to excite the devotion of carnal folk by spiritual things, do so by bodily ornaments. But we [monks] who have now come forth from the people; we who have left all the precious and beautiful things of the world for Christ's sake what profits, I say, do we expect therefrom? . . . [Men's] eyes are feasted with relics cased in gold; and their purse strings are loosed. They are shown a most comely image of some saint, whom they think all the more saintly that he is the more gaudily painted. Men run to kiss him, and are invited to give; there is more admiration for his comeliness than veneration for his sanctity. Hence the church is adorned with gemmed crowns of light—nay, with lustres like cart wheels, girt all round with lamps, but no less brilliant with the precious stones that stud them. Moreover, we see candelabra standing like trees of massive bronze, fashioned with marvelous subtlety of art, and glistening no less brightly with gems than the lights they carry. . . . The church is resplendent in her walls, beggarly in her poor; she clothes her stones in gold, and leaves her sons naked; the rich man's eye is fed at the expense of the indigent. . . . For God's sake, if men are not ashamed of these follies, why at least do they not shrink from the expense?

But long-standing tradition had made such sumptuous objects a real and necessary part of the Christian ritual. A miniature in the Uta Gospels (fig. 105) produced at Saint Emmeram in Regensburg between 1002 and 1025 shows the role of liturgical objects in the ecclesiastical hierarchy. Above the high altar hangs a small votive crown and below it leans a rectangular object, actually the Codex Aureus of Saint Emmeram, which was originally made for Charles the Bald, with its bejeweled cover. Next to it is the architectural form of the two-story ciborium of King Arnulf (fig. 106), today in the Treasury of the Residenz, Munich, which was meant to house the paten with the Host (shown to the right) and the chalice with the wine beneath another votive crown. These were all real revered objects bequeathed to Saint Emmeram by King Arnulf of Bavaria at the end of the ninth century and used in the celebration of the Mass. Through the persons of the deacon and of the high priest one had access to God ultimately through the divine objects that housed his word, his flesh and his blood. No luxury was too great to adorn these visual manifestations of a higher purpose.

The most effective statement of the higher value of lavish altar furnishings, which serves as a rebuttal to Saint Bernard's point of view, was made by his illustrious contemporary, Abbot Suger of Saint-Denis. His patronage was responsible for the rebuilding of the royal Abbey of Saint-Denis, resulting in the first example of the Gothic style. Suger's desire to embellish the new abbey went beyond the mere architectural fabric to the provision of new liturgical objects, new reliquaries, chalices, and altar frontals. The abbot recorded all his accomplishments in his book, *On What Was Done Under His Administration.* In this he reflected typically twelfth-century views, but his reasons given for the rich adornment of the new furnishings of the abbey reflect the traditional attitude concerning the decoration of religious objects. According to Suger, the new cast and gilded doors "being nobly

Fig. 105. Liturgical objects on high altar of Saint Emmeram, Regensburg. Mass of St. Erhard, Uta Codex. Regensburg. 1002–1025. 15" x 10⅝". Bayerische Staatsbibliothek (Clm. 13601, fol. 4), Munich.

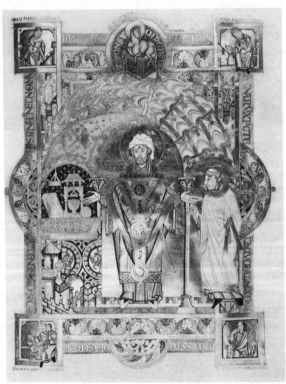

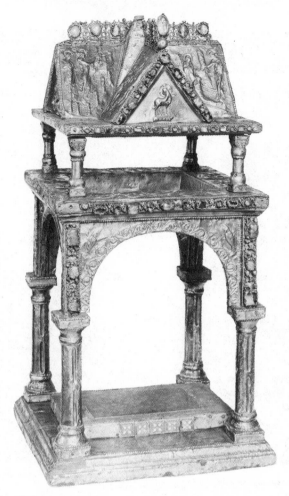

Fig. 106. Ciborium of King Arnulf of Bavaria. Reims (?). c. 870. Gold and precious stones, H. 23¼". Schatzkammer, Residenz, Munich.

bright . . . should brighten the minds so that they may travel through the true lights to the True Light where Christ is the true door." Such embellishment to illumine the mind and to encourage lofty thoughts was also carried out on the high altar, of which Suger wrote:

> Often we contemplate out of sheer affection for the church our mother, these different ornaments, both new and old. . . . Thus, when—out of my delight in the beauty of the house of God—the loveliness of the many colored gems has called me away from external cares, and worthy meditation has induced me to reflect, transferring that which is material to that which is immaterial, on the diversity of the sacred virtues; then it seems to me that I see myself dwelling, as it were, in some strange region of the universe which neither exists entirely in the slime of the earth nor in the purity of Heaven; and that by the grace of God, I can be transported from this inferior to that higher world in an anagogical manner.

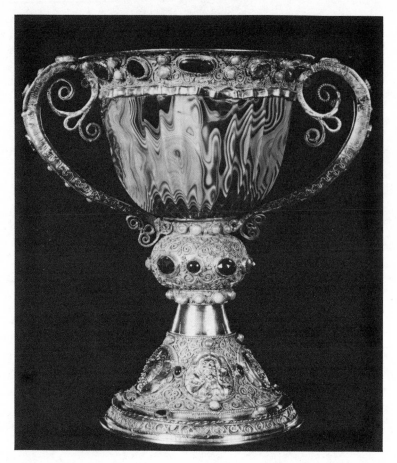

Fig. 107. Chalice of Abbot Suger of Saint Denis. French. c. 1140. Sardonyx, gold, silver gilt, gems, and pearls, H. $7\frac{17}{32}$". National Gallery of Art (Widener Collection, 1942), Washington, D.C.

The chalice of Abbot Suger (fig. 107), now in the National Gallery in Washington, D.C., was acquired by the abbot and its carved Roman sardonyx bowl was reset into a new mount. This object, set upon the high altar, as well as the resplendent reliquaries, gleaming processional crosses, multicolored enamel eucharistic doves, or the sparkling lights of a bishop's crosier, was appropriately "nobly bright" and served to "brighten the minds" of the beholder.

But these objects, too, must be seen in the context of the Romanesque church for which they were intended. Not only were they ceremonial and symbolic objects serving at the very focal point of private devotions and of the Mass, they, too, were vehicles of communication, relating the stories of martyrdoms and restating dogma. Indeed, the workmanship of some of these artifacts, small in comparison with the scale of a building or of a portal, nevertheless constitutes some of the most important stylistic and iconographical statements of the medieval period. They embody the higher significance of Christian ritual.

19. MOSAN METALWORK

Nowhere is metalwork more important than in the productions of another school of artists situated in the Meuse and Rhine valleys along the borders of present-day France, Belgium, and Germany, particularly at Liège and Cologne. Here, in the twelfth century, we find innovations in sculptural form that foreshadow stylistic developments on a more monumental scale well into the thirteenth century. Although we have seen nascent forms of relief used on caskets from southwestern France around Limoges, Mosan artisans developed a new sensitivity to human anatomy and volumetric forms and new ways of using champlevé enamel.

The ciborium of King Arnulf and the bookcover of the Codex Aureus of Saint Emmeram, mentioned previously, although produced in the late Carolingian period are both fine examples of the delicate technique of *repoussé* work, the manner of modeling or articulating the surface of the metal by pushing out the image from behind. On the sloping roofs of the ciborium (fig. 108) the relief is very slight, and the figures are agile and subtle. The "Temptation of Christ," where Christ refuses to turn stones into loaves of bread and tells the Devil that Man cannot live by bread alone, is a fitting symbolic complement to the function of the ciborium, which houses the bread of the Eucharist.

The golden altar frontal (*antependium*) executed around 1019 for the Basel Cathedral (pl. 12) is a monumental example of repoussé metalwork. Scaled larger than the other figures, Christ stands in the center arch flanked by three archangels, Michael, Gabriel, and Raphael, and Saint Benedict in smaller arcades while the diminutive figures of Emperor Henry II and his Empress Kunigunde kneel at his feet. The elongated forms of the standing figures swell smoothly out from the surface of the gold, their gently curving surfaces in turn articulated by eddying circles of folds about smooth ovoid islands over the knees or thighs. The scale is larger and the relief considerably deeper than the repoussé work on the ciborium. Although the volumes curve behind the figures before abutting the background and the heads are practically detached, the forms seem held in by an invisible force in the same manner as the early Romanesque sculpture at Toulouse. Nevertheless, as in stone sculpture, a process of detachment has begun, as well as an ability to evoke an overwhelming sense of ethereal presence and monumentality with restricted means in a precious metal.

In contrast with these earlier Carolingian and Ottonian works, a large bronze baptismal font (figs. 109, 110) commissioned by Abbot Hellin between 1107 and 1118 for the Cathedral of Notre Dame in Liège from the Mosan metalworker, Rainer of Huy, broke away from the spiritualized abstractions of the Romanesque style and introduced a new sensitivity to the human form. The large basin was originally supported upon the backs of twelve oxen (only ten survive), a reference to the lustral fountain by Hiram of Tyre in the court of the Temple of Solomon

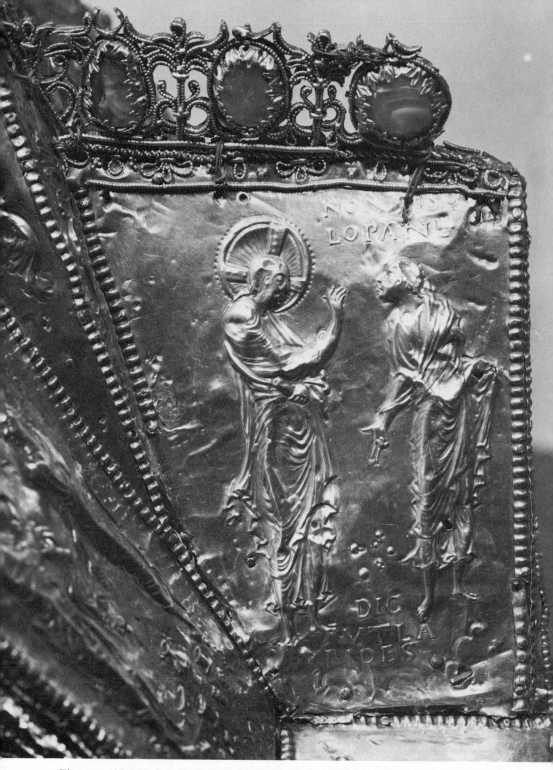

Fig. 108. "Temptation of Christ," detail. Roof of ciborium of King Arnulf. Reims(?). c. 870. Repoussé gold. Schatzkammer, Residenz, Munich.

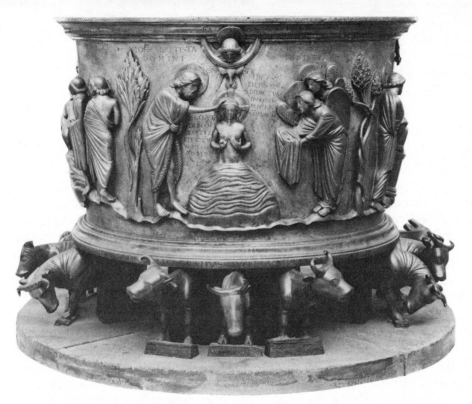

Fig. 109. Rainer of Huy: "Baptism of Christ." Baptismal font from Notre-Dame-aux-Fonts. 1107–1118. Bronze, H. 23⅝", Diam. 31½". Saint-Barthélemy, Liège. (Marburg)

Fig. 110. Rainer of Huy: "John the Baptist Baptizing Publicans." Baptismal font from Notre-Dame-aux-Fonts. 1107–1118. Bronze, H. 23⅝", Diam. 31½". Saint-Barthélemy, Liège. (Rheinisches Bildarchiv)

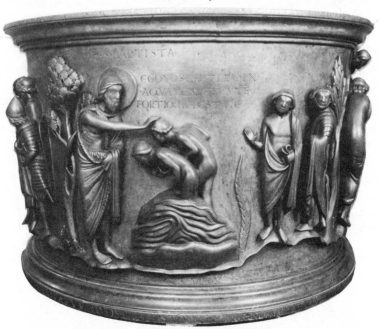

in Jerusalem, and perhaps also to the twelve apostles. The basin contains reliefs of ministry and baptism: "Saint John Preaching in the Desert," "Saint Peter Baptizing the Centurion Cornelius and the Philosopher Craton," symbolizing Rome and Greece receiving the Word of God, and "Saint John Baptizing Christ," which begins his Christian ministry. The figures are executed in high relief, and the smooth, buttery modeling of their bodies accurately reflects soft human flesh. Draperies are pulled taut over legs and shoulders, revealing the volumes of limbs beneath. The movements and gestures of the figures are natural, and the apprehensive, inquisitive glances of publicans waiting to be baptized reveal a psychological understanding of human reactions. Although the scene of the "Baptism of Christ" closely follows compositions in Byzantine art, with the frontal placement of Christ, the skirtlike arrangement of the River Jordan, and the two attendant angels holding his clothing, the forms are suffused with a generalization of features and idealization of form that approximate the effects of classical art of which Rainer of Huy may have been aware.

Undoubtedly the most innovative of the Mosan metalworkers was Nicholas of Verdun. In 1181 Provost Werner of the Abbey of Klosterneuburg dedicated a large champlevé-enamel pulpit containing a vast array of enamel plaques of Old and New Testament scenes. After a fire in 1331, the plaques were rearranged into a large *retable,* or altarpiece, which today is placed behind an altar. The fifty-one plaques are arranged to read in seventeen vertical rows of three scenes each. The top row presents Old Testament scenes *ante legem,* before Moses brings the Ten Commandments to the Israelites, and the bottom row contains Old Testament scenes after that moment. Both rows offer prefigurations for the middle row, which contains scenes from the life of Christ, when, during his ministry, he establishes the new order of the Christian church. Thus in one of the vertical rows we have scenes that prefigure the "Baptism of Christ" (figs. 111–113): in the upper row the miraculous salvation of the Israelites by the parting of the waters of the Red Sea as they flee from Egypt, and in the bottom row, the "Lustral Basin" for purification on the backs of twelve oxen. This latter, of course, was the underlying iconography of the Liège font of Rainer of Huy, and refers to the purification of the devout before entering the Temple. The "Crossing of the Red Sea," resulting in the subsequent salvation of the Israelites, is referred to as a "mystical baptism" in the accompanying inscription. The scene anticipates the Baptism of Christ by which he is received into grace and establishes the Sacrament by which man can also attain salvation. The entire altarpiece, therefore, is a vehicle for the intricate interweaving of two Old Testament precedents that serve to amplify and explain a Christological episode.

The iconographical program is sophisticated and the scale is immense. In addition, Nicholas of Verdun used the technique of champlevé enamel in a new way. Backgrounds were filled with blue enamel, and although the figures were left in reserve, they were articulated by incising them with broad tapering lines for draperies and filling them with enamel. The effect is one of a painted surface in which agile lines and elastic, tapering folds modulate the form, giving the illusion

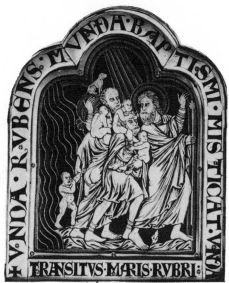

Fig. 111. Nicholas of Verdun: "Crossing of the Red Sea," detail of the Klosterneuburg altarpiece. 1181. Gold with enamel, 8″ x 6⁷⁄₁₆″. Stiftsmuseum, Klosterneuburg.

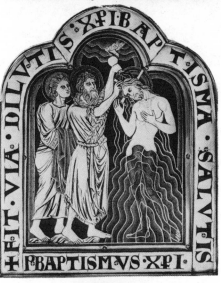

Fig. 112. Nicholas of Verdun: "Baptism of Christ," detail of the Klosterneuburg altarpiece. 1181. Gold with enamel, 8″ x 6⁷⁄₁₆″. Stiftsmuseum, Klosterneuburg.

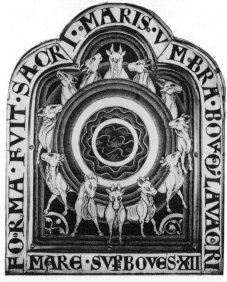

Fig. 113. Nicholas of Verdun: "Twelve Oxen and Lustral Basin," detail of the Klosterneuburg altarpiece. 1181. Gold with enamel, 8″ x 6⁷⁄₁₆″. Stiftsmuseum, Klosterneuburg.

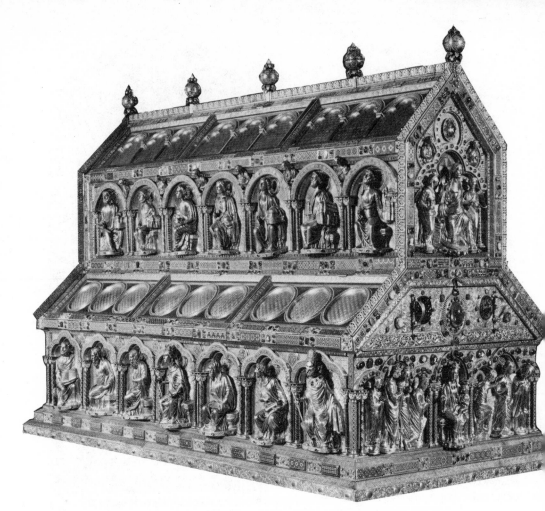

Fig. 114. Nicholas of Verdun and workshop: "Shrine of the Three Magi."
Cologne. c. 1181–1230. Silver and gilt bronze with enamel and gems, H. 68",
L. 72", W. 44". Cathedral Treasury, Cologne. (Rheinisches Bildarchiv)

of broadly modeled figures. The folds curve around the edges, giving the illusion
of depth, and shoulders, knees, and thighs seem to push through the drapery,
smoothing out the wrinkles and defining the form beneath. The breadth of forms,
the generalized features, and particularly the multiple-fold style of drapery closely
approximate the effect of classical statuary, and it is possible that Nicholas derived
inspiration from some examples of classical art that he saw in the twelfth century.

This style of enamelwork is a graphic equivalent of the intense, powerful
figures Nicholas created as virtually three-dimensional figures in silver and gilt
bronze for the "Shrine of the Three Magi" (fig. 114), which he and his workshop
worked on in Cologne from 1181 into the thirteenth century. This large, sumptuous
reliquary casket, now in the Cathedral Treasury in Cologne, is a two-story structure with figures of prophets and apostles set into the three-lobed arcades of the
sides. The features are heavily modeled (fig. 115), the pupils of the eyes drilled,

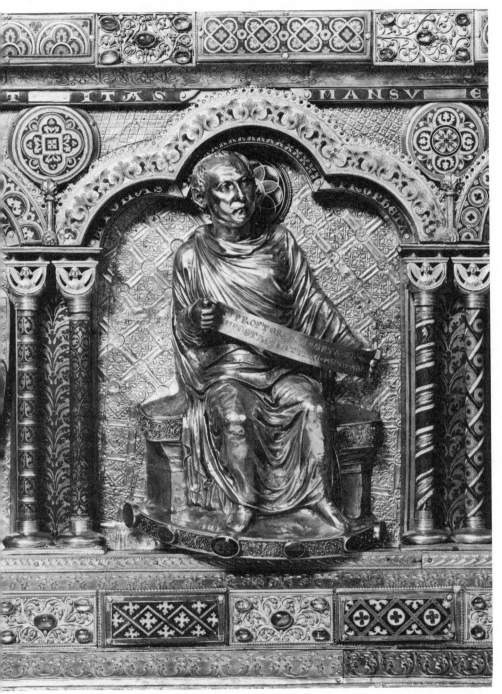

Fig. 115. Nicholas of Verdun and workshop: "Prophet Jonah," detail of "Shrine of the Three Magi." Cologne. c. 1181–1191. Silver and gilt bronze with enamel and gems. Cathedral Treasury, Cologne. (Rheinisches Bildarchiv)

and the faces often surrounded by cascades of curly hair and beards, as is often found in Late Roman portraiture. The draperies are corrugated with restless but meaningful folds pulled taut over projecting limbs and revealing the form beneath. The bodies are boldly modeled, only slighty engaged against the decorative background, and they frequently twist, lean, or gesticulate out from the enclosing arcade. The effect of detachment is further increased by the contrast of the activated contours of the figures with the geometric or foliate designs of the background. These figures have become three-dimensional pieces of sculpture, placed within the blind arcades. The monumental casket still combines the connotations of sepulcher and church as reliquary, but has become more recognizable as architecture. The new depth of relief, freedom of movement, and intense projection of personality remove these figures from the opposition of constraint and energy that characterizes so much of Romanesque sculpture.

These works by Nicholas of Verdun exist in neither the Romanesque period nor the Gothic, but in a transitional area between them. The energy and robustness of the Romanesque are still evident, but with a new sense of humanity, compassion, and psychological content that heralds the beginning of the new era. In fact, this classicizing style spread throughout northern Europe in the last decades of the twelfth and the first decades of the thirteenth century and is reflected in the monumental stone sculpture on the portals of such major Gothic cathedrals as Chartres, Strasbourg, and Reims.

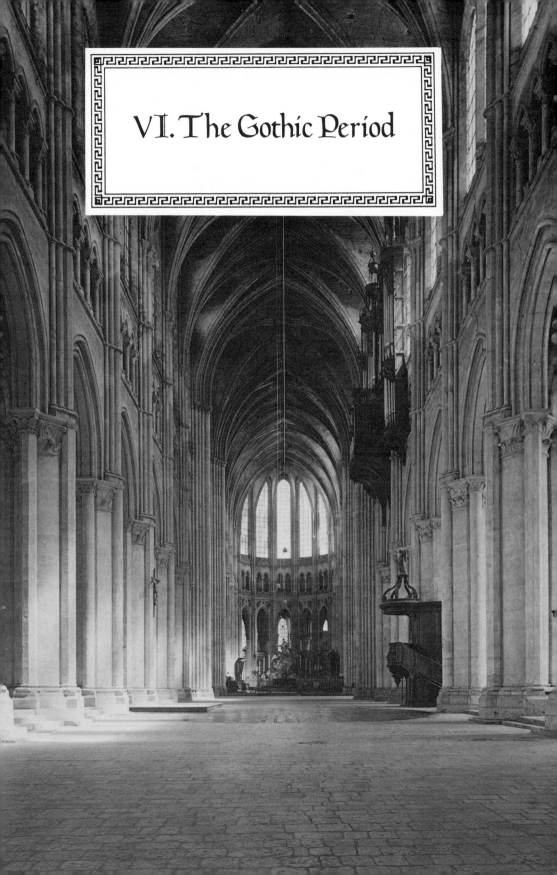

VI. The Gothic Period

20. Urbanization and Secularization

hen Italian Renaissance humanists applied the term *Gothic* to the period from around 1200 to their own era, they indicated their contempt for what they considered to be the barbarian art forms of the Germanic Goths, the principal manifestations of which were the great cathedrals of northern Europe. Although its disparaging connotations have fallen away, the term is still used to refer to the last two or three centuries of the Middle Ages.

The limits of this period, however, are imprecise, and its artistic manifestations diverse. The Gothic era may be considered to begin around 1140 to 1144 with the construction of the choir of the Abbey of Saint-Denis under Abbot Suger. Although this construction resulted in an entirely new spatial effect, it made use of devices such as pointed arches and rib vaults that had existed in Romanesque architecture. Abbot Suger, in the long discussion of his accomplishments at Saint-Denis, never singled out the most extraordinary achievement of his abbacy: the revolutionary quality of the architecture in the choir of his church. But throughout the remainder of the twelfth century all of the major churches, particularly those that were urban cathedrals, the site of the bishop's throne (*cathedra*), were erected in this new architectural style. While ecclesiastical architecture developed through this Early Gothic stage, however, the arts of painting and sculpture lagged behind and did not evolve, with the exception of the transitional developments influenced by Mosan metalwork, into an identifiable new style until around 1200.

In the same way, the termination of the Late Gothic and beginning of the Renaissance are equally vague. A courtly, "international Gothic" style coexisted with early Renaissance developments in Italy during the first third of the fifteenth century; Late Gothic gave way to the Renaissance in France around 1450 with the importation of Italian motifs by Jean Fouquet, and Albrecht Dürer made the dramatic transition from Late Gothic to Renaissance in Germany in his painted and graphic works after two trips to Italy in the beginning of the sixteenth century.

The Gothic cathedral is not only a new manifestation of architectural form, spatial experience, and spiritual effect, it is also symptomatic of major changes in ecclesiastical power and socioeconomic conditions. It looms above the neighboring rooftops as the Romanesque church did above its village, but it is the crown jewel of an urban environment rather than a beacon in a rural landscape. The cathedral is a monument not only to the power and organizational abilities of the bishops who saw these immense buildings through various stages of their construction but also to the economic support of prospering craft and trade guilds and the growing bourgeois population.

Increasing trade and its attendant spread of wealth throughout broader segments of the population were in part encouraged by the crusades of the thirteenth century and the opening up of new trade routes throughout Europe and the Mediterranean. Civic governments were formed; in Italy city-states fiercely maintained their independence and identity in constant rivalries, and a heightened concern for the proper administration of the municipalities sometimes found its expression in art, as in the frescoes, *Allegories of Good and Bad Government,* by Ambrogio Lorenzetti for the Town Hall of Siena.

Major calamities and disruptions occurred, the most severe of which was the outbreak of the bubonic plague in 1348 that reduced the population, according to some estimates, by almost a third. Recurrent outbreaks occurred into the fifteenth century. The papacy became discredited in the early fourteenth century, and from 1309 to 1378 a new papal court flourished at Avignon in southern France. Restored briefly to Rome in 1378, the papacy was then disrupted by the Great Schism during which two popes reigned, one in Rome, the other at Avignon, until 1414. The Hundred Years War (1337–1453) between France and England ravaged city and countryside alike and impeded economic development. When not actually locked in combat with each other on the battlefield, these countries were disrupted by internal struggles and revolts.

Although diverse feudal enclaves were slowly being united under the control of national monarchies in England and France from the twelfth century onward, the process was slow and often brutal, as events in Laon in 1111 illustrate. A particularly corrupt bishop had exploited the bourgeois in the town and the serfs in the countryside to the breaking point and had even had a baron murdered in the church. The townspeople revolted, invaded the bishop's palace, and massacred everyone within. King Louis VI supported the bishop and dispatched his troops and put down the revolt. The landed nobility then counterattacked and finally the peasants from the surrounding countryside sacked and burned what little had been left by the king's troops.

The Gothic period also witnessed the transferral of centers of learning from the monastic communities to the urban cathedral schools and to newly formed universities. Universities were founded in Paris and Bologna in the twelfth century, at Oxford in the thirteenth, and with increasing rapidity throughout all of Europe after that. Although the church still had powerful influence over the curriculum, the universities began to develop a more secular emphasis and to provide a haven for freedom of inquiry not strictly tied to prevailing dogma.

As a result of the social changes that took place from the thirteenth through the fifteenth centuries, the structure of the church, the nature of worship, and the basis of artistic patronage were transformed. Once the great cathedrals were constructed, by around 1275, the pace and scale of building decreased. Instead smaller parish churches were built in neighborhoods of the cities and in smaller towns. Emphasis turned away from aloof ceremonial services in the cathedrals to the more intimate performance of the Divine Offices and private devotion. The desire for greater immediacy in religion was further encouraged by the appearance of mendicant and preaching orders, the Franciscans and Dominicans, in which monks went out from the monasteries to preach and to do good works among the people.

The cult of the Virgin, which had its origins in the twelfth century, flowered in the thirteenth, and brought with it new attitudes about the role of the Virgin as the human Mother of God as well as the Intercessor for Man's salvation. The growth of Mariolatry also paralleled the development of courtly love within the chivalric tradition. A growth in mysticism accompanied increased preoccupation with the suffering and pathos of Christ's sacrifice and decreased concern with the triumphal theophanic manifestations of the Romanesque period. Religious images were made with less abstraction and more naturalism so that they would be more immediately equatable with the beholder's experience. At the same time the emotional content was heightened.

Nobles and the upper hierarchy of the church continued to patronize the arts, but as wealth filtered into the mercantile class and university education was available to more people, an increasing number of people in lower social strata bought or commissioned artifacts and manuscripts. Secular art existed, of course, throughout the Middle Ages, but in the Gothic period we find a proliferation of secular artifacts and an intrusion of secular themes into religious art. Vernacular languages had also existed throughout the medieval period, but in the thirteenth century they increasingly became vehicles for an expanding body of lay literature, and soon the Scriptures and books for private devotions were translated from Latin into the everyday tongues.

21. THE GOTHIC CATHEDRAL

The essential elements of structure—the pointed arch and vault, the flying buttress, and the rib vault—which when used together resulted in the Gothic style, all existed in Romanesque architecture. The pointed arch, perhaps inspired by the portico of Desiderius's Monte Cassino, had been used with slightly pointed barrel vaults in the nave at Cluny and in such Cistercian monasteries as Fontenay. These had the advantage of exerting a more vertical lateral thrust than semicircular arches and vaults, and therefore permitted less massive supporting walls and more openings for windows.

Even so, it was sometimes found necessary to provide a series of piers or raking external buttresses to support Romanesque vaults, and these took a variety of forms. The origin of the flying buttress was in the transverse arch bridging the gallery of the Romanesque church, sometimes semicircular beneath a quadrant vault, sometimes a quadrant arch conforming to the vault, and sometimes a segmental curved arch with a raking upper surface conforming to the slope of a timber roof over the gallery. The flying buttress evolved when this arch emerged above the roofline as an independent structural entity as at Notre Dame in Paris in the 1180s. Eventually it lost its massiveness and was reduced to skeletal form.

Massive diagonal ribs, usually square or semicircular in section, were used in conjunction with groin vaults in a few Romanesque churches. In contrast to the semicircular barrel vault exerting heavy forces all along its supporting walls, the groin vault (fig. 116), created by the intersection of two barrel vaults, exerts forces only upon its four supporting piers. It is possible, therefore, to void all four sides beneath the canopy of the vault and provide, on the sides, larger windows in the aisle walls and at the clerestory level. Seen from underneath, sharp angles (groins) marking the intersection of the two curving surfaces (fig. 117) become less pro-

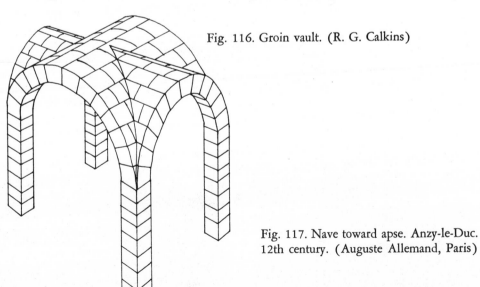

Fig. 116. Groin vault. (R. G. Calkins)

Fig. 117. Nave toward apse. Anzy-le-Duc. 12th century. (Auguste Allemand, Paris)

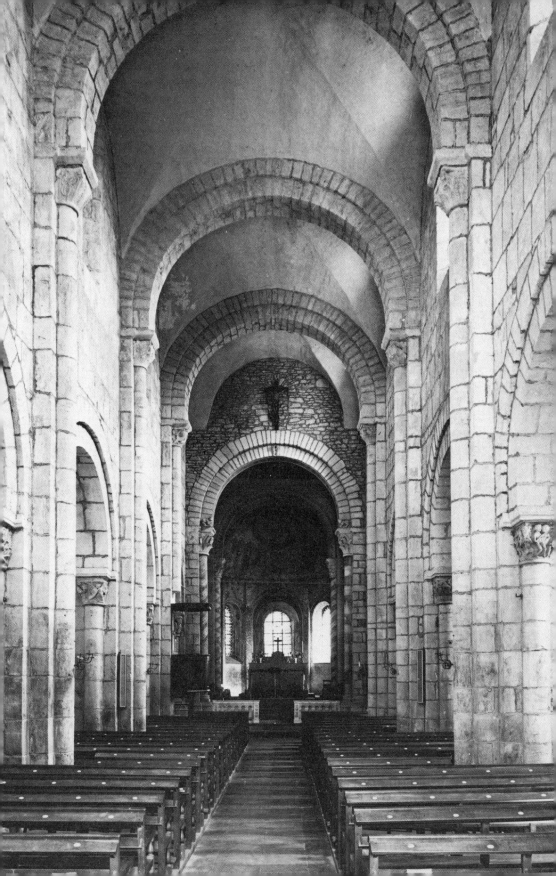

nounced and disappear near the crown of the vault. Medieval masons found it difficult to make these pronounced angles even, as evidenced by many surviving examples, such as the nave of Anzy-le-Duc. Groin vaults were mostly used in aisles and ambulatories, and only a few monumental examples over the main vessel of Romanesque churches have survived, notably Vézelay and the imperial Pantheon at Speyer. One of the uses of the diagonal rib, as a decorative cosmetic to hide the irregular angle of the groin, was a fortuituous solution to an aesthetic problem.

The exact origin and original purpose of the diagonal rib is still the subject of controversy. In any event, it was soon realized that the diagonal rib could serve two functions, structural and aesthetic. Structurally, it was possible to build a stone framework of arches (fig. 118) along the sides and across the nave, connected diagonally by ribs. This framework then served as a permanent centering to support planks in the individual cells of the vault, which would hold the cut and mortared stones of the thin, curved shells until the fabric cured. Aesthetically, the diagonal ribs provided a network of arches that continued the vertical accents of the supports into the vault and across the nave. When viewed down the center of the nave, the ribs also defined diamond-shaped areas of the vault (fig. 119) that visually unify sections of adjacent bays, even when interrupted by pronounced transverse arches. The nave vault of such a Gothic cathedral as Chartres thus appears as a continuous expanding and contracting canopy down the length of the building. The skeletal structure also permitted a succession of parallel lateral vaults, leading to the high clerestory windows, and thereby created an open, expansive effect. The resultant light, airy interior of Chartres is in marked contrast to the dark, heavy, compartmented barrel vault of Saint-Étienne at Nevers (fig. 120) with its pronounced transverse arches, or the succession of domical groin vaults, also demarcated by heavy transverse arches, at Anzy-le-Duc.

The statement of a new architectural style occurred when all these elements were fused into a cohesive, mutually sustaining structural system. This happened in the choir of Saint-Denis, constructed by Abbot Suger from 1140 to 1144. A new kind of space was required to accommodate the throngs of pilgrims on holy days and to permit them to observe the holiest moment in the celebration of the Mass, the elevation of the Host. The invention of a vaulting system that permitted thin, widely spaced supports, in turn allowed an easy flow of the crowds and easy visibility of the high altar.

Once formulated at Saint-Denis, the principle of the groin vault, in conjunction with the skeletonization of the repetitive bay system and the structural advantages of the rib vault, formed the basis of the Early Gothic style. The naves of the Early Gothic cathedrals were based on square bays with a lesser intermediate support, corresponding transverse arch, and resultant six-part vault. Because the different dimensions of the sides and diagonals of trapezoidal bays in ambulatories and square six-part bays in naves required different radii for semicircular arches and ribs, pointed arches were an essential element to avoid the excessive stilting of smaller arches or the depressing of the longest curves in the diagonal ribs. The Early Gothic style evolved with the increased use of the pointed arch in every element of the rib vault, until only a slightly undulating canopy was achieved and

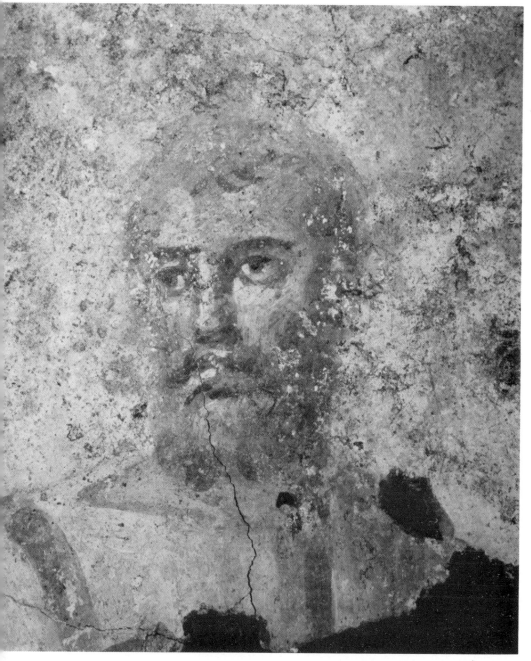

1. Head of an Apostle (?). Tomb of the Aurelians, Rome. Mid-3rd century.
(Pontificia Commissione di Archeologia Sacra, Rome)

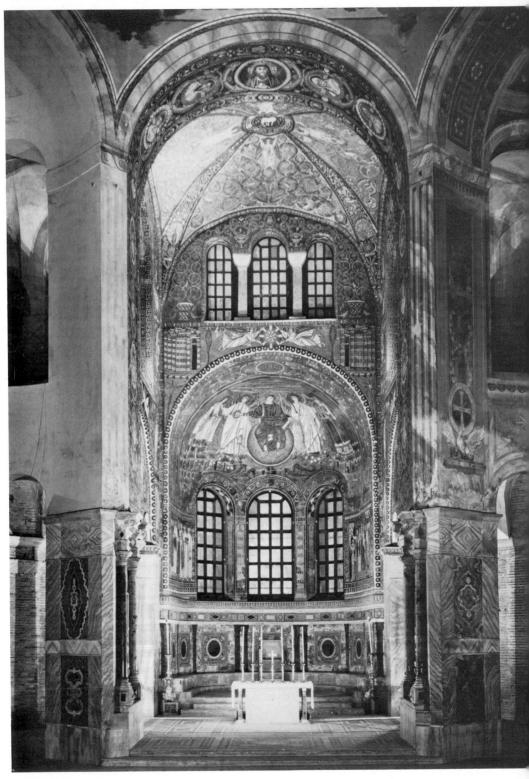

2. Sanctuary. S. Vitale, Ravenna. 548. (Scala/E.P.A.)

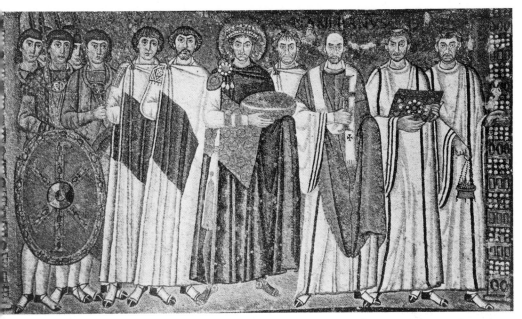

3. "Emperor Justinian and His Court," mosaic. S. Vitale, Ravenna. 548. (Scala/E.P.A.)

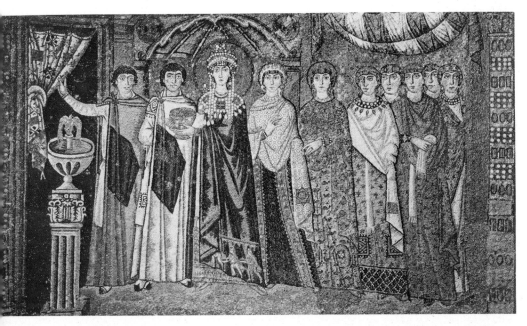

4. "Empress Theodora and Her Court," mosaic. S. Vitale, Ravenna. 548. (Scala/E.P.A.)

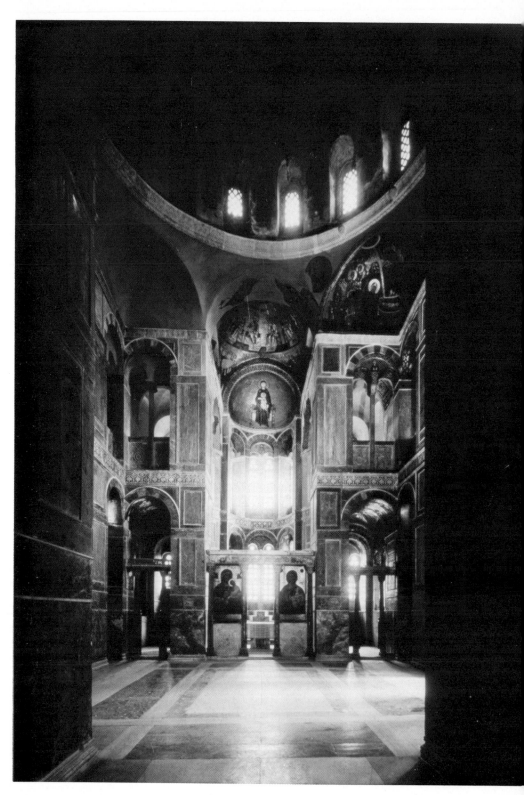

5. Interior toward sanctuary. Katholikon, Hosios Lukas, Greece. 1011 or 1022.
(Erich Lessing/Magnum)

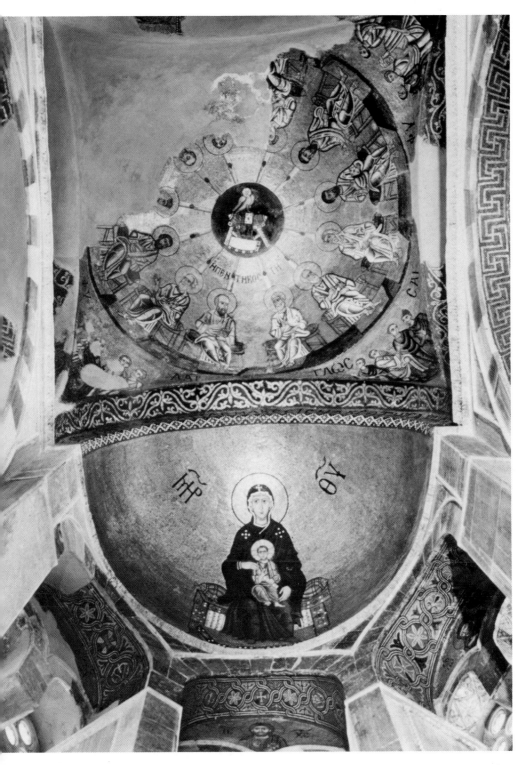

6. Apse and sanctuary mosaics. Katholikon, Hosios Lukas, Greece. 1011 or 1022.
(Erich Lessing/Magnum)

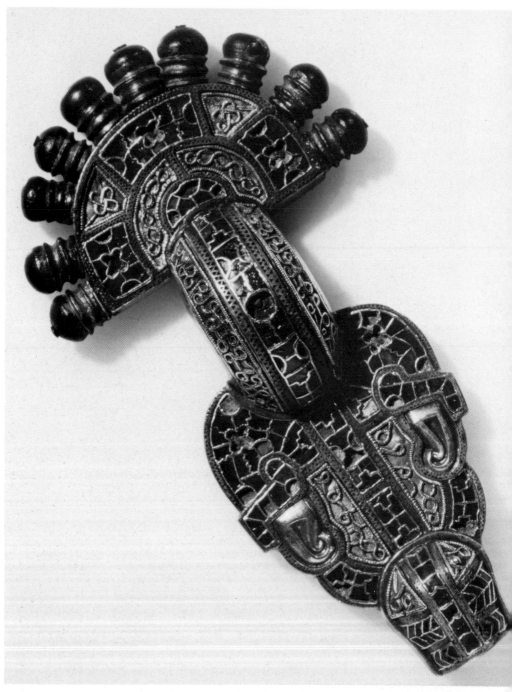

7. Wittislingen Fibula. 7th century. Silver gilt with niello, filigree, enamel, and precious
stones, 6¼″. Prähistorische Staatssammlung, Museum für Vor- und Frühgeschichte,
Munich. (Hirmer Fotoarchiv, Munich)

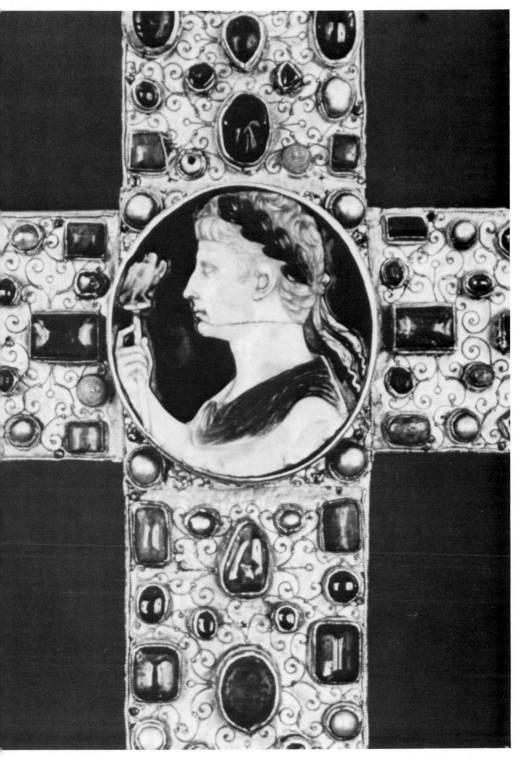

8. The Cross of Lothair II of Lotharingia with cameo of Augustus. Cologne. c. 1000.
Gold with precious stones, 19¾″ x 15¼″. Aachen, Schatzkammer. (Ann Münchow, Aachen)

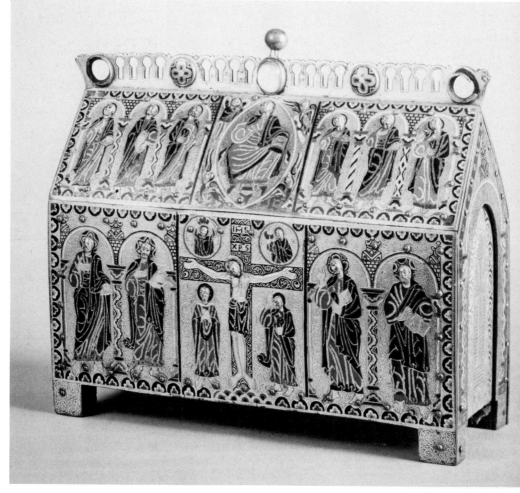

9. Reliquary casket. Limoges. Third quarter 12th century. Champlevé enamel on copper gilt, H. 10½″, L. 11¾″, W. 4½″. The Metropolitan Museum of Art (Gift of J. Pierpont Morgan, 1917), New York.

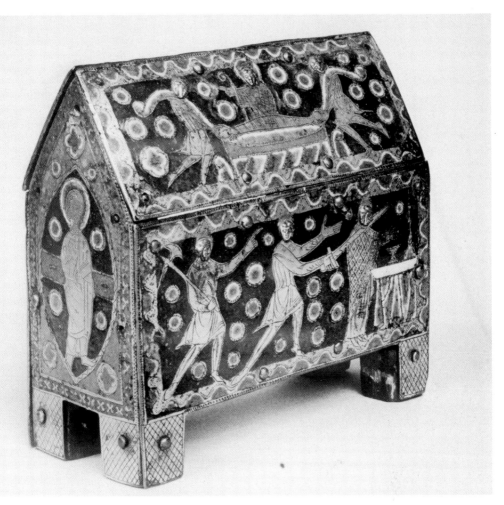

10. Reliquary casket with scenes of martyrdom of Thomas à Becket. Limoges. 13th century. Champlevé enamel on copper gilt, 5⅛″ x 5¼″. Musée de Cluny, Paris. (Clichés Musées nationaux, Paris)

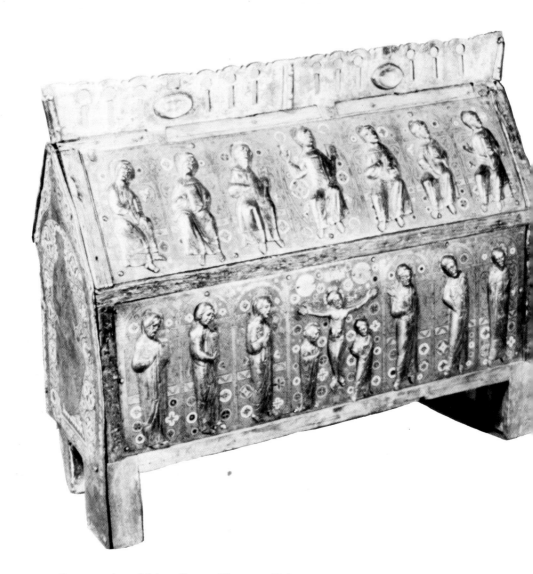

11. Reliquary casket of Sainte Fauste. Limoges. 13th century. Champlevé enamel on copper gilt, 17⅛″ x 20⅛″. Musée de Cluny, Paris.

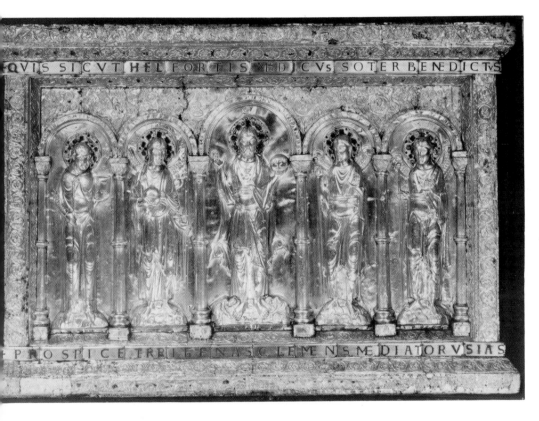

12. Basel Cathedral antependium. Fulda (?) c. 1019. Repoussé gold with gilt copper and niello, 47″ x 70″. Musée de Cluny, Paris. (Clichés Musées nationaux, Paris)

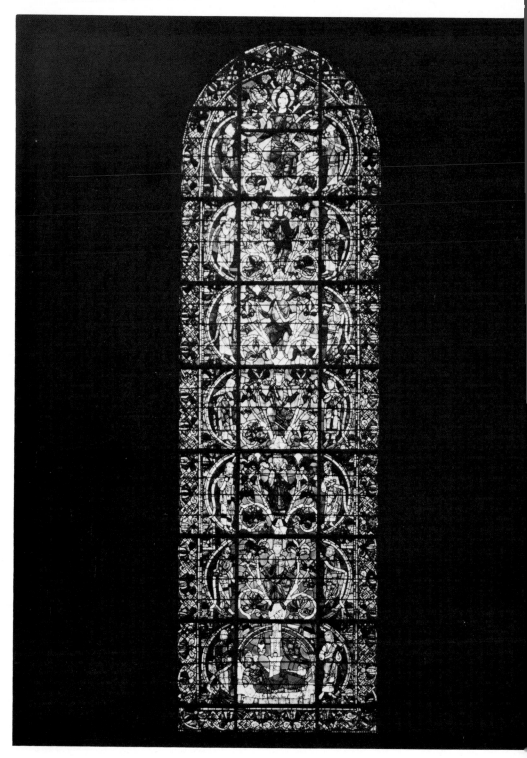

13. "Tree of Jesse" window. West facade, Chartres Cathedral. c. 1145. (Maurice Babey, Basel/Joseph Ziolo, Paris)

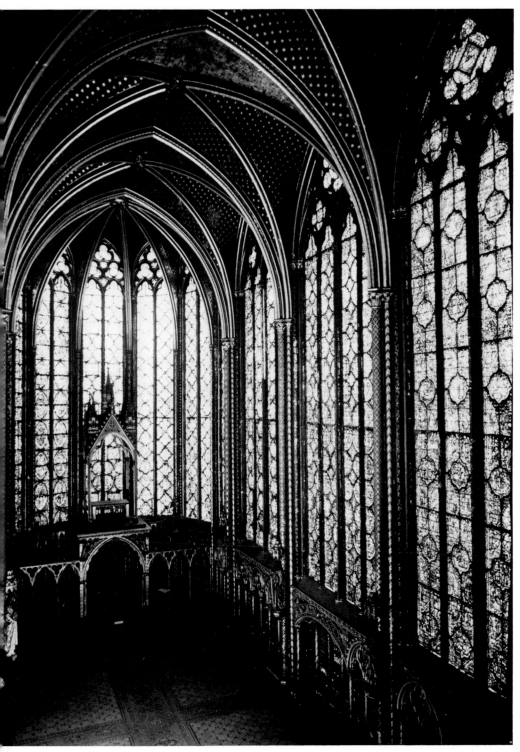

14. Interior of upper chapel toward apse. Sainte-Chapelle, Paris. 1243–1248. (Lauros-Giraudon)

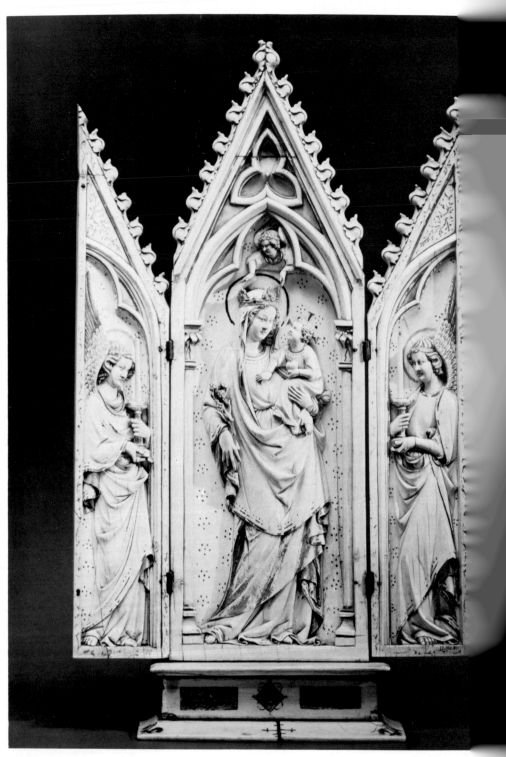

15. Ivory tabernacle with Virgin and Child and attendant angels. France. Second half 14th century. 15½″ x 9″. The Metropolitan Museum of Art (Gift of J. Pierpont Morgan, 1917), New York.

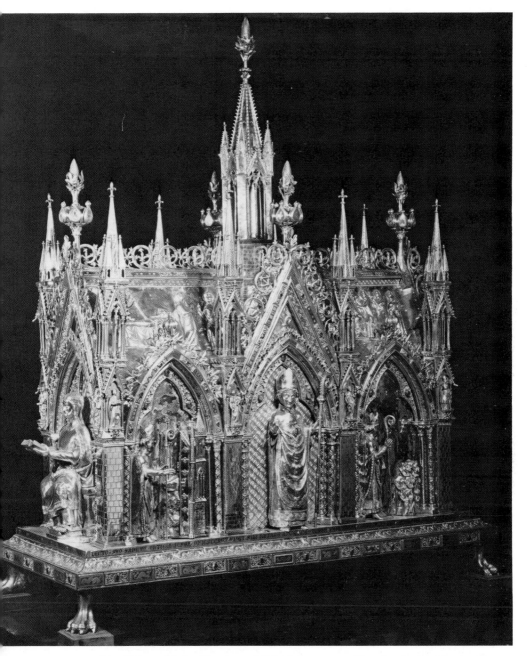

16. Shrine of Saint Taurinus. Mid-13th century. Church of Saint Taurin, Evreux.
Copper and silver gilt with enamel plaques, H. 27⅝″, base 41″ x 17¾″.
(Maurice Babey, Basel/Joseph Ziolo, Paris)

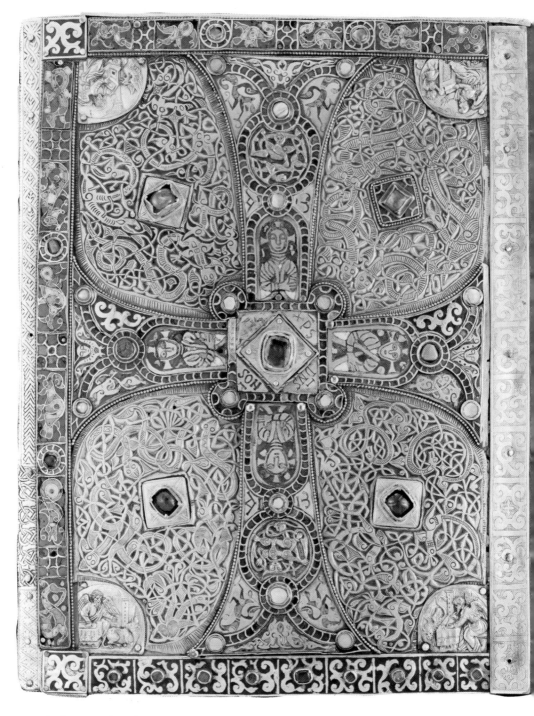

17. Back cover of Lindau Gospels. c. 800. Silver gilt with enamel and precious stones, 13⅜″ x 10⅜″. The Pierpont Morgan Library (MS 1), New York.

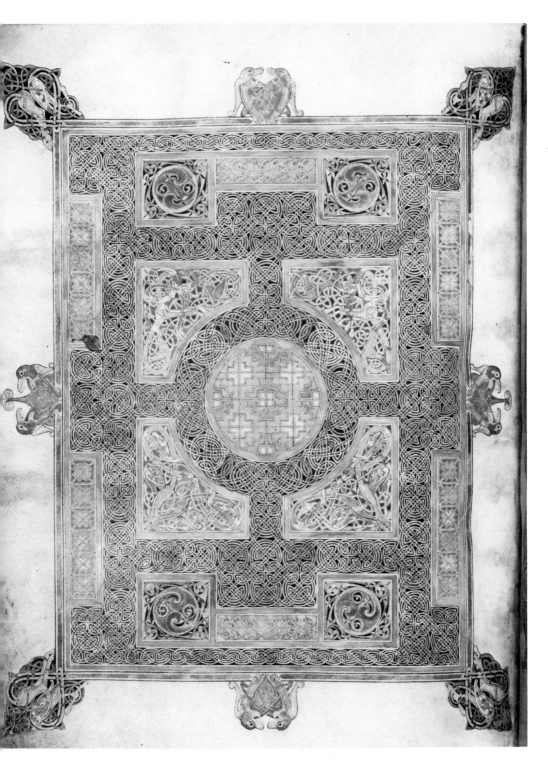

18. Carpet page. Lindisfarne Gospels. Before 698. 13½″ x 9¾″. The British Library (MS Cotton Nero D. IV, fol. 94v), London.

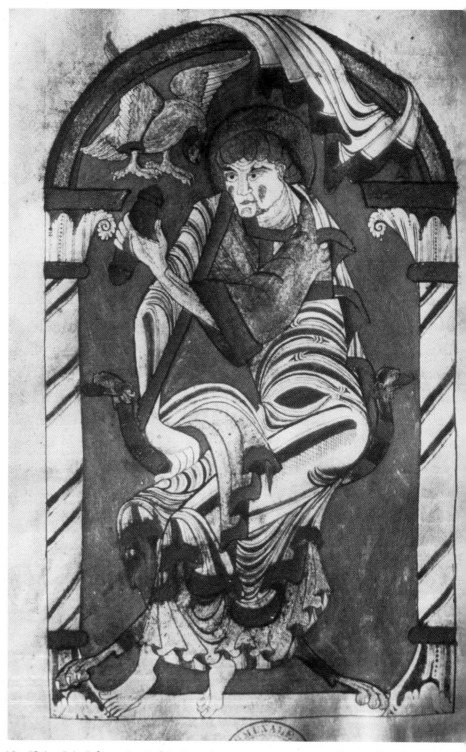

19. "Saint John" from the Corbie Gospels. France. c. 1090. 10¾″ x 7⅞″. Bibliothèque municipale (MS 24, fol. 118v), Amiens.

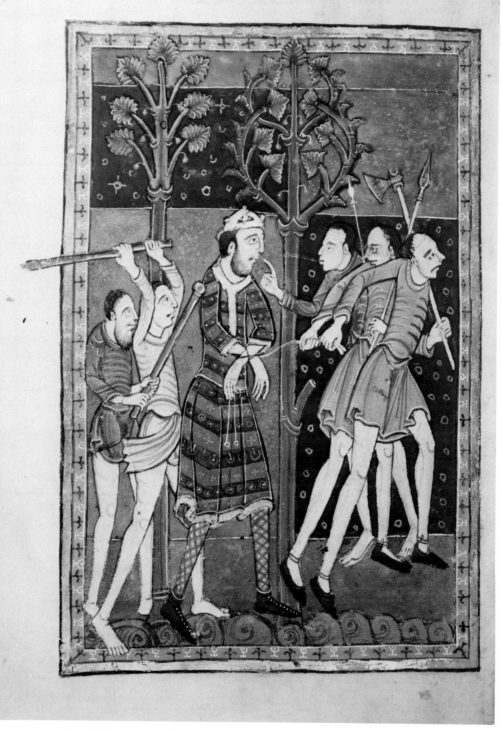

20. "Saint Edmund Led into Captivity" from *The Life of Saint Edmund*. England. Second quarter 12th century. 10¾" x 7¼". The Pierpont Morgan Library (MS 736, fol. 12v), New York.

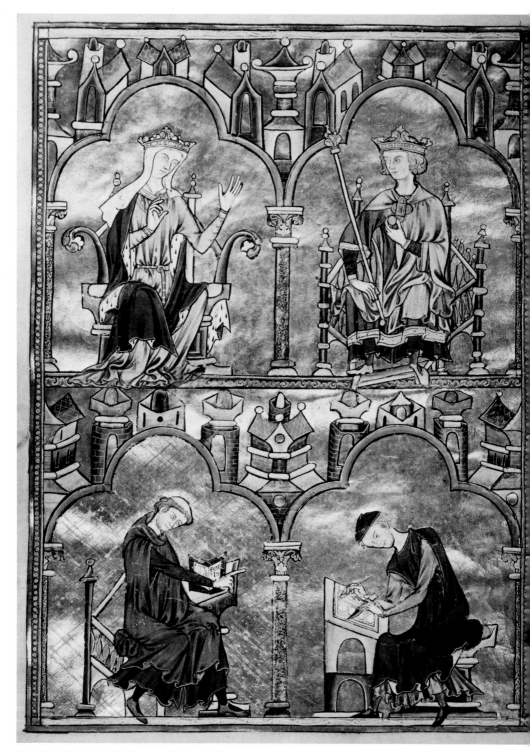

21. Frontispiece with Queen Blanche of Castile, King Louis IX, cleric dictating and scribe. Toledo Bible. Paris (?) 1226–1234. 14¾" x 10⅜". The Pierpont Morgan Library (MS 240, fol. 8), New York.

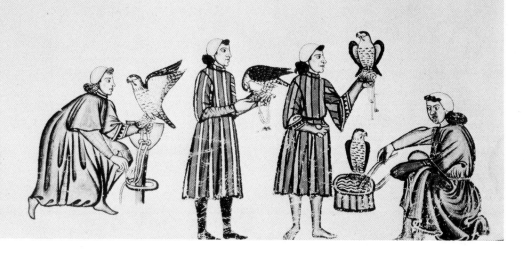

22. "Care and Training of Falcons," detail of bottom margin. Frederick II, *De Arte Venandi cum Avibus*. Italy. c. 1260. Biblioteca Apostolica Vaticana (MS Pal. lat. 1071, fol. 79), Vatican City. (Scala/E.P.A.)

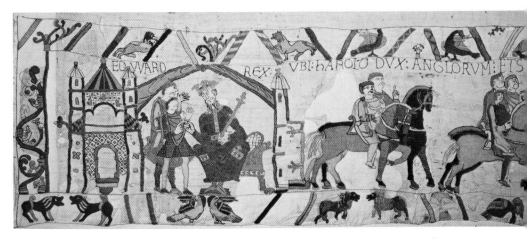

23. "Edward the Confessor Giving Instruction to Earl Harold the Saxon." Detail from the *Bayeux Tapestry*. 1070–1080. H. 19½". Musée de la Ville de Bayeux.

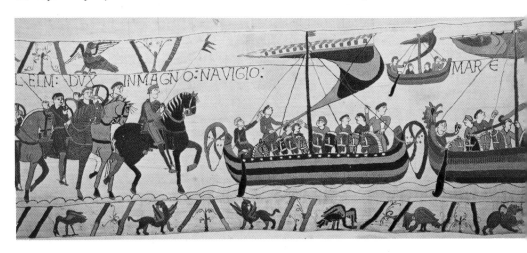

24. "Duke William Leads the Norman Army down to the Ships." Detail from the *Bayeux Tapestry*. 1070–1080. H. 19½". Musée de la Ville de Bayeux.

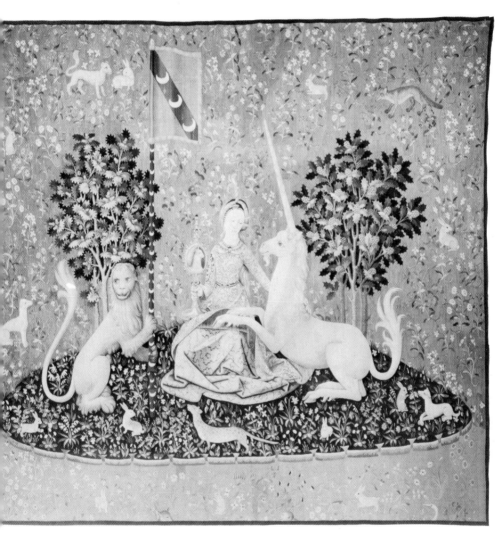

25. "Sight" from *La Dame à la licorne* tapestries. France. End of 15th century. Wool and silk, 122″ x 130″. Musée de Cluny, Paris. (Clichés Musées nationaux, Paris)

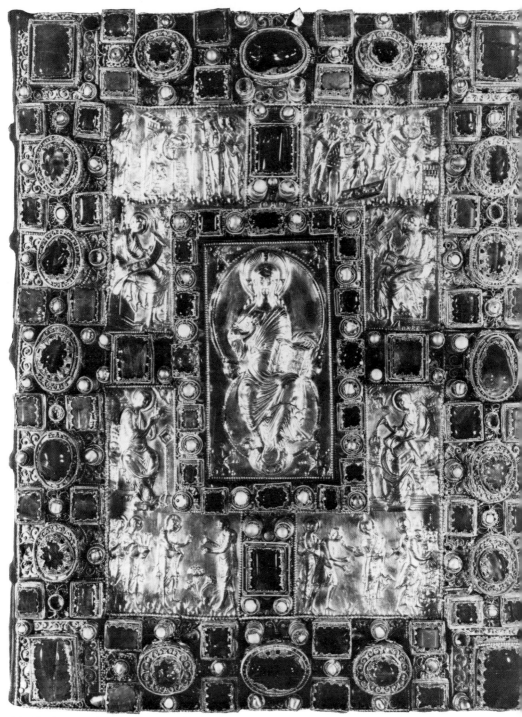

26. Bookcover of Codex Aureus of Saint Emmeram. France. c. 870. Repoussé gold with precious stones and pearls, 16½″ x 13″. Bayerische Staatsbibliothek (Clm. 14000), Munich.

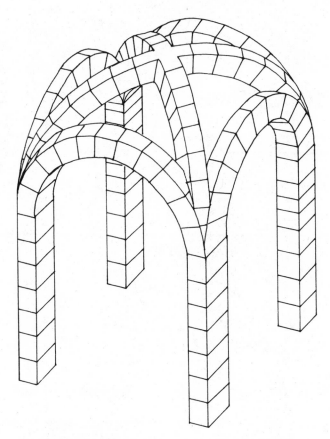

Fig. 118. Rib-vault construction. (R. G. Calkins)

it was no longer necessary to create square six-part vaults with transverse ribs supported by alternate less pronounced nave shafts and piers.

At the end of the twelfth century, with the introduction of the rectangular quadripartite bay and the exclusive use of pointed arches and ribs, the High Gothic style was crystallized. To the interior structural canopy were added the external flying buttresses. First appearing on a Gothic cathedral on the nave of Notre Dame de Paris in the 1180s as massive raking walls of masonry above arches, they abutted the wall of the building at that point where the congregating forces of the vaults met and exerted outward pressure on the piers. These forces were then transmitted down the flying buttress to its supporting pier and contained within it. Sometimes, as at Chartres, a secondary buttress rose to stabilize the wall above the clerestory windows and acted as wind bracing when the tall building was buffeted by gales.

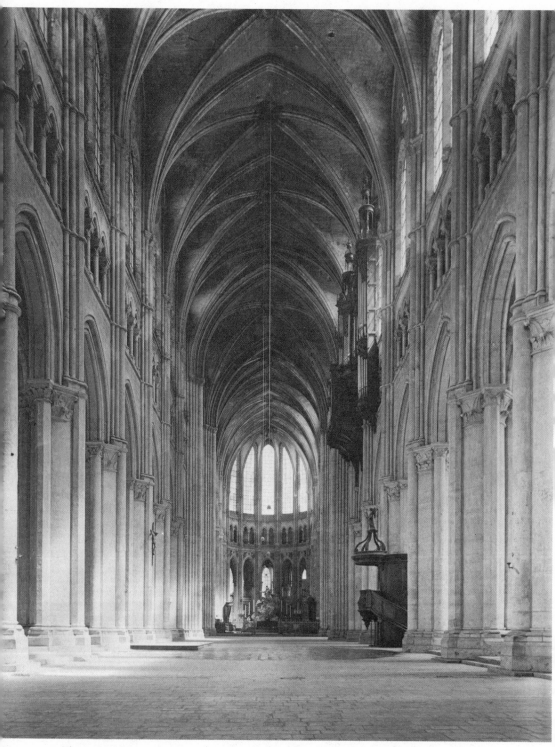

Fig. 119. Nave toward apse. Chartres Cathedral. 1194–1220. (Marburg)

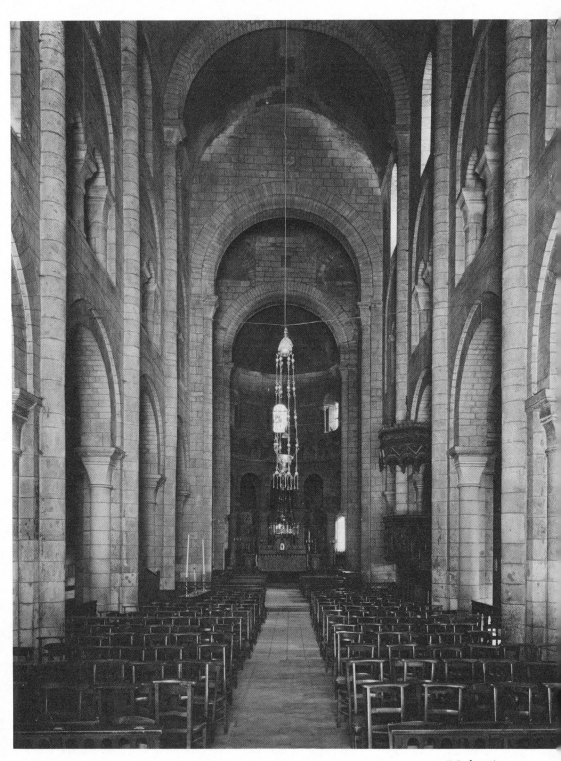

Fig. 120. Nave toward apse. Saint-Étienne, Nevers, Burgundy. 1083–1097. (Marburg)

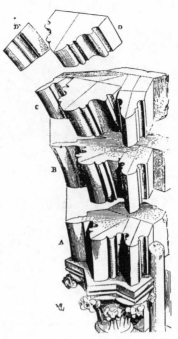

Fig. 121. Drawing of a tas-de-charge. (After Viollet-le-Duc)

The key point in this structural system was the point at which the two diagonal ribs, the transverse arch, the nave shafts responding to them, the wall, and the inner end of the flying buttress all joined. An intricate arrangement of carefully cut stones (*tas-de-charge,* fig. 121) tied these elements together. As the ribs and arch spring from the cluster of nave shafts and their capitals, they are too close together to be differentiated, and all were therefore carved on a single block of stone as three intricate moldings. In Viollet-le-Duc's hypothetical drawing of the tas-de-charge, the ribs diverge further on the second and third stones, but are still carved from a single block. At the fourth course of masonry the angles of the ribs and arch are sufficiently separated so that each member is carved separately. The critical stone, according to Viollet-le-Duc's drawing, however, is the third one. Its inner edge is beveled so that the separate ribs spring firmly from it, and it extends into the wall at a level corresponding to the end of the flying buttress (fig. 122). Thus, forces are converged, directed, and transmitted at this critical juncture. At Chartres, this occurs at the eighth and ninth courses above the spring line.

As the first fully developed example of the High Gothic style, Chartres Cathedral not only incorporated the rectangular quadripartite bay but also revived the three-story elevation. In Romanesque churches (fig. 123) the vertical elevation of the nave usually consisted of the nave arcade, a gallery, and sometimes a clerestory, as at Nevers. In some Early Gothic churches a fourth division (*triforium*), consisting of a series of arcades opening into a narrow passage in the thickness of the wall, was added. This was often placed above the gallery and corresponded to the dead area under its raking roof. At Chartres (figs. 122, 124)

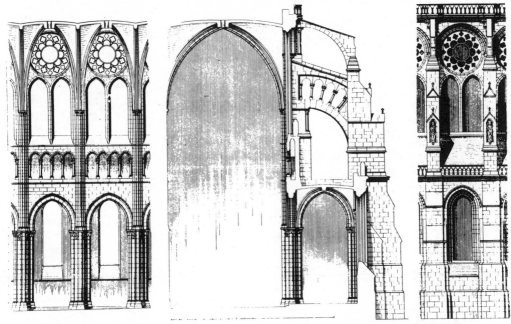

Fig. 122. Section, interior and exterior elevations of nave. Chartres Cathedral. 1194–1220. (After Dehio and Bezold)

the gallery was omitted and the triforium became an articulating, space-holding arcade between nave arcade and clerestory, corresponding to the area under the roof of the aisle. The width and height of the nave arcade and clerestory window were nearly identical, giving not only a harmonious balance to the composition of the wall but also providing an immense area for stained-glass windows. The upper wall thus became a translucent diaphragm, made possible by the skeletonization of the entire structure.

The nave wall was strongly articulated in relief. In contrast to the massive piers and frontally oriented nave shafts, facing across the nave and responding to the transverse arch at Nevers, a cluster of five bold nave shafts (*responds*) rise from the top of the nave pier and respond to the various members in the vault. The outside shafts rise up past the springing of the main vault and respond to a molded arch (*formeret*) over the clerestory window. The intermediate shafts respond to the diagonal ribs: their reference is made clear by the diagonal placement of the plinths of their bases and the abaci of their capitals in contrast to the orientation of the bases and abaci of the outside shafts set parallel to the wall. The middle shaft responds to the transverse arch, emphasized again by the square-set placement of its capital abacus. This bundle of colonnettes, tied into the wall by the horizontal accents of stringcourses at the triforium and clerestory levels, provides continuous vertical accents leading logically into the structural members of the vault and dividing the wall into distinct vertical panels.

Anomalies appear at Chartres, however, that link the design with discarded past traditions and that point forward to further refinements in the High Gothic style. Subtle variations in the nave piers (fig. 124) and the central colonnette above are created by placing polygonal shafts against a cylindrical column on one

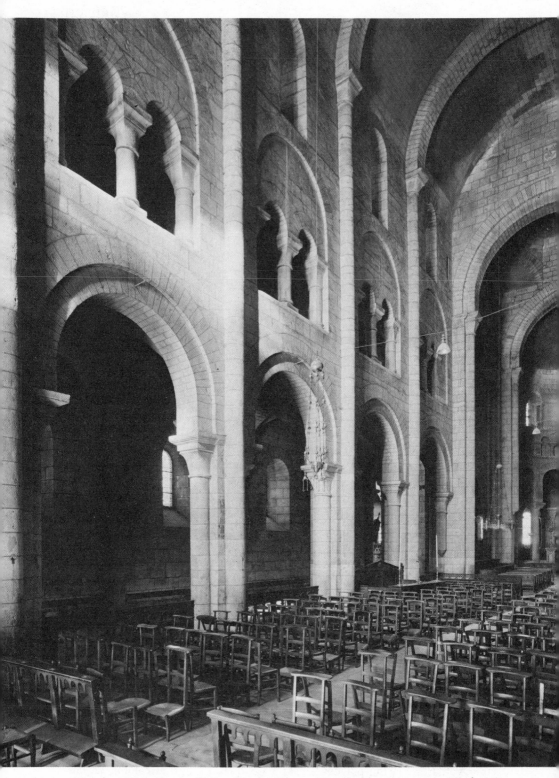

Fig. 123. Nave elevation. Saint-Étienne, Nevers, Burgundy. 1083–1097. (Marburg)

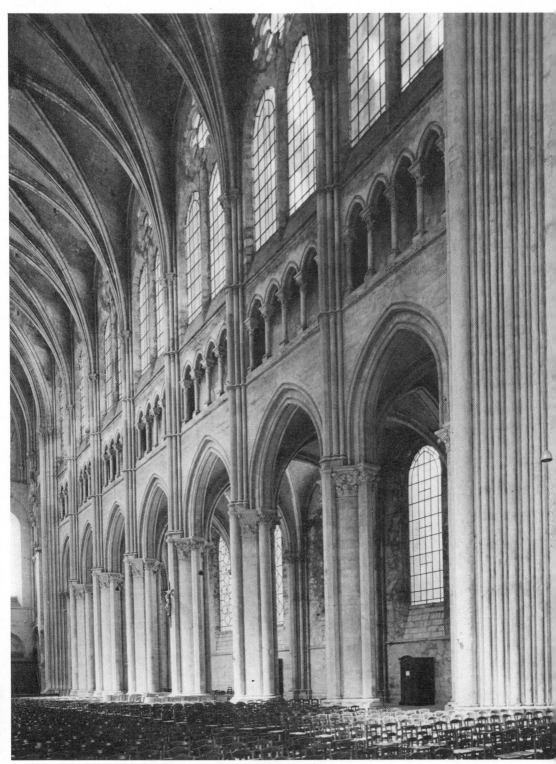

Fig. 124. Nave elevation. Chartres Cathedral. 1194–1220. (Marburg)

pier and cylindrical shafts against a polygonal column on the next. This system reflects the earlier alternation of supports accentuating the major and minor piers supporting the six-part vaults of Early Gothic architecture. Although not needed at Chartres, their presence establishes a minimal alternate rhythm down the nave. This alternation is carried upward into the base and main colonnette above. In an effort to distinguish between the larger diameter of the central pier and the smaller ones of the engaged columns responding to the nave and aisle arcades, the capitals of the lesser members were made only half the height of the one on the major pier. The column on the nave side, however, was not given a capital because it serves as visual support for the principal respond above. Although the bundle of responds begins on top of the nave pier, this detail indicates that the designers of Chartres were concerned with creating a logical statement of supporting functions in the lowest level of the elevation relating to the membering of the vault above. It was not until further refinements had been developed at Reims, and in the thirteenth-century naves of Saint-Denis and Amiens, however, that we find a full, coherent cluster of responds at floor level accurately reflecting their duties at the vault level.

All of the interior elements of wall articulation and structure worked together to produce a unified, expansive, soaring space (see fig. 119, p. 142). The vertical emphasis of wall shafts flowed easily into the arching ribs. Horizontal accents of stringcourses tying the shafts lightly to the wall and triforium arcades provide longitudinal continuity down the nave. The diagonality of the responds and corresponding ribs emphasizes the relief of the bundled colonnettes and the spreading, unifying canopy of vault above, composed of adjacent sections of rectangular bays. So strong is the visual effect of these diamond-shaped areas of vault that they, rather than the bay, read as the continuous vaulting surface, boldly penetrated by the triangular voids of the side vaults leading to the clerestory windows. Vaults are voided as walls are voided, and we are left with the impression of a soaring vertical space supported by the minimum of skeleton and enclosed by translucent, diaphanous skin. The nineteenth-century architectural historian Dehio equated the effect of such a building with the principles underlying the process of Scholastic thought, which permeated the thinking of the thirteenth century:

> As scholasticism begins its doctrinal structure at the top, as it were, from whence it derives everything else deductively, so in Gothic, everything is the result of a particular system of vaulting. As scholasticism proves the unprovable with the help of the authority of revelation lying outside thought, so Gothic produces the miracle of its vaulted halls resting on incredibly weak supports with the help of a system of buttresses lying outside the building itself.

Erwin Panofsky, in *Gothic Architecture and Scholasticism*, developed this theme further, and showed how the actual orderly, deductive process of Scholastic reasoning was developed and reflected in the ordered membering of Gothic windows and wall elevations, culminating in the final resolution at Amiens and

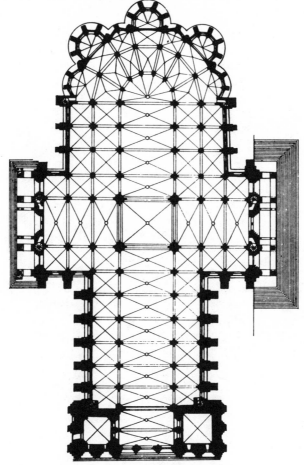

Fig. 125. Plan of Chartres Cathedral. 1194–1220.
(After Dehio and Bezold)

Saint-Denis in the mid-thirteenth century. Although both of these views may be
overstatements of the effect of an erudite process of philosophical reasoning on
the designers of Gothic cathedrals, they are based upon persuasive similarities.

The ground plan of Chartres Cathedral (fig. 125) reveals a three-aisled basilican structure, with square bays in the aisles, rectangular bays in the nave, and
rib vaults throughout. The choir is flanked by two aisles, and the ambulatory con-
tinues this double passageway around the apse. Alternately shallow and deep
chapels radiate off the outer ambulatory providing an undulating, unified chevet.
In contrast with Romanesque churches where the transept boldly projected from
the volume of the church at the eastern end, at Chartres it extended only one bay
beyond the choir and was situated more toward the center. At Reims and Amiens
the transept was placed even farther forward. Massive pier buttresses project from
the wall of the nave (fig. 126) and choir at Chartres to support the flying buttresses arching above the roof of the aisles. Two heavy square foundations at the
western end of the building support the facade towers and four great piers at
the crossing of the nave and transept were intended to support a crossing tower
that was never built.

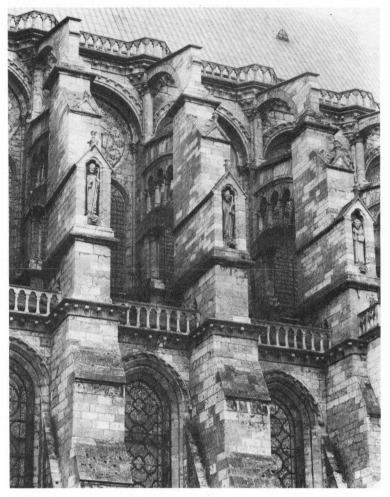

Fig. 126. South flank of nave with buttresses. Chartres Cathedral. 1194–1220. (Archives photographiques, Paris, S.P.A.D.E.M.)

An exterior view of the cathedral (fig. 127) reveals that it was originally intended to have a different appearance. Two facade towers were built, although the northern one was finished in the sixteenth century; but massive bases flanking the two transept facades suggest that another four towers were intended there and two additional bases next to the choir show that an additional pair of towers was intended to mark the beginning of the curve of the chevet. A tower was also planned for the crossing of the transept and nave. Thus, Chartres was intended to have nine towers and would have looked like the reconstruction drawing of a hypothetical seven-towered cathedral (fig. 128), perhaps reflecting the original design for Reims. This configuration was rooted in a northern European tradition of many-towered Romanesque and Early Gothic cathedrals, of which Tournai and Laon are but two partially intact examples.

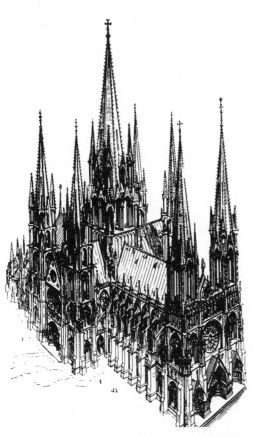

Fig. 128. Reconstruction of
a seven-towered cathedral.
(After Viollet-le-Duc)

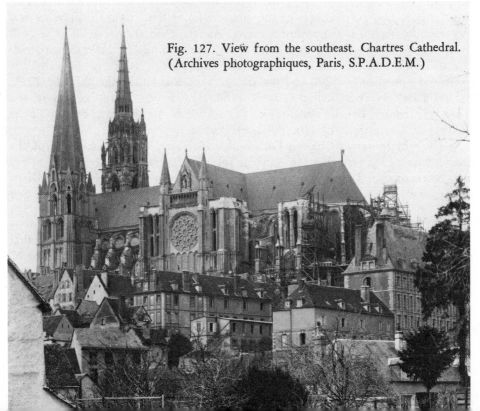

Fig. 127. View from the southeast. Chartres Cathedral.
(Archives photographiques, Paris, S.P.A.D.E.M.)

In contrast to the measured, additive buildup of solid geometric forms that characterized the exterior of the Romanesque church, the Gothic cathedral presents a more unified but ethereal mass. The volume of the building is the sum of the external edges of the pier buttresses along the nave and around the apse. The wall of the inner core is largely glass, a diaphanous skin between bold skeletal elements. In later Gothic buildings, particularly in the chevets of Le Mans or Amiens cathedrals, the structure is even more dissolved than at Chartres, a multitude of buttresses and piers project out into space and state a false exterior, while space permeates the structure and leads us inward to a transparent shell. As intended, with its many towers, the exterior of the building would have possessed a vertical emphasis even more dramatic than that of the interior, and the interplay of pinnacles, towers, and spires would have led both the eye and the spirit upward.

Each Gothic cathedral arose from its own special circumstances and held special meaning for the populace of the town. Chartres was no exception, for from Carolingian times the church had possessed the relic of the tunic of the Virgin and in the Romanesque period obtained a miraculous statue of the Virgin and Child. The Virgin thereby became the patron of the church and the protector of the city. Many miracles were believed to have been caused by her relics, and the cathedral and the city prospered as a result of the pilgrimages they attracted. An important early Romanesque church begun by Abbot Fulbert after a fire in 1020 occupied the site of previous Christian buildings as well as of pagan shrines. Another fire in 1134 destroyed the western end of Fulbert's church, but work was begun immediately on a new north tower and around 1144 on the south tower and facade sculpture. In 1194 an even more disastrous fire destroyed the remainder of Fulbert's church, but the discovery of the intact relics of the Virgin in the ashes was construed to mean that she wished a greater and more beautiful church to be built in her honor. The result was the Gothic church that assimilated the known technology of the day into the first statement of the High Gothic synthesis. Although the vaults were finished by 1220 and the canons were able to use the choir by 1221, the cathedral was not dedicated until 1260. The towers were finished in the thirteenth century, but the north tower was rebuilt in the sixteenth century in the Flamboyant Gothic style by Jean Texier de Beauce.

The rebuildings of Chartres Cathedral, particularly the reconstruction of the facade after 1134, provided the occasion for popular participation in virtually a civic enterprise. In a famous letter from Abbot Haimon of Saint-Pierre-sur-Dives in Normandy to the monks of Tutbury in England, he recounted:

> . . . Who has ever seen! Who has ever heard tell in times past, that powerful princes of the world, that men brought up in honor and in wealth, that nobles, men and women, have bent their haughty necks to the harness of carts, and that, like beasts of burden, they have dragged to the abode of Christ these waggons, loaded with wines and grains, oil, stones, wood and all that is necessary for the wants of life or for the construction of the church? But while they drew these burdens, there is one thing admirable to

observe; it is that often when a thousand persons and more are attached
to the chariots—so great is the difficulty—yet they march in such silence
that not a murmur is heard, and truly if one did not see such a thing with
one's eyes, one might believe that among such a multitude there was hardly
a person present. When they halt on the road, nothing is heard but the con-
fession of sins and pure and suppliant prayer to God to obtain pardon. At
the voice of the priests who exhort their hearts to peace, they forget all
hatred, discord is thrown far aside, debts are remitted, the unity of hearts
is established. . . . After the people, warned by the sound of trumpets and
the sight of banners have resumed their road, the march is made with such
ease that no obstacle can retard it.

It has been observed that Haimon's description of the so-called cult of carts
may have been exaggerated from hearsay information and that the motives of
the participants may have been more to perform an act of penance to further their
salvation than to further the reconstruction of the cathedral. Nevertheless, the
building was both a civic and an ecclesiastical monument. Participation of the
guilds in furnishing stained-glass windows attests to their pride in embellishing
the church. As a visible landmark, the cathedral embodied the wealth and organizational ability of the community to erect such a magnificent structure. Ultimately,
however, the cathedral was the earthly symbol of the spiritual church built of
"living stones." Durandus, a thirteenth-century Bishop of Mende and a professor
of canon law at Modena, wrote,

> The word church hath two meanings: the one a material building where-
> in the divine offices are celebrated; the other a spiritual fabric which is a
> collection of the faithful. The church, that is the people forming it, is assem-
> bled by its ministers and collected together into one place by "Him who
> maketh man to be of one mind in a house." For as the material church is
> constructed from the joining together of various stones so is the spiritual
> Church by that of various men. . . . For the material church, wherein the
> people assemble to set forth God's Holy praise symbolizeth that Holy Church
> which is built in Heaven of living stones.

And Abbot Suger, in summing up the significance of his reconstructed choir
at Saint-Denis, varied this idea in his own inimitable way:

> . . . Jesus Christ Himself being the chief cornerstone which joins one
> wall to the other; in whom all the building—whether spiritual or material—
> groweth unto one holy temple in the Lord. In whom we, too, are taught to
> be builded together for an habitation of God through the Holy Spirit by our-
> selves in a spiritual way, the more loftily and fitly we strive to build in a
> material way.

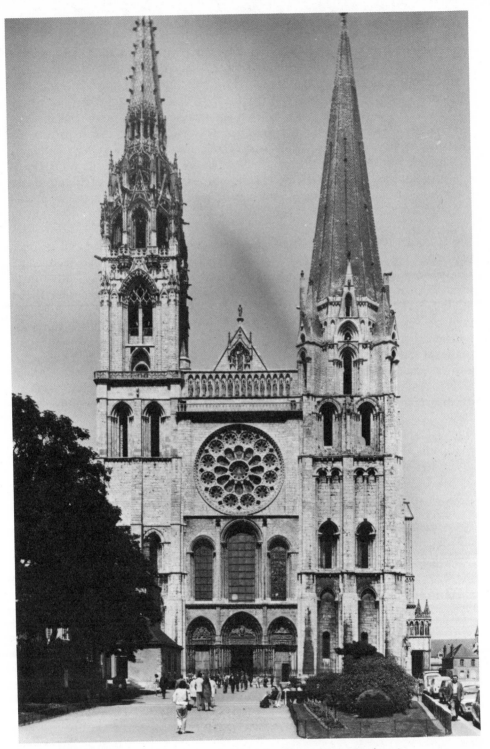

Fig. 129. West facade. Chartres Cathedral. 1134–16th century. (Marburg)

22. The Gothic Portal

When work was begun on the rebuilding of the facade of Fulbert's church at Chartres in 1134, plans were made for an elaborate sculpted triple portal known since the thirteenth century as the *porta regia* or *portail royal* (fig. 129). Originally, it is believed, this portal may have been intended to be recessed under a porch between the two facade towers that were under construction by 1142, but by 1144 the plan was changed and they were brought forward, even with the outer face of the towers. Three roundheaded windows were placed above them in the new harmonious facade. The western portals at Chartres are unusual because they all open into the nave; in Romanesque churches of just a decade or so before, such as Vézelay, the major portal opened into the nave and smaller doorways opened into the aisles. The massive walls and buttressing for the towers at Chartres precluded this possibility, but the result was fortunate, for it permitted a closely integrated visual and iconographical ensemble. The "portail royal" contains a highly developed and coherent symbolic program. In its complexity and careful organization it reflects the sensibilities of a new Gothic age; its stylistic and formal properties, however, retain many characteristics of Romanesque form.

The Chartres portals (fig. 130) combine all of the sculpted elements we found in Romanesque doorways. Carved archivolts surround sculpted tympanums and lintels. The doors are set into the fabric of the facade; the doorjambs are splayed and are articulated with engaged columns against which are placed thin columnar figures. No longer is a planar surface a mere field for inset sculpted reliefs; instead, the deep embrasures permit space to penetrate into the fabric along the undulating carved surfaces of the archivolts and jambs, the figures of which project into that space. The effect is consistent with the architecture itself, where space penetrates structure and structure projects into space. We are gently focused inward toward the open doorway. A continuous frieze of historiated capitals visually and thematically ties all three portals together.

The right ("Incarnation") portal (fig. 131) contains, in the tympanum, the image of the Virgin Enthroned with the Christ Child in her lap, flanked by two angels. This static, frontal image, with an equally frontal Christ Child, is similar to the Byzantine icon of the Hodegetria Madonna, the Virgin as the Indicator of the Way to Salvation, and was often repeated in wooden and stone cult images of the Virgin in the Romanesque period. Below, in the bottom lintel are narrative reliefs depicting the "Annunciation," "Visitation," "Nativity," and the "Adoration of the Shepherds," while above is the "Presentation of Christ at the Temple." Adolf Katzenellenbogen pointed out the axial relationship between the Christ standing on the altar in this scene and the infant lying in his crib on the manger below, as though there too the child were placed upon the altar table. Since these reliefs narrate the Incarnation, the sacrificial implications of this placement, signify-

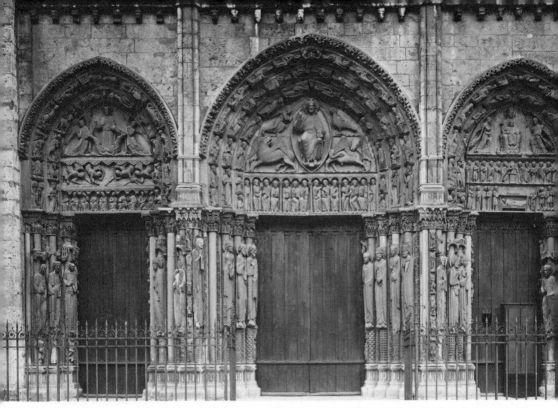

Fig. 130. "Portail royal." West facade, Chartres Cathedral. 1134–1150. (Marburg)

ing Christ's ultimate sacrifice for mankind, is appropriate. Both poles of Christ's mission on earth are stated, the First Coming explicitly and the climax of his mission implicitly. In the archivolt around the portal are personifications of the seven liberal arts: grammar, dialectic (logic), and rhetoric constituting the *trivium,* and arithmetic, music, geometry, and astronomy constituting the *quadrivium*. They are accompanied by the seven major authors in these fields of knowledge, such as Cicero for rhetoric, Aristotle for dialectic, and Pythagoras for music. Angels accompany them on the inner archivolt. Reading all of the elements of the portal together, we find that the seven liberal arts, the sum of human wisdom, are complemented by the figures of the Virgin and Child, who are seated on the throne of Solomon, the Throne of Wisdom (*Sedes Sapientiae*). The Virgin is the means by which Divine Wisdom was made incarnate in the person of Christ and upon whom human wisdom depends. In the Incarnation the *Logos* or Word is made flesh. Although this theme has a long tradition in medieval art, for the church of Hagia Sophia in Constantinople was dedicated to the Virgin as the personification of Divine Wisdom, it attained its fullest explanation in the teaching of Scholasticism at the cathedral school at Chartres in the mid-twelfth century. This portal also makes explicit the role of the Virgin, to whom Notre Dame of Chartres was dedicated, in making Divine Wisdom incarnate. This erudite representation of the theme of the Incarnation on several levels and subtle elaboration of interwoven themes indicate a new sophistication of symbolic programs in the Gothic period.

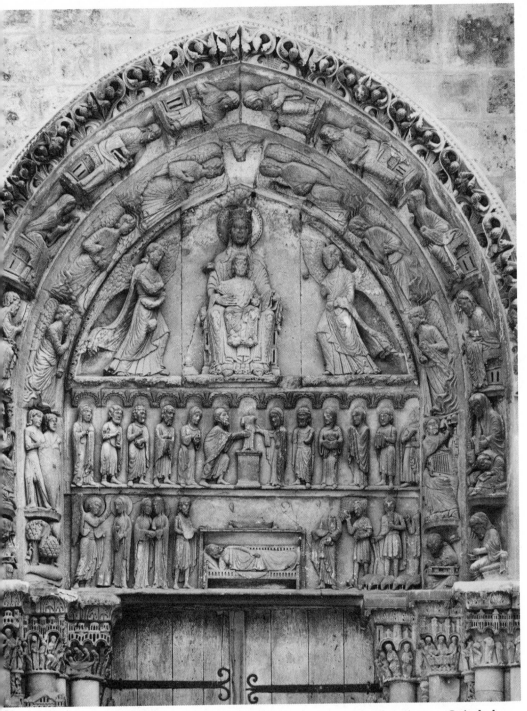

Fig. 131. "Incarnation." Right portal, west facade, Chartres Cathedral. 1134–1150. (Hirmer Fotoarchiv)

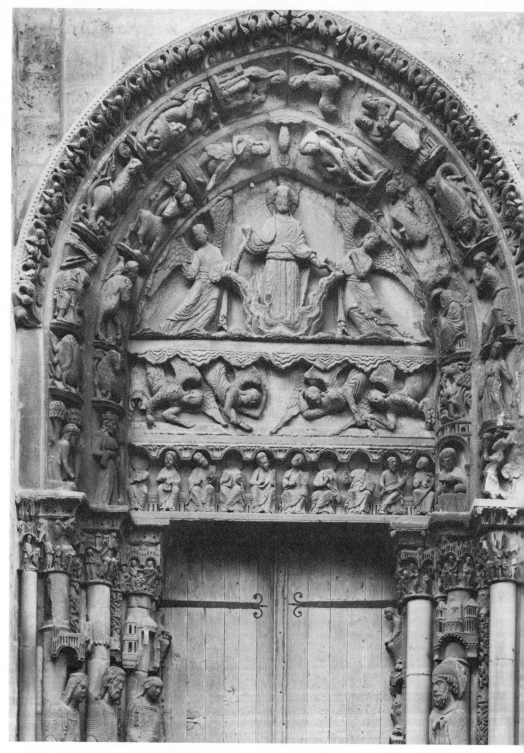

Fig. 132. "Ascension." Left portal, west facade, Chartres Cathedral. 1134–1150. (Hirmer Fotoarchiv)

The tympanum in the left portal is usually thought to depict the "Ascension." Christ is between two angels who lift him upward in an undulating cloud (fig. 132). In the bottom lintel the apostles witness the event, while above them four angels predict the "Second Coming." In the archivolt are representations of the signs of the zodiac and labors of the months, signifying the passage of cosmic and terrestrial time between the "Ascension" and the "Second Coming." Thus this portal terminates the ministry of Christ begun in the right portal. The flesh returns to spirit, but it also prepares the way for the event depicted in the central portal.

The vision of the "Second Coming" according to the fourth chapter of Revelation appears in the central portal (fig. 133). This portal is higher, wider, and deeper by one archivolt and one doorjamb than the flanking embrasures. Christ, making a gesture of benediction, looms almost detached from the mandorla flanked by the four attributes of the Evangelists. In the archivolts the seated elders and standing angels surround the heavenly vision. Below, in an arcaded lintel, stand the apostles with the prophets Elijah and Enoch who also had ascended into heaven without dying.

The impact of the figure of Christ in this Second Coming has changed from that at Moissac. The Chartres Christ is executed in bolder and more varied relief, with knees pushing forward and an upraised arm completely detached from the ground. The drapery style is a mixture of a new form-defining series of multiple folds, particularly on Christ's right knee, and the Romanesque surface articulation, found at Autun and particularly at Vézelay, in the eddying of concentric folds on the upraised arm and upper torso. Likewise the head is completely detached and instead of the blocklike massiveness of Moissac, it is subtly and naturalistically rendered. Gone also is the severe, staring quality. Instead we find an introspective, saddened gaze implying a more compassionate and forgiving attitude about the sinfulness of mankind.

Below the lintels the intricately carved frieze of capitals narrates the life of the Virgin, or the pre-Incarnation events, and the ministry and Passion of Christ, linking the Incarnation with the Ascension, and tying the themes of the portals together.

In the embrasures below, a series of elongated columnar figures (fig. 134) stands against the columns of the doorjambs. Stiff and frontal, they echo the function of the column even though they appear as separate volumes engaged in front of them. They have been found to be representations of prophets and kings and queens of the Old Testament who were the ancestors of Christ. In the twelfth century, among such writers as Bernard of Clairvaux, considerable emphasis was placed upon the terrestrial genealogy of Christ in an effort to stress his dual nature —human and divine—in opposition to prevalent twelfth-century heresies that denied this duality. In manuscript illumination and stained glass this theme took the form of the "Tree of Jesse" (pl. 13), a vision of the genealogical tree of Christ prophesied by Isaiah. But on the western facade of Chartres Christ's ancestors become the Old Testament antecedents, ushering the beholder to the door of the church and serving visually as the supports for the New Testament incidents related above. Their presence heightened the impact of the Incarnation of

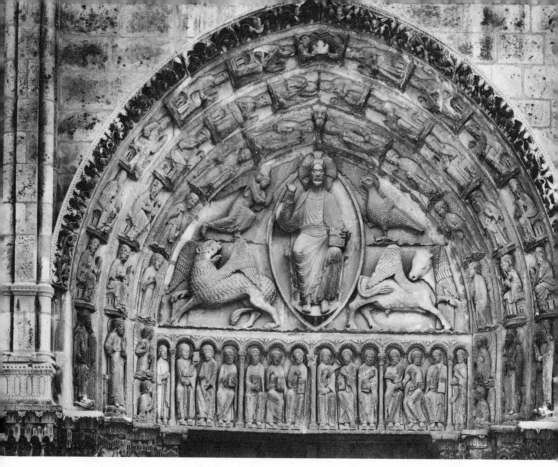

Fig. 133. "Second Coming." Central portal, west facade, Chartres Cathedral. 1134–1150. (Hirmer Fotoarchiv)

the Spirit and of Divine Wisdom in the person of Christ above by reminding the beholder of Christ's human as well as his divine nature.

The column figures also combine elements of Romanesque form with a new Gothic sensibility. The excessively attenuated canon of proportions and the tight constraint of the figures as though within an invisible tube heighten the rigidity of their frontal positions. Arms are held close to the body, and draperies contain the figures within parallel and concentric folds. The column figures are by different hands, and some of them have the circular eddies and blocklike treatment of heads that is close to the sculpture of Autun and Vézelay. Others, however, combine the rigidity of pose with softer and more generalized features and almond-shaped eyes to create an effect of introspective serenity and majestic self-assurance.

The column figures serve dual architectural and decorative functions. Engaged with and part of the column behind, they are subjugated to the function of architecture, assuming the shape of an architectural member even more than the trumeau figures at Moissac. But the Chartres jamb figures also exist in front of the columns and are relieved of all supporting duties. Some of the column figures

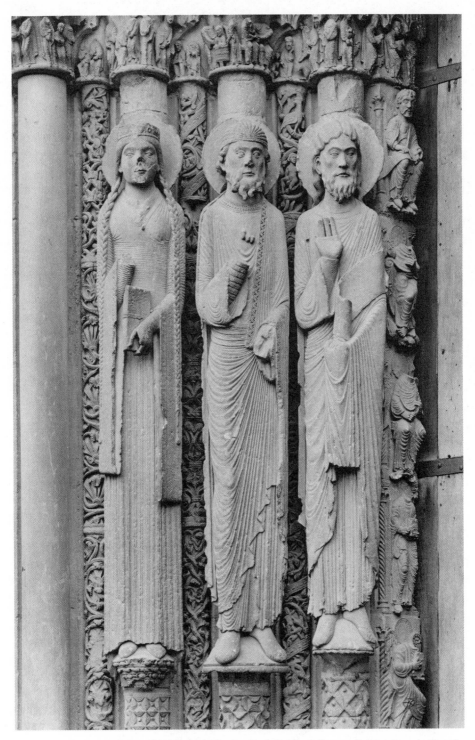

Fig. 134. Column figures. Left jambs of central portal, west facade, Chartres Cathedral. 1134–1150. (Hirmer Fotoarchiv)

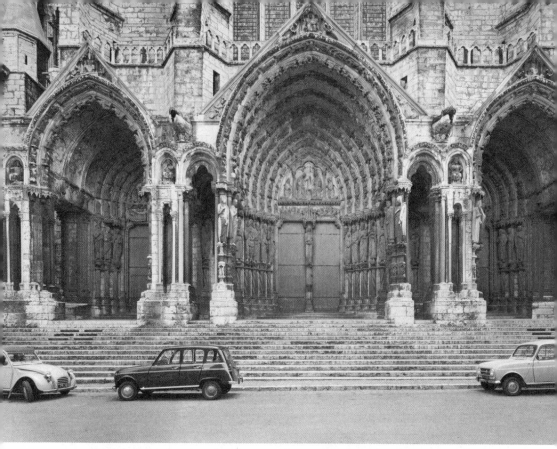

Fig. 135. Portals. North transept, Chartres Cathedral. 1200–1220.
(Hirmer Fotoarchiv)

stand on projecting bases beneath projecting canopies, in their own cylindrical space before the column. In their imaginary imprisonment they assert a volumetric independence that later leads to freestanding, freely moving jamb figures in architectural niches. Individually, each of the Chartres column figures is different in physiognomy, demeanor, and even in size, but when seen from a distance (see fig. 130, p. 156) they act together as an undulating screen, partially obscuring the embrasure as the edges of the pier buttresses obscure the core of the church, and ushering the beholder inward toward the door.

Both transepts of Chartres Cathedral were under construction between 1200 and 1220, and further innovations in portal arrangement and style took place at this time. Both transept ends were designed with fully developed tripartite facades and projecting porches over deeply recessed portals (fig. 135). Here the side portals opened into the aisles of the transept while the central portal entered into its nave. In the transept facades projecting architectural elements alternate with deeply penetrating spaces. The number of articulated elements was multiplied: nine bands of carved archivolts surround the central tympanum of the north transept. The myriad of repetitive details resembles the profusion of pinnacles, buttresses, and traceries in the fabric of the building as a whole.

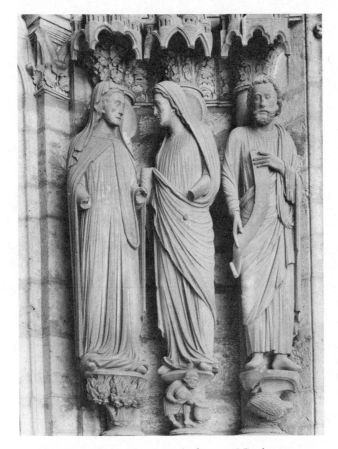

Fig. 136. "Visitation," jamb figures. North transept,
Chartres Cathedral. c. 1220. (Hirmer Fotoarchiv)

The central portal of the north transept is devoted to the Virgin, the tympanum containing the "Coronation of the Virgin" above a lintel depicting her
"Death and Assumption into Heaven." The figures appear even more detached
from the background; they are no longer frontal and they are clothed in draperies
with multiple folds, perhaps derived from the style of Nicholas of Verdun, which
pull taut over the body and reveal the volumetric form beneath.

The jamb figures (fig. 136) reveal the extent of transformation in Gothic
sculpture by the beginning of the thirteenth century. Although still elongated,
they have assumed more normative proportions. Standing on carved figures or
monsters beneath boldly projecting canopies, they assert their almost total independence from the column behind them by twisting and turning in a variety of
postures. This freedom of movement and more volumetric treatment is most boldly
stated in the group of the "Visitation" jamb figures of the left doorway, where
Saint Elizabeth and the Virgin pivot dramatically in their places to face each
other. Executed around 1220, they also reflect the full effect of a combination of
attention to natural detail in the older visage of Saint Elizabeth, and classical feeling for the form-defining properties of multiple-fold drapery, which was widely
current at that time.

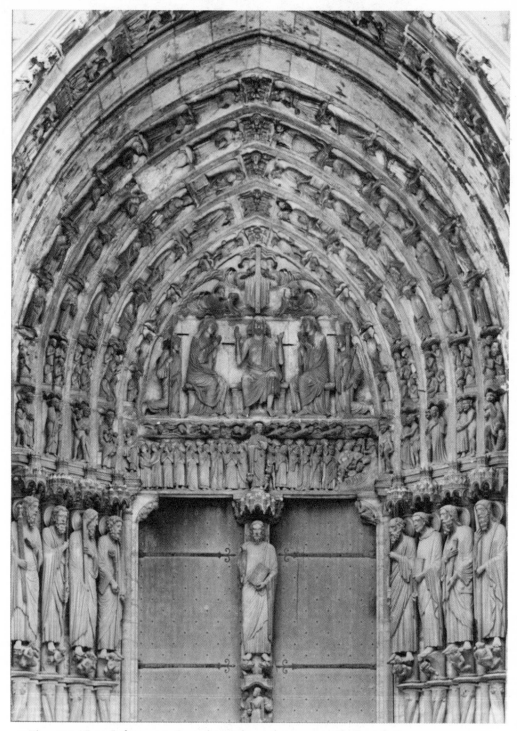

Fig. 137. "Last Judgment." Central portal, south transept, Chartres Cathedral. c. 1200–1220. (Hirmer Fotoarchiv)

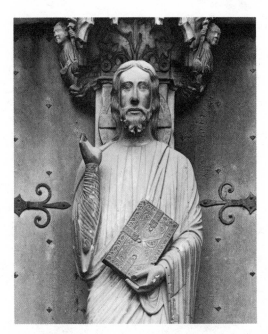

Fig. 138. "Beau Dieu," trumeau. Central portal, south transept,
Chartres Cathedral. 1200–1220. (Hirmer Fotoarchiv)

The portals of the north transept were dedicated to the Virgin, depicting to
the left of the "Coronation" the "Nativity" and "Adoration of the Magi," and
on the right Old Testament precedents for the *Sedes Sapientiae* with the "Judgment of Solomon," and of the suffering of the Virgin with the story of Job. On
the south transept the central tympanum was devoted to the "Last Judgment"
(fig. 137), while the flanking portals contained the stories of the lives of Saints
Martin, Nicholas, and Stephen. The number of decorative elements in these later
portals is multiplied, and the repertoire of motifs is increased beyond the theophanic and eschatological themes of the Romanesque period.

The treatment of the "Last Judgment" has changed considerably from the
earlier representation of Autun. In the tympanum of the central portal Christ is
enthroned, surrounded by angels holding the instruments of the Passion, the cross,
the crown of thorns, the lance, and the sponge—all the implements of his torture
before and during the Crucifixion. At the moment of Judgment these serve as
reminders of Christ's sacrifice for mankind. The Virgin and Saint John serve as
intercessors for mankind. In the lintel below Saint Michael with a scale presides
over the separation of the blessed and the damned. The damned—kings, bishops,
nobles, and clergy alike—are shunted to the right where they are devoured by
a Hell mouth, and in the adjacent lower archivolts, devils take away the sinners.
Opposite, Abraham receives three souls in his bosom and angels receive the blessed.
In the archivolts above, souls rise from their sarcophagi and above them a heavenly
choir of angels and seraphim preside. On the jambs below the tympanum, the
apostles flank the doorway.

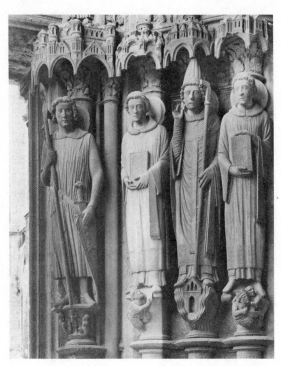

Fig. 139. "Saint Theodore" or "Roland" and jamb figures. Left portal, south transept, Chartres Cathedral. c. 1220–1230. (Hirmer Fotoarchiv)

A trumeau also contains the figure of Christ (fig. 138), but this time he does not act as judge. His placement next to the doors to his church reflects the passage from Saint John, "I am the door: by me if any enter in, he shall be saved" (John 10:9). Although he stands on a lion and a basilisk, symbolic of his triumph over evil, Christ's demeanor is humane and compassionate, welcoming, not condemning. The emphasis on Christ's passion and suffering above and on the receptiveness of his attitude below show that the Christian faith in Gothic era became a more emotional and immediate experience for the worshiper.

Another jamb figure on the south transept of Chartres Cathedral epitomizes another aspect of the Gothic era. "Saint Theodore" (fig. 139), a military saint who lived in Roman times, or possibly Roland, is depicted in contemporary thirteenth-century chain mail; he is dressed as a Christian knight and is the personification of a youthful chivalric ideal. He is also the embodiment of the Church Militant, for this was the period of continuing crusades to the Holy Land. His sure, easy stance, aristocratic demeanor, and the meticulous detail of his armor reflect a greater assimilation of actual observation mixed with a new courtly ideal that was to transform Gothic art by the middle of the thirteenth century.

Whereas Romanesque sculpture had pronounced certain didactic messages reinforced with biblical narrative in selected places in the pilgrimage church, Gothic cathedral sculpture soon became encyclopedic in its scope. On its three facades and nine portals Chartres itself manifested the expanding narrative and multiplication of details that were to continue throughout the thirteenth century.

23. THE GOTHIC STAINED-GLASS WINDOW

Stained-glass windows had been used in Romanesque churches of the eleventh century, but they had been restricted to small roundheaded openings set in thick walls. The perfection of a structural system that concentrated the load of the vaults onto a skeletal framework in the choir of Saint-Denis allowed the nonbearing walls beneath to become increasingly voided. In the ambulatory chapels at Saint-Denis the windows filled, on the inside, almost all of the available wall space. The building was not, however, filled with light. Because rich, deep tonalities of blue, red, and green predominated, enlivened with light blue, white, yellow, and orange, a soft purple light pervaded the interior. Although Abbot Suger did not mention the new quality of architecture that had been created during the reconstruction of the choir at Saint-Denis, he did mention the "splendid variety of new windows, both below and above . . . which are very valuable on account of their wonderful execution and profuse expenditure of painted glass and sapphire glass." He valued them so highly that he appointed a special master for their maintenance.

An artist's manual, *On Divers Arts,* written by the German monk Theophilus around 1100, explains the procedures for making stained glass, or "pot metal," as it is sometimes called after the large caldrons used for melting the glass. Glass was colored by adding a variety of metal oxides, such as iron or manganese, and the color would vary from saffron to purple depending on the length of time it was heated. Flat panes of glass were made by blowing a bubble with a long tube and then forming it into a cylinder. This cylinder might be dipped into a caldron of red pot metal, allowing a colored film to fuse with the surface. The cylinder would then be cut and flattened out on a panel of wood. Meanwhile the design of the window or panel would then be marked out on a board, and, when cooled, colored pieces of glass would be cut and fitted as though in a jigsaw puzzle. These panes would then be joined with lead strips and fixed within a larger armature in the window. Onto the colored panes that were used for areas of flesh, drapery, and background, vitreous pigment was applied to indicate features, folds of cloth, and foliate designs.

The earliest stained-glass windows in Romanesque and Early Gothic churches were placed in simple vertical openings called *lancets.* Roundheaded openings were used in Romanesque, and pointed arches in Gothic churches. Horizontal armatures, and sometimes vertical ones if the window was wide, stabilized the leaded design. In lancets placed high in the clerestory, or in the transepts under the rose windows as at Chartres Cathedral, tall, thin figures were usually placed as in the lancets of King David (fig. 140) and Saint Anne and the Virgin, as though in a translucent homme-arcade. These large figures ensured maximum visibility and could be "read" easily from the main pavement.

A similar window of around 1150 in the south ambulatory of Chartres Cathedral, known as "La Belle Verrière" (fig. 141), depicts a monumental iconlike image

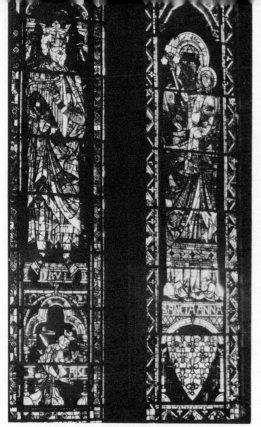

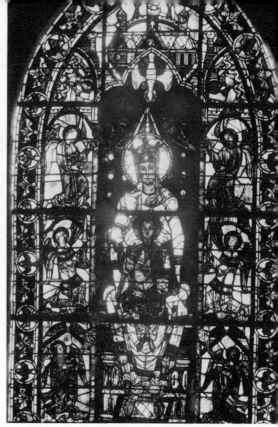

Fig. 140. King David and Saint Anne and the Virgin. Lancet windows, north transept, Chartres Cathedral. c. 1200. (Editions Houvet, Chartres)

Fig. 141. Virgin and Child ("La Belle Verrière"). Window, Chartres Cathedral. c. 1150, angels added c. 1200. (Editions Houvet, Chartres)

of the Virgin and Child enthroned in majesty in the central panel. She is a stained-glass equivalent of the *Sedes Sapientiae* on the western portal, clothed in a light-blue robe marked with decorative folds in the Romanesque manner. When the window was placed in a larger opening around 1200, two vertical rows of three kneeling angels were added. Executed in deep, rich, glowing reds and blues, although lightened by the Virgin's light-blue garment, the window has the bold, hieratic impact of Romanesque art.

Other, more complicated designs were also used in the twelfth century. Although these were usually placed in the aisles and ambulatory chapels where they could be seen more closely, they also were placed in the upper levels. The right lancet below the rose of the west facade of Chartres contains the "Tree of Jesse" (pl. 13), perhaps patterned after a similar window that had been made for Saint-Denis. This is the genealogical tree envisioned by Isaiah (11:1): "There shall come forth a rod out of the stem of Jesse, and a branch shall grow out of his root." Jesse reclines in the lowest medallion and a leafy tree grows upward from his loins, containing representations of David and other Old Testament kings, culminating with the Virgin and Christ at the very top. Old Testament prophets

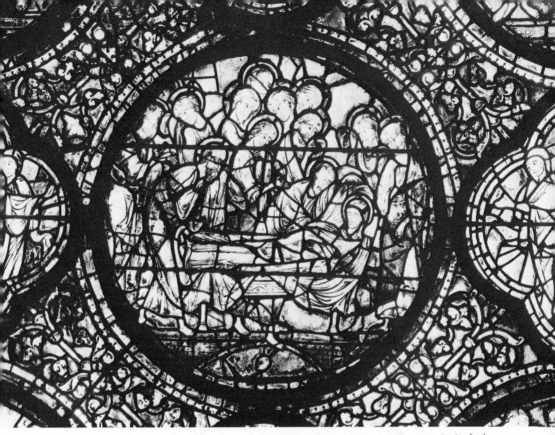

Fig. 142. "Death of the Virgin." Aisle window, Chartres Cathedral. 1200–1220. (Giraudon)

occupy the segmental medallions along the sides of the window. Because individual figures filled each compartment, they were visible from the pavement below, and the entire scheme filling the lancet served, in the same way as the column figures flanking the portals, to remind the observer of the human as well as the divine nature of Christ.

With increasing frequency large lancet windows were subdivided into medallions of various geometric shapes that were filled with a multitude of figures relating a profusion of narrative incidents on a given theme. Such windows were often donated to the cathedral by various trade guilds in Chartres, such as the "Window of the Life of the Virgin" with scenes of her life, death (fig. 142), and Assumption, donated by the cobblers guild. This window of around 1200 to 1220, designed for a large aperture, reflected the expansion of iconographical programs and multiplicity of scenes also manifested by the contemporary portal sculptures at Chartres. Whereas the earlier twelfth-century glass had contained a balance of lighter blues and whites with the deeper reds, blues, and greens, the early thirteenth-century windows became even darker and richer in their overall impact with the increased use of a deep manganese blue instead of the lighter cobalt blue.

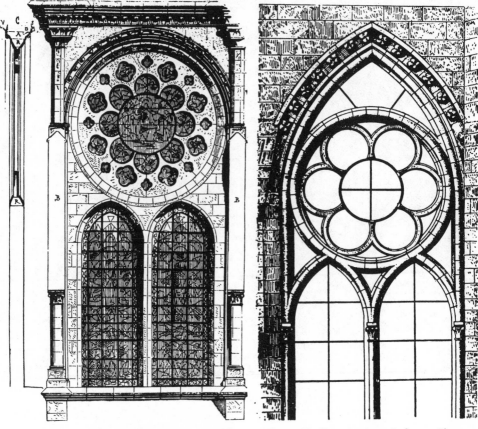

Fig. 143. Plate-tracery window. Clerestory of nave, Chartres Cathedral. c. 1200. (After Viollet-le-Duc)

Fig. 144. Bar-tracery window. Clerestory of choir, Reims Cathedral. 1211–1236. (After Charles H. Moore)

With the possibility of using larger areas of the clerestory for window openings at Chartres than had been possible under the six-part vaults of previous Gothic cathedrals, a new elaborate arrangement was designed. Two pointed lancets were placed beneath a circular rose window. The rose was composed of *plate tracery* (fig. 143), flat stones cut to form, in the overall design, a series of petallike circles around a central roundel that was surrounded by quatrefoils. The rose neatly filled in most of the wall area under the curved vault.

Between 1211 and 1236 a new development occurred in the design of the windows for the choir of Reims cathedral (fig. 144). Stone armatures, called *bar tracery,* were fitted together to form arches and roundels in a skeletal manner. Some of the stone bars performed a dual function, forming the upper curve of the lancet as well as a segment of the lower curve of the rose. Residual areas were voided and filled with glass. Thus, two lancets and a rose now were placed within a single encompassing lancet.

The ultimate disintegration of the wall and the orderly multiplication of subunits took place at the Sainte-Chapelle (fig. 145, pl. 14), built by Saint Louis in

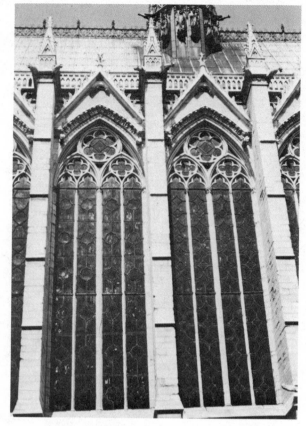

Fig. 145. Exterior of windows. Sainte-Chapelle, Paris.
1243–1248. (R. G. Calkins)

Paris between 1243 and 1248 as an elaborate architectural reliquary for the Thorn
from the Crown of Thorns and other relics, which he purchased in Constantinople.
The upper story of this chapel is a cage of glass. Tall lancet windows contain a
rose surmounting a pair of lancet windows, each with its own rose and two smaller
lancets. This logical division of units reflects the orderly membering of responds
that had been perfected in the 1230s in the nave of Saint-Denis. Within the four
lancets a variety of geometric forms—circles, half circles, diamonds, and quatrefoils—form medallions for an astonishing number of pictorial representations of
Old and New Testament scenes, the lives of the saints, and the story of the obtaining of the relics by Saint Louis. With the virtual mass production that was
necessary to produce this much glass, the quality of the drawing of the figures
declined, facial types became stereotyped, and decoration became less elaborate
and more formulaic. The colors of the glass, still predominantly red and blue,
suffused the interior with a purplish light.

By the end of the thirteenth century and throughout the fourteenth and fifteenth centuries, however, changes in coloration led to different interior effects.

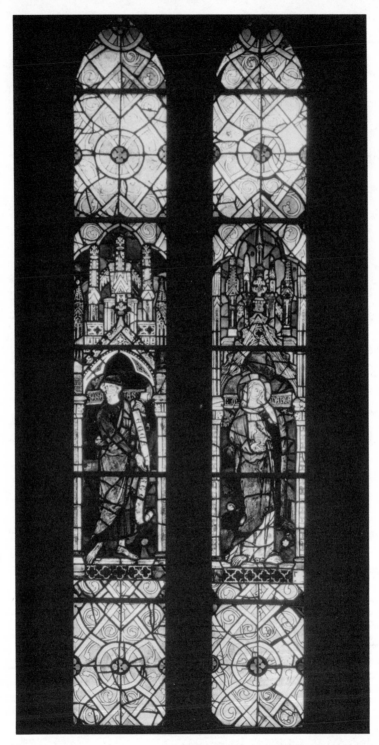

Fig. 146. Window with the prophet Isaiah and Mary Magdalene.
Évron, northern France. c. 1315. The Metropolitan Museum of Art,
The Cloisters Collection (Fletcher Fund, 1928).

A window of around 1315, believed to be from Évron (fig. 146) near Évreux and now in The Cloisters in New York, contains lighter tonalities and an increased use of yellowish accents on white glass. The two panels depict on the left Isaiah holding a scroll with the word *Ecce*: "Behold a Virgin shall conceive and bear a son" and on the right Mary Magdalene holding a jar of unguent, with which she had anointed Christ's feet (Luke 7:37–38). The robes are a red-brown for the Magdalene and light green over a reddish-brown robe for Isaiah. The figures, in comparison with those at Chartres, are elongated, insubstantial, and willowy in their gently curving postures and are representative of the courtly style that predominated in the later thirteenth and the beginning of the fourteenth century. They are placed in architectural canopies of white glass touched with yellow that fill the remainder of the lancet. Above and below the colored panels, circles and lozenges of white glass lightly shaded with touches of gray and touched with yellow (*grisaille*) reflect the contemporary tradition of stained glass current particularly among the Cistercians, who spurned figurative, richly colored glass in the Gothic period as they had the costly gold artifacts and distracting capitals of the Romanesque. The figures and colored areas are therefore small in relation to the entire window, and more light thus suffused the interiors of the churches, permitting greater visibility of their increasingly intricate architectural detail and furnishings.

In the fifteenth century the stained-glass window lost its role as a field for glowing flat images and became a vehicle for volumetric figures in illusionistic architectural settings. The large window at Bourges Cathedral, donated by Jacques Coeur in 1450 (fig. 147), is placed in a vast flamboyant tracery ensemble incorporating a fleur-de-lis and heart-shaped medallions, symbols of the donor's family name. Depicting an "Annunciation" in the two center lancets, with Saint James the Elder and Saint Catherine of Alexandria in the flanking ones, the window is unified by a coherent architectural setting rendered in perspective. Separate vaults, as though for aisles, occupy the side lancets and a single vault unites the two center panels. The figures are modeled to give the illusion of three-dimensional bodies. With the imposition of the spatial qualities of Renaissance painting on this window, we have the final dissolution of the earlier aesthetic of stained glass as a planar translucent surface.

The stained-glass window played an essential role in the functioning of the Gothic cathedral and provided important aspects of its meaning. In writing of the windows at Saint-Denis, Abbot Suger pointed out that they had a threefold function. First, they were the bearers of holy images: they related, as had the historiated capitals in the Romanesque churches, an encyclopedic array of biblical narratives, allegories, and lives of the saints. Second, Suger noted that the windows were made of intrinsically rich materials resembling precious stones. Third, he noted that the light emitted by these windows was a mystery, for it glowed without fire. They were the source of a divine light, for natural light passed through them and was transformed into a mystical icon-bearing light. Suger marveled at his choir "shining with wonderful and uninterrupted light of most sacred windows,"

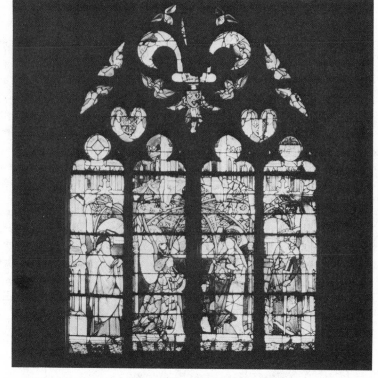

Fig. 147. Window of Jacques Coeur. Bourges Cathedral. c. 1450.
(Archives photographiques, Paris, S.P.A.D.E.M.)

and noted that "the noble edifice . . . is pervaded by the new light." As Suger had observed about his building and about the precious objects he had commissioned for its high altar, the contemplation of the windows led one "from the material to the immaterial."

This dictum would have been particularly true at Saint-Denis, Chartres, or the Sainte-Chapelle, where the purplish glow of the windows shone on the stone structure and dissolved its materiality in a rainbow of color. Vaults soar in a mystical ambience, walls glow with rich variegated light, and structure itself is rendered visually immaterial. That the Gothic cathedral was often considered to be the earthly equivalent of the heavenly city of Jerusalem is not surprising, for the twelfth- and thirteenth-century preoccupation with the mystical light within these edifices surely evoked the vision of the heavenly city of Jerusalem as described in the Book of Revelation:

> . . . that great city, the holy Jerusalem, descending out of heaven from God, having the glory of God; and her light was like unto a stone most precious, even a jasper stone, clear as crystal. . . . The wall of it was of jasper and the city was of pure gold, like unto clear glass, . . . And the city had no need of the sun, neither of the moon, to shine in it: for the glory of God did lighten it, and the Lamb is the light thereof. (Rev. 21:10–23)

24. The Gothic Altarpiece

In contrast to the antependium, which was placed below the altar table, the altarpiece or retable was usually placed upon or behind it. Altarpieces were made in a variety of mediums, but we shall be concerned here with those that were painted on panels. The Romanesque and Gothic panel paintings were similar in technique to, and perhaps derived in inspiration from, the Byzantine icon. The process of preparing the wooden panel, smoothing it, coating it with gesso, applying bole where gold leaf was to be used, making an underdrawing, and then building up areas from basic tonalities in modulated shadows and highlights was generally the same. In Italy in the thirteenth and fourteenth centuries *tempera* paint, a mixture of ground pigments with the yolk of egg, was used. This dried quickly in brilliant but opaque tonalities. In contrast, in Flanders in the fifteenth century, artists perfected a manner of painting with oil-based paints. Although Jan van Eyck has been traditionally credited with this invention, this view is now regarded as erroneous, for Italians and sometimes others used touches of oil glazes on their tempera paintings in the fourteenth century. Oil paints permitted the use of transparent oil glazes, which allowed artists to obtain subtle gradations of tones and luminous highlights in painted jewels, brocades, and even hair.

Some of the early Italian altarpieces have the simple format and stark impact of the Byzantine icon, by which they were undoubtedly influenced. In an early panel representing Saint Francis of Assisi (fig. 148), signed by the artist, Bonaventura Berlinghieri, and dated 1235, only nine years after the saint's death and seven years after his canonization, he is depicted in an attenuated, stiff, frontal form in the center of a gabled panel. The face with high cheekbones and caved-in cheeks, the domed cranium, and the staring quality of the eyes, even the somber tonalities of the flesh, are all derived from the manner of Byzantine icon painting. This panel can, in fact, be considered an icon of Saint Francis, but with one important difference. It is flanked not by attendant saints, but by narrative scenes of the life of Saint Francis, such as the "stigmatization," when he received the wounds of Christ, and the engaging scene of the "Sermon to the Birds." There had been no precedent for these scenes, and they reveal a liveliness of narration that contrasts with the intense stylized image of the saint in the central panel. Such panels, placed upon altars dedicated to the saints represented, invoked the devotions of the beholder.

The large, almost twelve-foot-high panel of the *Madonna and Child Enthroned with Angels and Prophets* (fig. 149) in the Uffizi Gallery, Florence, painted by Cimabue for the church of S. Trinità in Florence around 1285 to 1300, is a monumental variant of the theme of the Mount Sinai icon of around 700 years before. With the enthroned Virgin flanked by eight standing angels, the panel reiterated the revised composition of "La Belle Verrière" at Chartres and was used, with variations in style, in other monumental panels by the contemporary Italian

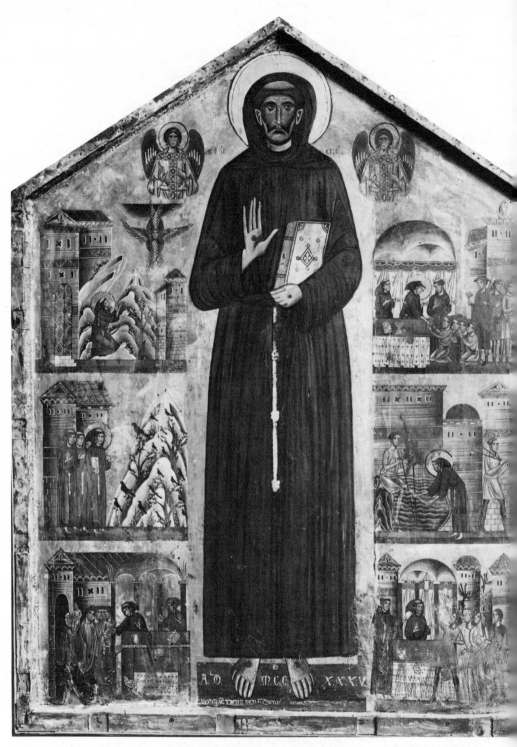

Fig. 148. Bonaventura Berlinghieri: "Altarpiece of Saint Francis." 1235.
Tempera on panel, 60" x 46". S. Francesco, Pescia. (Alinari)

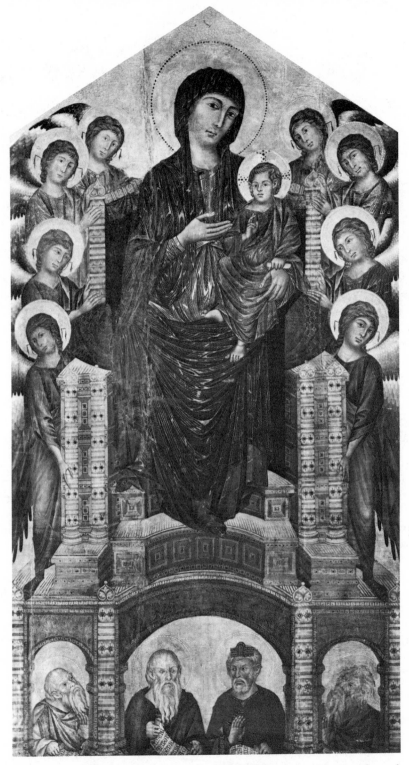

Fig. 149. Cimabue: *Madonna and Child Enthroned with Angels and Prophets.* c. 1285–1300. Tempera on panel, 139″ x 88″. Uffizi Gallery, Florence. (Alinari)

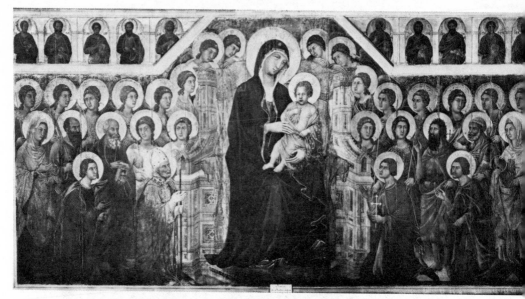

Fig. 150. Duccio di Buoninsegna: *Maestà*, altarpiece. 1308–1311. Tempera on panel, 7′ x 13′. Museo dell' Opera del Duomo, Siena. (Alinari)

artists, Duccio and Giotto. The Virgin's robe is articulated by the shimmering golden striations of Byzantine icons or mosaics, such as the "Pantocrator" at Cefalù. The greenish tonalities of the faces, caused by the terra verde of the underpainting from which the highlights of the features were built up, also recall Byzantine painting, but we find a more emphatic modeling and massiveness that herald future developments in Italian painting. The iconography is still that of the Byzantine Hodegetria Madonna, but she is also crowned and enthroned as Queen of Heaven, and the flanking angels imply the levitation of her "Assumption" into heaven. In the niches under the throne are the prophets Jeremiah, Isaiah, Abraham, and David, with scrolls prophesying the coming of the Messiah.

In the early fourteenth century both the form of the altarpiece and the theme of the Virgin in Majesty were elaborated and magnified. In 1308 the Commission of the Works of the Cathedral at Siena contracted with Duccio di Buoninsegna to paint for the high altar a large retable of the *Maestà* ("Virgin in the Court of Heaven," fig. 150). Completed in 1311, it was carried in triumph to the cathedral "accompanied by members of the congregation, the government, the clergy and the people carrying lighted candles and torches, to the sounds of all the bells of the city, and the music of trumpets and bagpipes." The central panel measured seven by thirteen feet and was surrounded by pinnacles above and narrative panels below in the *predella*. Because the altarpiece was set upon a freestanding altar, the back contained twenty-six scenes of the Passion of Christ.

On the main front panel the enthroned Virgin was placed in an expanded celestial context, attended by adoring saints and angels. This glorified image of the Virgin was a fitting depiction, as the people of Siena believed that she had protected them and aided in the victory of Montaperti against the Florentines in 1260. In the foreground four kneeling saints—Asanus, Savinus, Crescentius, and Victor—the patron saints of Siena, act as intercessors for the favor of the Virgin and Child on behalf of the beholder. Still dependent upon Byzantine formulas for facial types, greenish modeling of features, and the theme of the Hodegetria Madonna, Duccio has nevertheless combined these elements with a refinement, sumptuousness, and Gothic lyricism that transforms the scene into an elegant courtly vision. Rhythmic gestures lead the eye inward to the central figures of the Virgin and Child, while colored robes are arranged to create balancing patterns in the composition.

In the predella and pinnacles, which have now been dispersed, were representations of scenes of the childhood of Christ and the life of the Virgin with additional figures of apostles, prophets, and angels. On the back the predella contained the "Baptism" and "Temptation of Christ" and his miracles, while the pinnacles appropriately contained scenes of Christ's appearances after the Resurrection. In the *Maestà,* the Byzantine formula of the twelve liturgical feasts often found in the iconostasis was amplified by Duccio into a detailed account of the Incarnation, Ministry, Passion, and Resurrection of Christ and focused on the ethereal presence of the Virgin indicating that her son is the way to salvation.

With the increasing elaboration of the Gothic altarpiece in the thirteenth and fourteenth centuries, a variety of new forms and functions were developed. In the thirteenth century, simple rectangular, horizontal or vertical, or gabled forms were used, as in the Saint Francis *paliotto* (frontal), a large figure was flanked by narrative scenes. Sometimes half-length figures of saints were placed in arcades on either side of a half-length figure of the Virgin and Child. When two panels were hinged together, a diptych was formed. The triptych usually had two hinged side panels that folded over and covered the central panel. A polyptych had many panels, sometimes with predella and gables, sometimes fixed in a rigid framework, as in the *Maestà* by Duccio, and sometimes with several movable wings as in the famous polyptych of the *Adoration of the Mystic Lamb* finished by Jan van Eyck in 1432. Some movable altars were painted on the exterior wings, which covered a sculpted ensemble in the center panel, and were set within an elaborate carved architectural framework, as in the intricate altar painted and sculpted by Michael Pacher between 1471 and 1481 for the small parish church of Saint-Wolfgang, Austria.

One of the finest examples of a functioning Late Gothic altarpiece is the polyptych painted by Matthias Grünewald for the hospital chapel of a monastery at Isenheim, about twenty miles south of Colmar in northeastern France. Completed in 1515, it contains two sets of wings on each side providing for three sets of representations for specific purposes.

In its closed position (fig. 151), the altarpiece shows the "Crucifixion" flanked by Saint Anthony, the patron saint of the monastery, on the left, and Saint Sebastian on the right. Both of these saints were painted on fixed wings. Below

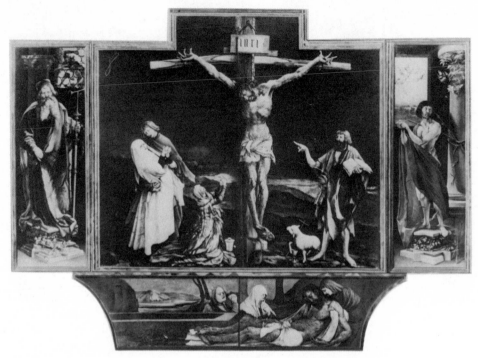

Fig. 151. Matthias Grünewald: Isenheim altarpiece, closed position. 1515.
12′ 3″ x 16′ 10″. Musée d'Unterlinden, Colmar. (Bruckmann: Art Reference
Bureau)

the "Crucifixion" is a narrow, horizontal predella with the "Entombment of
Christ." The "Crucifixion," depicted in a barren landscape barely visible in the
dark background, is charged with emotion, heightened by the darkness, which
refers to the eclipse and earthquake at the moment of Christ's death. The kneeling
Mary Magdalene, the swooning Virgin, and the bending Saint John trying to
support her form a group united in their grief and emotional recoil from the
gruesome spectacle of the crucified Christ before them. Christ's body is a sickly
green, flecked with bleeding sores from the flagellation. It hangs heavily on the
cross, bending the ankles and causing the fingers to curl grotesquely. The roughly
cut timbers of the cross, particularly the bowed crosspiece with the appearance
of a minimally shaped branch, refer to the Cross as the Tree of Life. In contrast
with the grief-stricken figures on the left, Saint John the Baptist stands on the
right pointing didactically to Christ and holding a book that states "He must in-
crease, I must decrease" (John 3:30), a reference to the fact that John's ministry was
but a prefiguration of the ministry of Christ and the growth of the church in his
name. The Paschal Lamb at John's feet is bleeding, symbolizing Christ's sacrifice.
The entire panel is imbued with a stark pathos and strident emotionalism that reflect
the description in the *Revelations* of Saint Bridget, a fourteenth-century Swedish
mystic, whose visions had widespread influence on fifteenth-century northern
European art.

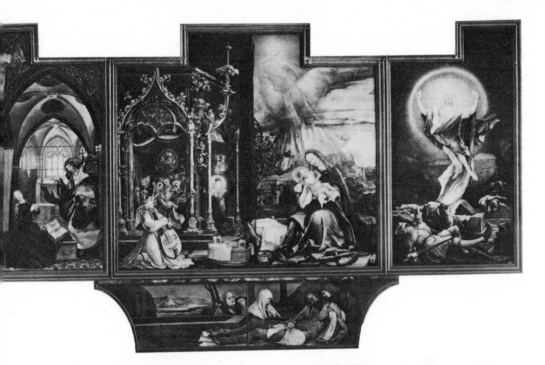

Fig. 152. Matthias Grünewald: Isenheim altarpiece, intermediate position. 1515. Musée d'Unterlinden, Colmar. (Bruckmann: Art Reference Bureau)

Saint Anthony in the left wing holds his symbol, a tau cross, while a demon breathes the breath of pestilence upon him through a window. In the right wing Saint Sebastian stands pierced with arrows, echoing the gesture of Saint John the Baptist in the central panel. The predella contains an equally stark and emotive image of the "Entombment." These images held a special relevance for the members of the monastic order of Saint Anthony at Isenheim. The monastery administered a hospital that tended sufferers of many skin diseases, including leprosy and syphilis. Both Saints Anthony and Sebastian, because of his bleeding wounds, were the patron saints of those afflicted with such maladies. Indeed, the pocked sores of Christ's dead body equated their suffering with his and made the emotional impact of the scene even more immediate. Placed in the chapel where the sick could see it, the altarpiece remained in this closed position on weekdays, in Lent, and during Holy Week, as a reminder of the enormity of Christ's sacrifice.

The "Crucifixion" is painted on two hinged panels, which, when opened, obscure the fixed wings with the saints and reveal a strikingly different panoply of scenes. This intermediate position (fig. 152) contains representations, from left to right, of the "Annunciation," a "Concert of Angels" and "Nativity" (Incarnation), and the "Resurrection." In contrast with the somber exterior, these panels are filled with brilliant, glowing colors. Light fills the chapel where the "Annunciation" takes place and the Virgin recoils, not in grief, but in joy

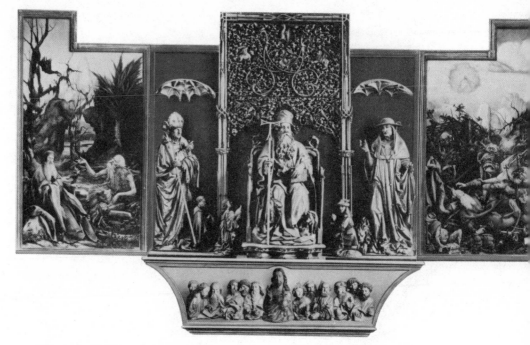

Fig. 153. Matthias Grünewald: Isenheim altarpiece (1515), interior with sculptures by Nicholas von Hagenau (1503). Musée d'Unterlinden, Colmar. (Bruckmann: Art Reference Bureau)

at the appearance of the Angel Gabriel. The "Concert" has a festive air as joyous angels make music, and the maternal, tender Virgin cuddling her Child sit in a landscape bathed with golden radiance. In the portal of the Flamboyant Gothic chapel between the angels and the landscape kneels another image of the Virgin, crowned and almost dissolved in light. The Virgin's dual nature as affectionate, human mother and as Queen of Heaven are therefore juxtaposed. Again, the praying gesture of the celestial Virgin and the extended arms of the musical angels recall the pointing hand of Saint John the Baptist on the exterior.

In the right wing an unearthly levitation of Christ takes place. His head and shoulders are dissolved in light and his flesh is made whole again, except for the five wounds, in contrast with the sores evident in the "Entombment" still visible below. The presence of the predella below these scenes, and particularly in contrast with the "Resurrection," heightens the joyousness of these scenes. The intermediate position, therefore, was reserved for joyous feasts such as Christmas and Easter, as well as appropriate Sundays throughout the liturgical year.

The "Concert of Angels" and "Nativity" were also painted on hinged wings. When these were opened to the third position (fig. 153), their reverse sides contained painted representations that flanked a central ensemble of wooden, polychromed sculptures. The predella panels also opened to reveal a group of sculpted busts of Christ and the apostles. This sculptural group of the Isenheim altarpiece had been carved by Nicholas of Hagenau in 1503 as an earlier altar commissioned by the previous preceptor of the monastery. Grünewald's paintings were therefore an ingenious addition, amplifying the program of the altar but conforming to the stepped-up frame of the original shrine. Seated enthroned in the middle section and holding his tau cross is Saint Anthony, while dense, elaborate foliate tracery fills the area above his head. He is flanked by Saint Athanasius, the biographer of Saint Anthony, and Saint Jerome, who wrote a life of Saint Paul.

The painted wings by Grünewald are devoted to the two hermit monks, Saint Anthony and Saint Paul, meeting in the desert on the left, and the "Temptation of Saint Anthony" on the right. In the "Temptation" the saint is beset by horrid demons, some covered with pustulant sores, an affliction similar to the trials of Job in the Old Testament. Saint Anthony's struggle, reiterated in the luminous sky by angels battling demons, symbolized the continuing conflict of the virtues over the vices and temptations of the world, and Saint Anthony's ultimate triumph over the demons with the aid of Christ. In contrast with this frenzied scene the "Visit of Saint Paul to Saint Anthony in the Desert" brings the promise of peace and salvation, symbolized by the doe and stag drinking from the water of eternal life. A crow miraculously brings food for the hermits, a traditional symbol for the miraculous meal of Holy Communion. Medicinal plants growing in the foreground imply the possibility of cures for the afflicted who viewed the altar. It is thought that the visage of Saint Anthony is a portrait of Guido Guersi, the preceptor of the monastery who ordered the painted wings from Grünewald, and that Saint Paul is a self-portrait of the artist. This last opening of the altar was reserved for the feast day of Saint Anthony. The Isenheim altarpiece, like many other Late Gothic altarpieces, served as a changeable, functioning liturgical object emphasizing specific moments in the liturgical calendar.

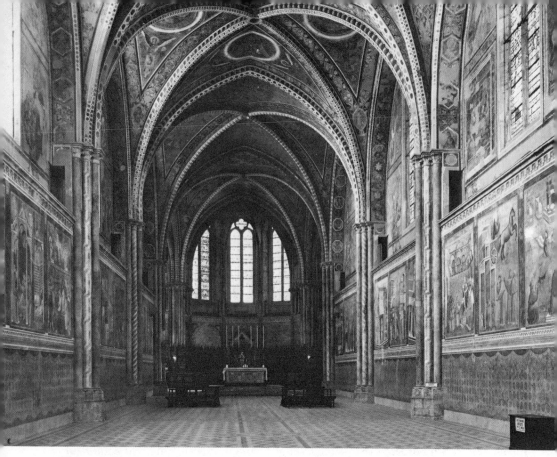

Fig. 154. Upper church, S. Francesco, Assisi. c. 1250. (Alinari)

25. The Gothic Fresco

Since Roman times the painting of pictures on walls had been a major form of architectural decoration. The Early Christians had continued the Roman tradition in the catacombs and basilicas, and surviving vestiges in Carolingian, Ottonian, and particularly Romanesque churches testify to the widespread continuance of this form of mural decoration. In the thirteenth and fourteenth centuries, and especially in Italian Gothic churches and cloisters, this tradition reached its apogee and was to continue to be a major art form in Italy through the Baroque period.

The Gothic church of S. Francesco at Assisi (fig. 154), dedicated to Saint Francis, is one of the early major examples of the concert of architecture and fresco in the Italian Gothic period. Completed in the last decade of the thirteenth century upon a vast bastion because of its situation on the steep slopes of a mountain, it consists of an upper and lower church of single naves with boldly projecting transepts. The building is representative of the Italian translation of the Gothic style. The interior of the upper church is rib-vaulted, but the diagonal ribs are semircircular, and the bays are lower in proportion to their height than in northern Gothic buildings. Moreover, ribs, transverse arches, engaged responds, and wall surfaces are all painted so that the tectonic quality of masonry structure is reduced to a decorative armature. A tall pair of narrow lancets of stained glass in each bay leave ample wall surface for wall decoration, retaining the mural tradition of the Early Christian basilica. The recessed panel of the clerestory wall and the provision of a wall passage behind the engaged columns at that level at Assisi only approximate the northern aesthetic of the structural skeleton. Whereas the increasing dissolution of the wall and increasing skeletonization of French Gothic churches required that pictorial representation be placed in stained-glass windows, the continuing mural tradition of Italian churches permitted the development of vast cycles of frescoes.

The process of fresco painting on a large scale required a number of stages. First, the rough stone or brick of the walls had to be covered with a layer of preliminary plaster (*arriccio*). Usually a rough sketch of the general outline of the composition was executed on the arriccio with a reddish-brown substance called *sinopia*. At the Campo Santo at Pisa, and elsewhere where the finished frescoes were either badly damaged or removed for preservation, the vivacious sinopia designs remain. A final layer of smooth plaster (*intonaco*) was then applied. If the painting was to be done in *buon fresco* or *fresco* with the intonaco still damp, only enough plaster was applied for one day's work (*giornate*). The buon fresco method had the advantage of allowing the pigment to permeate the surface of the plaster, which became bonded to the wall and made it more durable. Frequently added touches of pigment were applied to the dried painting or to dry intonaco. This method of painting (*a secco*) was less durable. Both techniques were used at Assisi.

On the final layer of plaster heavy brown lines of sinopia were used to designate the contours of the forms and some of the features. Facial tones were modulated from a greenish base of terra verde to white highlights. In the execution of the pictorial panels as a whole, the artists started at the top and worked downward in irregular areas of giornate, the size depending upon the amount of intricate detail that had to be painted before the intonaco dried. In the *Miracle of the Spring* (fig. 155), one of the twenty-eight panels in the cycle of pictures telling the life of Saint Francis in the lower area of the wall, the smallest giornate was executed on the fifth day when the artist had not only to articulate the face of Saint Francis but also to mold in relief the angled disk of the halo with its corrugated rays. Throughout all of these frescoes in the upper church at Assisi the divisions of the picture into giornate are clearly evident in the abutting or overlapping layers of plaster.

Both the Old Testament scenes on the upper wall surfaces and the cycle of the life of Saint Francis are controversial concerning their dating and attribution, although both have been connected with the Florentine painter Giotto di Bondone and his workshop. Both cycles manifest, in varying degrees, an early appearance of a new volumetric style of painting in which broadly modeled figures are placed in spatial landscapes and architectural settings. The best demonstration of an overall iconographical program of a frescoed interior and of Giotto's innovations

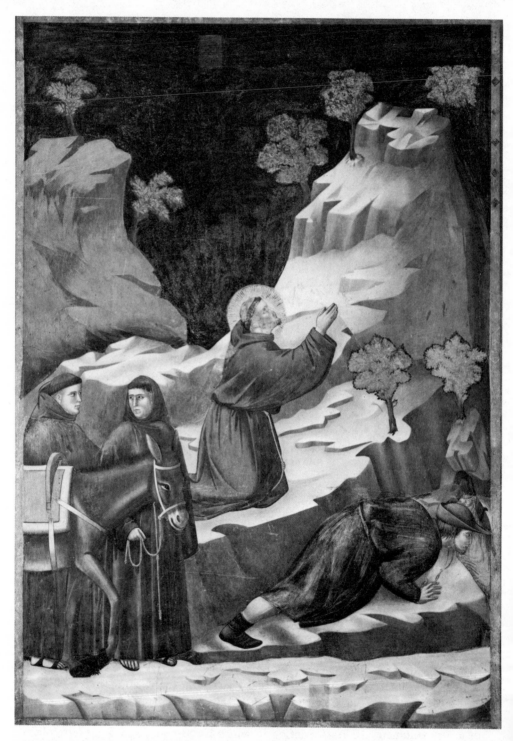

Fig. 155. Giotto di Bondone(?): *Miracle of the Spring.* Upper church,
S. Francesco, Assisi. c. 1290? (Alinari)

in style and content, however, is to be found in the frescoes of the Scrovegni Chapel in Padua, documented to be by Giotto's hand from 1304 to 1306.

Although Gothic in a few of its details, the Scrovegni Chapel, also known as the Arena Chapel because of its placement on the circumference of what used to be a Roman arena, is merely a rectangular gabled box with six lancet windows in the south wall. Except for the decorative pilaster strips and arched corbel table, the exterior is nondescript. The barrel-vaulted interior (fig. 156), however, is a field for three rows of pictorial narration in fresco on each wall, prefaced, on the west wall over the entrance, with a vast painted *Last Judgment*. The chapel was commissioned by Enrico Scrovegni and dedicated to the Virgin of the Annunciation in expiation of the sins of his father who was a notorious usurer. In the *Last Judgment*, Enrico is shown kneeling and presenting his chapel to three angels. Behind him the blessed are received into Heaven, while in front of him the damned souls are dispatched to Hell where a large grotesque figure of Satan devours some hapless figures. Above, Christ appears in a burst of light, surrounded by angels and the seated apostles. This composition reflects the Italo-Byzantine tradition of placing the Last Judgment on the inside of the west wall, as at Torcello and Sant-Angelo in Formis, and is an Italian equivalent of the French Romanesque Last Judgment portal on the exterior of the building.

Along the nave, the upper register of frescoes contains scenes of the life of the Virgin, commencing on the south wall next to the chancel and reading to the facade, and then toward the chancel again along the north wall. Below are two rows of paintings devoted to the life of Christ, the upper row of which tells of the infancy and ministry of Christ, and the lower of the Passion, beginning with the *Last Supper* and finishing with the *Pentecost*. At the eastern end of the chapel above the chancel arch leading into the sanctuary is the *Coronation* and below, separated by the arch, but almost on the level of the life of the Virgin is the *Annunciation*. Below, on the right, the *Visitation* provides a link between the life of the Virgin, the *Annunciation,* and the sequence of infancy scenes that are adjacent. Opposite, on the left side of the chancel, the *Hiring of Judas*, adjacent to the *Cleansing of the Temple,* the final act of Christ's ministry, links that row with the lower ones of the Passion. Symbolic and compositional references between the two rows of Christological scenes tie them together. The *Nativity*, or Incarnation, is equated with the *Last Supper,* when Christ institutes the transubstantiation of the bread and wine into his flesh and blood; the *Adoration of the Magi,* the kingdoms of the world paying homage to Christ is paired with Christ humbly washing the feet of his disciples; the *Baptism* in which the water of the Jordan was traditionally considered to be a prefiguration of Christ's shedding blood on the Cross is paired with the *Crucifixion;* the *Raising of Lazarus* is appropriately paired with the combined scene of the *Three Marys at the Tomb* being informed by the angel of Christ's resurrection and the *Noli me tangere* when the Magdalene sees Christ walking in the garden; and Christ's triumphal entry into Jerusalem is equated with his *Ascension* into heaven. Thus, the interior of the Arena Chapel contains a finely organized symbolic program in which the Christian message is heightened, as on Bernward's bronze doors at Hildesheim, by apt juxtapositions of scenes. Giotto's innovation

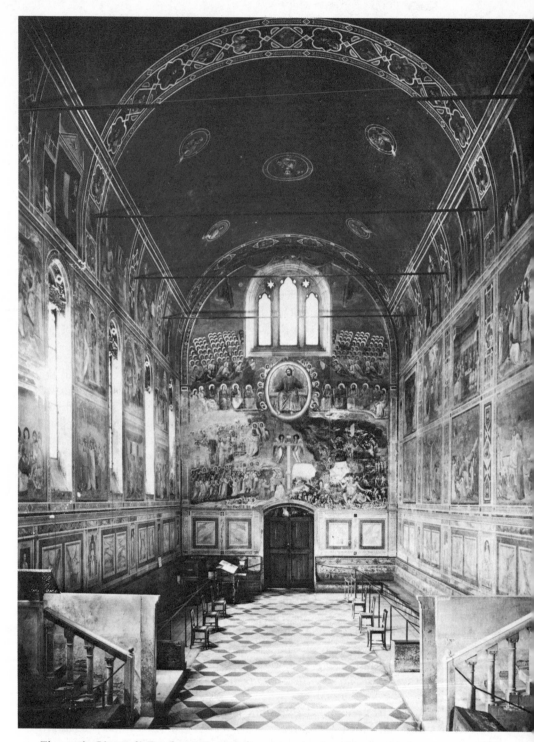

Fig. 156. Giotto di Bondone: *Last Judgment* and other frescoes. Arena Chapel, Padua. 1304–1306. (Alinari)

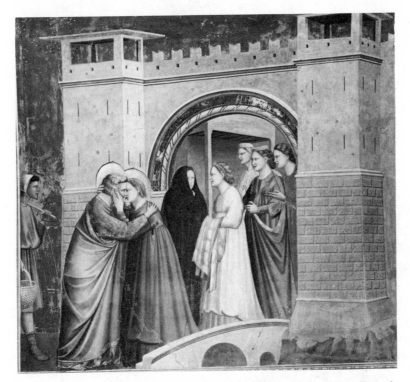

Fig. 157. Giotto di Bondone: *Meeting at the Golden Gate*. Arena Chapel, Padua. 1304–1306. (Alinari)

was in the juxtaposition of New Testament scenes rather than the traditional Old–New Testament typologies.

Below the entire ensemble of narrative scenes is a series of panels with figures painted in monochromatic tonalities simulating the effect of stone sculpture. These are the fourteen allegories of the virtues and vices, a reminder of the constant struggle between good and evil.

Innovations in style, composition, and content abound in Giotto's frescoes at the Arena Chapel. In the *Meeting at the Golden Gate* (fig. 157), derived from the thirteenth-century *Golden Legend* (*Legenda Aurea*) of Jacobus de Voragine, Joachim returns to his aged wife Anne after learning from an angel that she will bear him a daughter. Giotto has captured a moment of tenderness and joy as they meet at the gate of Jerusalem. The effectiveness of the psychological and emotional portrayal results from the gentle embrace of the broadly modeled, herculean forms and the proximity of their eyes, magnifying the intensity of their glances. In addition, the massive bulk of the figures, created by smooth transitions between strong shadows and bright highlights and a simplification of drapery folds, implies a pictorial space that is further accentuated by the overlapping of these volumetric figures and by the diagonal placement of the city gate.

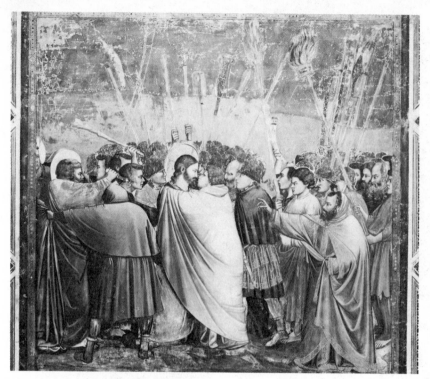

Fig. 158. Giotto di Bondone: *Betrayal of Christ*. Arena Chapel,
Padua. 1304–1306. (Alinari)

Fig. 159. Giotto di Bondone: *Lamentation*. Arena Chapel,
Padua. 1304–1306. (Alinari)

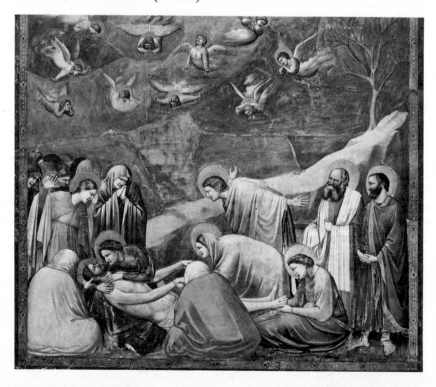

In contrast with the restrained joy of the *Meeting at the Golden Gate,* the *Betrayal of Christ* (fig. 158) is filled with compositional movement, which is largely the result of the varying angles of the lances and torches against the blue sky and the crowding of massive bodies toward the center. The gesticulating priest on the right, balanced by the violent slashing motion of Peter on the left as he cuts off the ear of Malchus, and the intense, leering, grotesque faces charge the scene with energy. Yet, in the center, the broad embracing figure of Judas about to kiss Christ provides a strong stabilizing accent. The evil grimace of Judas contrasts with the calm demeanor of the figure he is about to betray. Lances converge on this point in the composition and focus on the intense visual interchange between the two figures.

Similarly, in the *Lamentation* (fig. 159), the powerful compositional accents of the sloping rock and bending figures concentrate attention in the lower left corner where, face to face, the Virgin laments over the dead body of her son. Two massive seated figures with their backs toward the spectator incline inward toward the group of the Virgin and Christ. The degree of anguish is heightened according to the proximity of the bystanders to this group: those figures at the right standing calmly, the gestures of the figures immediately above, more contorted. Fluttering angels, convulsed by grief, fill the sky. Giotto has used massive figures bowed by grief and compositional devices to focus on the intense pathos of the moment. Perhaps the dramatic intensity of the gestures were in part occasioned by the frequent enactment of religious plays, which were performed in front of the Arena Chapel.

Giotto's innovations in placing his biblical scenes in settings made more immediate by virtue of their rocks, trees, and blue sky, albeit still schematic, in providing his figures with bulk and weight, and in endowing them with a new sense of psychological reaction and human emotion make his art a precursor of many elements that were to be developed further in the Italian Renaissance. His role, possibly in the upper church at Assisi, and most certainly in the Arena Chapel at Padua, constitutes the fruition of a medieval tradition of mural decoration with increasingly more elaborate symbolic programs and a wider range of meanings.

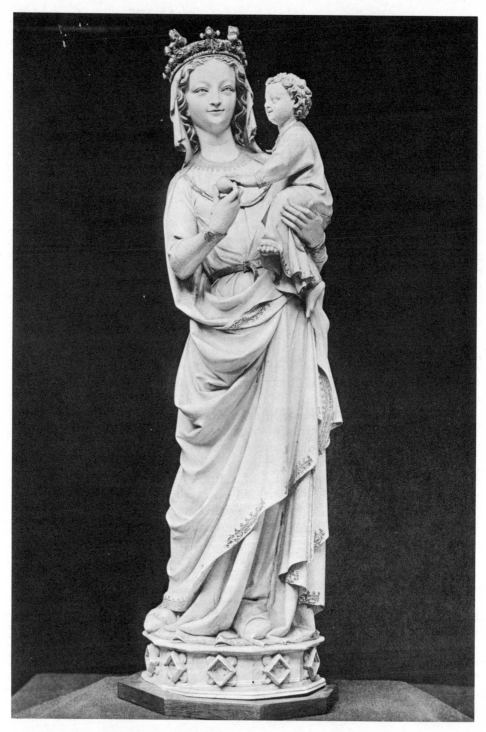

Fig. 160. Ivory Virgin and Child from Sainte-Chapelle. Paris. c. 1300.
H. 16⅛″. Musée du Louvre, Paris. (Giraudon)

26. GOTHIC DEVOTIONAL OBJECTS

In the fourteenth and fifteenth centuries increasing emphasis was placed upon private devotion in order to achieve more immediate and meaningful access to God. In part this trend was furthered by such mystics as Master Eckhart (1260?–1327?), who proposed personal and direct communion with God rather than through the intermediary of the sacraments. Although these preachings were condemned by the church in 1325, they were symptomatic of new attitudes in religious thinking. These attitudes were accompanied by changes in class structure and in the distribution of economic wealth. In addition to the clergy and the nobility, more members of the growing burgher class in the cities could afford to obtain a variety of objects upon which to focus their devotions.

An indication of the changes in attitudes toward the roles of the Virgin and of Christ in comparison with the Romanesque period has already been noted in the twelfth-century sculpture at Chartres. In the thirteenth and fourteenth centuries this new ideal of the Virgin evolved further, occasioned by the continuing cult of the Virgin and parallel developments in the chivalric attitude toward women. A small fourteenth-century statuette of ivory (fig. 160) made for the Sainte-Chapelle in Paris around 1300 epitomizes this evolution. This image, perhaps first stated on the trumeau of the south transept of Amiens Cathedral in the mid-thirteenth century, has here been couched in idealized aristocratic terms. The Virgin is depicted as a young, aristocratic girl with exquisitely refined features and a radiant smile. Bending slightly in her pose, she supports the infant Christ in the crook of her left arm while the voluminous, sweeping folds about her body direct the eye to him and lend visual support. The delicate golden hemline of her garment and her bejeweled crown indicate that she is the Queen of Heaven. In her right hand she holds an apple, which the child touches playfully. This attribute adds the connotation that the Virgin is the new Eve who has come to redeem the sins of the old Eve through her role as the Mother of God and as intercessor for mankind. The apple, a symbol for the Fall of Man, also carries connotations of Christ's impending sacrifice to redeem man from his loss of grace. Nevertheless, the pervasive impact of this ivory is of hope through the human, affectionate, and maternal aspect of the Virgin. The aristocratic demeanor, the idealization of the features, and the youthful radiance of the Virgin all reflect the courtly elegance and love of refinement that dominated Gothic art of the fourteenth century.

Throughout the fourteenth century the increased demand for such objects to adorn small chapels and family altars all over Europe resulted in a vast production of small, portable diptychs, triptychs, and tabernacles in metalwork and ivory. A major center of production was Paris, but many ivories were also carved in Cologne in the Rhineland, as well as in Italy and England. A folding ivory tabernacle (pl. 15) produced in the second half of the fourteenth century in France contains

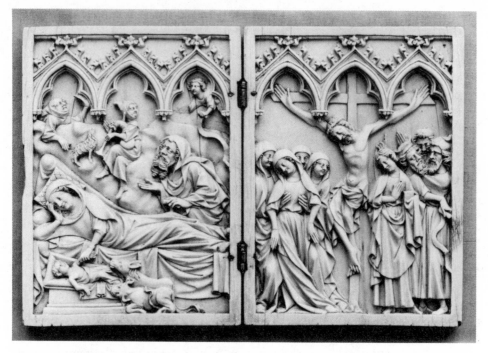

Fig. 161. Diptych with "Nativity" and "Crucifixion." France. Mid-13th century. Ivory, 4⅞" x 6¾". The Metropolitan Museum of Art (Rogers Fund, 1911).

the Virgin in the center flanked by angels holding candles in the folding wings. The Virgin firmly supports the child on her hip, imparting a pronounced, lyrical S curve to her pose. Two hovering angels crown her Queen of Heaven, and the child holds the apple, yet again the emphasis is on the tender interchange between mother and infant. This ivory retains vestiges of color on the robes as well as of painted decorative detailing on the hems and dotted background; the figures would have looked like painted sculpture against the ivory ground. The Gothic gable with tracery forming trefoiled and cusped arches reflects the delicacy of fourteenth-century architecture.

Frequently ivory diptychs contained certain essential narrative scenes that embodied the polarities of the Christian experience. A small ivory diptych at The Cloisters (fig. 161), depicting the "Nativity" with the "Annunciation to the Shepherds" above on the left wing, served as an appropriate reminder of the Incarnation and of the joy of Christ's birth. The "Crucifixion" on the right wing reminded the beholder of Christ's sacrifice and of the sorrow of his death. In the Gothic period the Crucifixion became a vehicle, as in the case of Giotto's frescoes in Padua, of intense emotionalism. In The Cloisters diptych, the dead body of Christ was bent into a sharp zigzag form to heighten the pathos of his agony. The Virgin swoons at the sight, her slumping body reiterating the diagonal of Christ's legs.

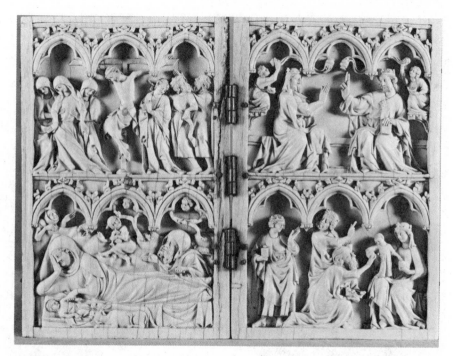

Fig. 162. Diptych with "Crucifixion," "Nativity," "Coronation of the Virgin," and "Adoration of the Magi." France. 14th century. Ivory, H. 6¼″ x W. 8⅜″ (open). Victoria and Albert Museum, London. (Crown Copyright)

Sometimes the number of scenes was multiplied, as in another diptych (fig. 162) in the Victoria and Albert Museum. The "Crucifixion" appears above the "Nativity" on the left wing, and the "Coronation of the Virgin" as Queen of Heaven above the "Adoration of the Magi" on the right. Although obviously by a different hand and workshop, this ivory demonstrates the similarity of compositions that became standardized and were constantly repeated. The figures are elegant, the gestures mannered, yet the scenes impart the simple joy and sorrow of the events depicted. The architectural gables of both these diptychs provide a unifying framework, like a miniature altarpiece, for each of the scenes regardless of their exterior setting.

The use of reliquaries did not lessen in this period, and the art of the metalworker became increasingly architectural in form. A reliquary casket of Saint Taurinus (pl. 16), made in the mid-thirteenth century for the Church of Saint-Taurin at Évreux, developed even further the churchlike characteristics of previous reliquaries. Fully modeled figures occupy the niches at the ends and at the transepts in the middle. Representations in the four other arcades depict various miracles performed by Saint Taurinus, who was the first bishop of Évreux, while reliefs on the roof narrate other incidents of his life. A delicate lantern tower rises above the crossing, and openwork pinnacles flank the end and transept gables, a miniature evocation of a nine-towered cathedral.

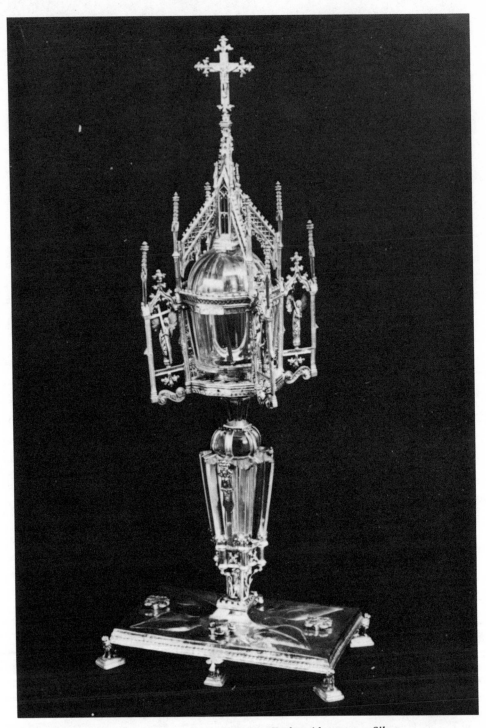

Fig. 163. Nicollet Paumars: Monstrance-reliquary. Early 16th century. Silver
gilt, H. 21¾": Parish church, Crespin. (Archives photographiques, Paris,
S.P.A.D.E.M.)

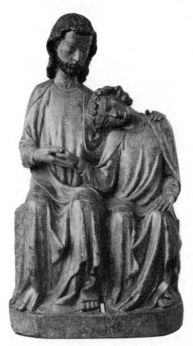

Fig. 164. "Saint John on the Breast of Christ." Upper Swabia. c. 1320.
Oak and polychrome, 35⅛″ x 17¾″. Skulpturengalerie, Staatliche Museen Preussischer Kulturbesitz, West Berlin. (Foto: Jörg P. Anders)

Fig. 165. Röttgen Vesperbild. Mainz? Early 14th century. Wood
and polychrome, H. 34½″. Rheinisches Landesmuseum, Bonn.

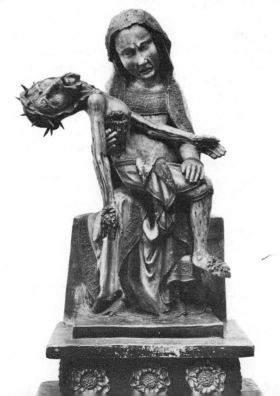

The need for greater immediacy with God and with the saints led to the increasing popularity of the *monstrance;* as the name implies, this object displayed either the Host or relics of saints. Although monstrances had existed before, the increasing desire to see the venerated relic, not just to contemplate the enameled casket in which it was enshrined, led to the development of tall vessels with rock-crystal containers supported on delicate armatures of metal. The early sixteenth-century monstrance (fig. 163) made by Nicollet Paumars, now in the parish church of Crespin, makes use of crocket finials and tracery buttresses to support a lantern tower and crucifix above the crystal vessel. This monstrance is considerably more restrained in form and decoration than numerous ones made for the nobility, which were decorated with charming figures and encrusted with pearls and precious stones.

The intensity of devotion that required the worshiper to look upon fragments of bone or shriveled skin enshrined in rock crystal also produced other forms of votive images. The enthroned, and later, the standing statue of the Virgin and Child had served as cult images on the altars of churches throughout the Middle Ages. But in the fourteenth century the heightened emotionalism of private devotions and the desire to make biblical incidents more meaningful in everyday experience resulted in the creation of small statuary groups excerpted from individual incidents, usually from the Passion of Christ. These devotional images, or *Andachtsbilder* as they were known in Germany where they were especially prevalent, frequently represented Christ with Saint John asleep on his shoulder (fig. 164). This was a detail taken from traditional representations of the Last Supper, depicting the incident recounted in the Gospel of Saint John (13:23) when the youthful apostle leaned on Christ's bosom. It was considered to be a reassuring and compassionate image symbolizing Christ's love for mankind, expressed at the very moment of his announcement of his impending sacrifice.

Another prevalent sculptural group was that of the seated Virgin with the dead body of Christ in her lap (fig. 165). Excerpted from the Lamentation, this *Pietà* or *Vesperbild* reminded the worshiper of similar, happier statues of the maternal Virgin and her playful child. The features contorted by grief, as in the Röttgen Vesperbild in Bonn, accentuated the sorrow and anguish of the moment of Christ's death, and the emaciated, bloody body of Christ made the horror of his sacrifice very real. These juxtapositions were made explicit in the devotional literature of the day, in the *Revelations* of Saint Bridget of Sweden, and in the *Meditations on the Life of Christ* by the Pseudo-Bonaventura.

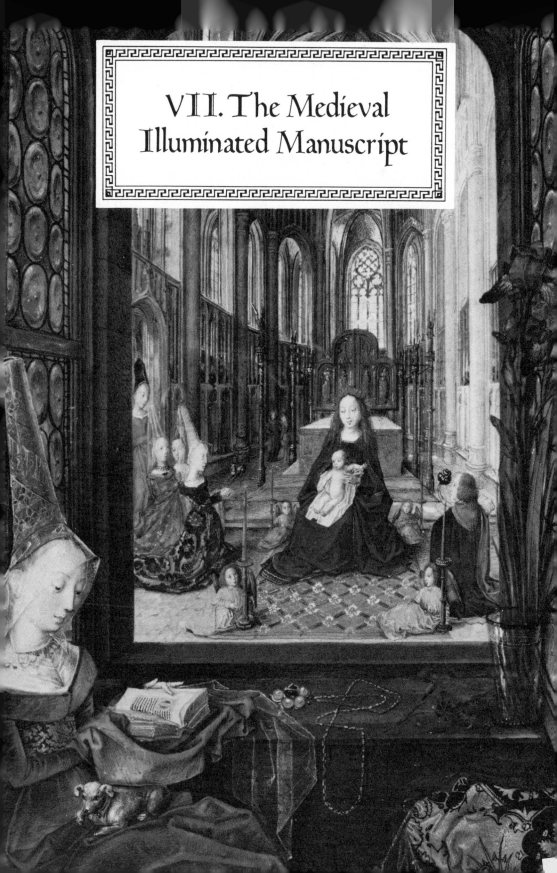

VII. The Medieval Illuminated Manuscript

27. The Illuminated Word

he book occupies a special place in the development of the Middle Ages, for it was the principal vehicle for the transmission of the Scriptures and commentaries upon them, dogmatic and theological treatises, as well as the means by which all classical knowledge and literature has been preserved. Medieval monasteries, first in Italy and then throughout Europe, formed their own *scriptoria,* or writing shops, and assiduously copied the Bible, liturgical books for use in the Mass and the Divine Office, and even books of classical literature and natural history—although avowedly for Christian purposes.

Many of these books were illustrated with scenes of biblical incidents, schematic and symbolic diagrams, and representations of plants and animals. In the early Middle Ages these followed, as is the case with the catacomb frescoes and Early Christian mosaics, the models of Roman painting, but soon new forms of decoration and new styles of painting evolved. These books were considered to be *illuminated,* a term that, in the narrow sense, referred to the application of brightly colored pigments and gold and silver in decorative initials, border decorations, and in the miniatures themselves. These bright colors and metallic surfaces both contain light and reflect it from the page. These qualities were especially appropriate, with reference to books of the Scriptures, for the divine light of the Word of God was made physically bright through the use of colors and gold. This was the essence of the illuminated Christian book, for two phrases justified the lavish decoration of these texts and their bindings throughout the Middle Ages. The opening passage from the Gospel of Saint John "In the beginning was the Word, and the Word was with God, and the Word was God" reminds us that in Christ the *Logos* was made flesh, and that therefore the Gospels are also an incarnation of the Divine spirit. This thought, reinforced by Christ's pronouncement "I am the Light," provides one of the reasons for the embellishment of the word, which, as stated in another context by Abbot Suger, "being nobly bright . . . should brighten the minds so that [the beholder] may travel through the true lights to the True Light. . . ." No embellishment was therefore too lavish, and the encrustation of bindings with gold and precious stones thereby provided a fitting container for the Word of God. Some Byzantine and Carolingian manuscripts were written in gold and silver letters upon purple-dyed parchment, reflecting, perhaps, imperial patronage and elevating the material text, by virtue of the costly dye and precious materials, into a symbolic, immaterial realm.

Large, elaborately decorated gospel books, the embodiment of the presence of Christ, were often carried in triumphal processions into the church at the beginning of the celebration of the Mass. They were then placed ceremoniously on the high altar, symbol of the Incarnate Christ on the sacrificial table. Mosaic representations of the book enshrined on the high altar and of the Cross enthroned, sacrificial and triumphal symbols of the presence of Christ, surround the fifth-century dome mosaic of the Baptistry of the Orthodox at Ravenna. Also, revered as a sumptuous liturgical object in its own right, the illuminated Bible combined functions as a resplendent container of the Word of God equivalent to the paten and chalice containing the bread and wine placed next to it. The resplendent cover of the Codex Aureus of Saint Emmeram (pl. 26) reflects this higher purpose alongside the liturgical objects on the high altar of Saint Emmeram depicted in the miniature in Abbess Uta's gospel book (see fig. 105, p. 122).

The Benedictine abbot Johannes Trithemius (1462–1516) recognized, in his treatise *In Praise of Scribes* (*De Laude Scriptorum*), the value of illumination, but in moderation:

> As far as possible, manuscripts should be decorated so that their appearance alone will induce perusal. We know that the ancients took great care to match contents and exterior beauty. Holy Scripture is deserving of all possible adornment. However, we should beware that this artwork does not become an end in itself. Otherwise, beauty might prevail over truth because only where honesty rules is the vain and spectacular repressed. This would prevent our being identified with those rebuked by Jerome, who reprimands the indiscriminate because they prefer their manuscripts full of decoration rather than free of mistakes. His judgment applies to a multitude of books.

Fig. 166. Diagram of a gathering of bifolios showing the relationship of the flesh and hair sides (shaded). (R. G. Calkins and M. Block)

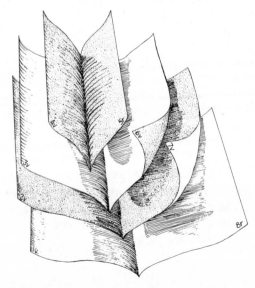

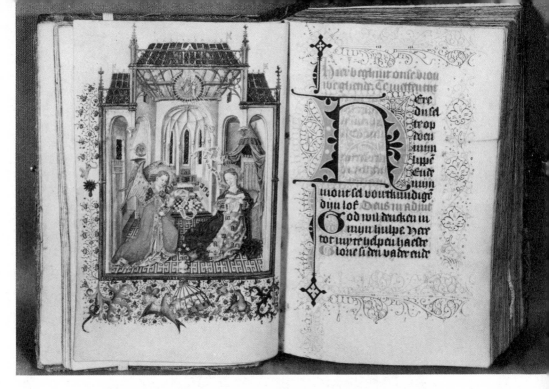

Fig. 167. *Book of Hours of Katharina van Lochorst.* Utrecht. c. 1450.
7½″ x 5⅛″ each page. Westfälisches Landesmuseum, Münster.

28. FORM AND SCRIPT

In the classical world the written word was usually inscribed upon scrolls made of sheets of papyrus glued together. The text was arranged in columns, sometimes with inset illustrations, and as the reader proceeded through the roll, he unwound it from the right and rolled it up on the left. Such a device proved to be awkward, for it was not easy to consult other passages of text, and the entire scroll had to be rewound before it could be read again. By around 200 B.C., however, another substance more durable than the fragile paperlike papyrus sheets was being used for writing. Skins of animals, usually calves or lambs, were carefully scraped and cured and then cut into sheets of vellum or parchment. The younger the animal, and the more carefully cured the skins, the whiter, thinner, and more silky the texture was, with the very finest vellum coming from unborn calves or lambs.

With the increased use of vellum in Roman times, another innovation resulted in the complete transformation of the early book into the form we know today. Perhaps partly occasioned by the hinged wax tablets used in Roman schools for practicing writing, vellum sheets were folded to form a *bifolio,* and bifolios were placed within each other to form quires or gatherings (fig. 166). These were then sewn together in the middle, stacked with other gatherings, and bound together to form a hinged accumulation of leaves or folios, which is called a *codex,* the form of the modern book (fig. 167). Both rolls and codices were used during the late antique period, but perhaps because of their practicality, the influence of the

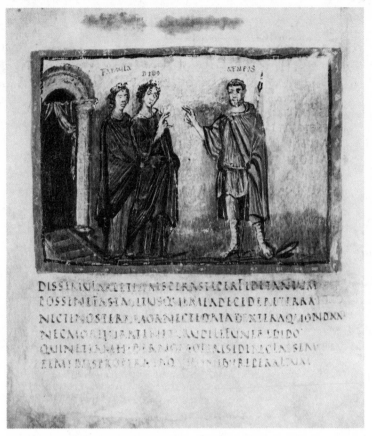

Fig. 168. "Aeneas and Dido." Vergil, *Aeneid*. Script in rustic capitals. Rome. End of 4th century. 8⅝″ x 7¾″. Biblioteca Apostolica Vaticana (MS Vat. lat. 3225, fol. 36v), Vatican City.

Early Christian Church, and the fact that early Bibles ordered by Constantine were codices, the parchment codex gained precedence over the papyrus scroll. Nevertheless, because of the traditional usage of papyrus and of scrolls, the use of this material and form continued, particularly for official pronouncements of the curia and for papal bulls, until the eleventh century. Although the invention of paper reached Europe through Moslem importation and was used by the eleventh century, it was not widely used as a writing material until the mid-fifteenth century when its production was simplified and encouraged by the demand created by the invention of printing.

As the word *manuscript* indicates, medieval books before the invention of printing were written by hand. Over the centuries the style of the script changed, and numerous regional variations manifested themselves. Different forms of script were also used for different kinds of books and documents. The study of the development of writing (*paleography*) can often help to date and localize medieval manuscripts. Although it is not possible to give a complete paleographical survey of medieval scripts here, certain general developments should be noted.

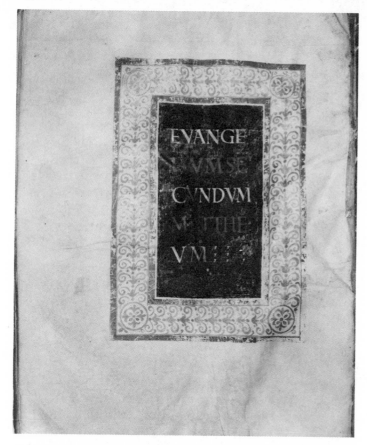

Fig. 169. Title page of the Gospel of Saint Matthew. *Gospels of Charlemagne* (fol. 19v). c. 800. 12⅛″ x 9½″. Cathedral Treasury, Aachen. (Ann Münchow)

The script found in a late fourth-century copy of the *Aeneid* of Vergil (fig. 168) consists of irregular capital letters with some projections of the ascenders above the line. This script is known as the rustic capital (*capitalis rustica*). A Roman cursive script, in subsequent centuries it became more irregular, verging almost on illegibility in some Merovingian manuscripts. In the eighth and ninth centuries, Carolingian scribes undertook to reform and reclarify this script.

A title page to the Gospel of Saint Matthew in the *Gospels of Charlemagne* in the Cathedral Treasury at Aachen (fig. 169) contains a Carolingian revival of Roman lettering. The capital letters, written in gold and silver on a purple-dyed page, copy the monumental, square-proportioned capital letters, with tapering terminals known as serifs, frequently found in the carved inscriptions on Roman monuments. Known as a *square* or *epigraphic* capital, this form of letter was revived by Carolingian scribes as another visual manifestation of the *renovatio romana*.

But even before the Carolingian reform of the style of script, other developments were taking place. Certain capital letters were changing in form: *a, d, e,*

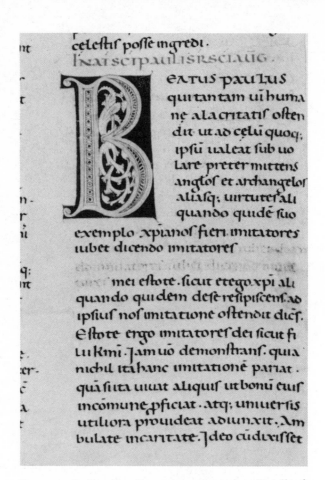

Fig. 170. Italian Caroline minuscule script. Detail of
leaf from Saint John Chrysostom, *Homily on Saint Paul*.
Italy. Early 12th century. Cornell University Library
(MS B. 63++c), Ithaca, New York.

and *m* gradually were transformed into what we recognize as lower-case letters
today, for the *a, e,* and *m* became rounded and the *d* was reversed and given an
ascender that projected slightly above the line of script. This form of writing, called
uncial, then became the basis for the development of an entirely lower-case alphabet,
the *Caroline minuscule* (fig. 170). The three forms of script were frequently used
together, the epigraphic capitals for titles, the uncial for subheadings, and the Caroline minuscule for the body of the text. These forms of script persisted, with
regional variations, until the advent of the Gothic period.

   In the twelfth century, particularly in English manuscripts, the rounded letters
of the Caroline minuscule became slightly pointed on the upper and lower curves.
In the thirteenth century all of the letters became pointed, with heavy, vertical,
dense strokes (fig. 171). Although perhaps a coincidence, the shift from the
rounded Caroline minuscule to the vertical pointed forms reflects the basic change
in architectural forms from Romanesque to Gothic. This *gotica textura* or *gotica*

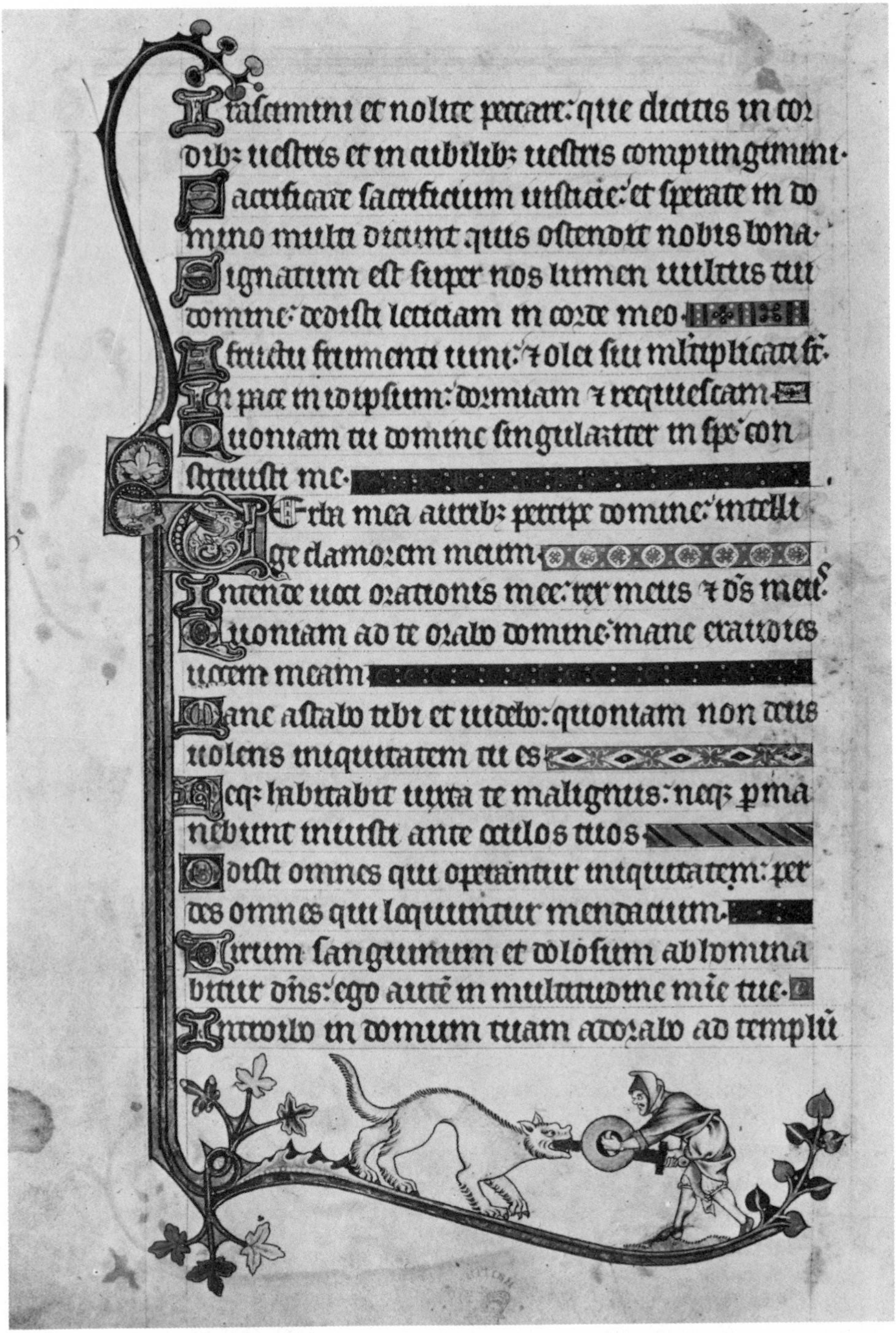

Fig. 171. Gotica textura script. Alfonso Psalter. England. Before 1284.
9½" x 6½". The British Library (MS Add. 24686, fol. 12v), London.

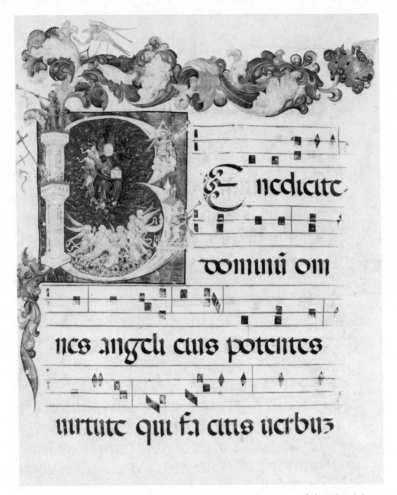

Fig. 172. Gotica rotunda script. Gradual illuminated by the Master of the Franciscan Breviary. Milan. c. 1450. 21¼" x 14½". Cornell University Library (MS B. 50++, fol. 65), Ithaca, New York.

formata script was widely used for ecclesiastical books and for formal texts. A more rounded variant of the Gothic script (*gotica rotunda,* fig. 172) was used in Italy and Spain. A sloping, informal, cursive hand (*bastarda* script, fig. 173), perhaps derived from some of the cursive hands used for legal and secular documents, gained popularity in the fifteenth century. It first became prevalent in vernacular literary manuscripts in France and Flanders, but was occasionally used in books for the Divine Office.

Another major form of writing known as *humanistic script* (fig. 174) was developed in Renaissance Italy. This was invented by Renaissance humanists who, despising the dense, angular forms of gotica textura, created a variant of what they considered to be the writing of antiquity, but which was actually Caroline minuscule. They used this script with quadrata capitals for titles and headings. This revived script served as the basis for many of the typefaces used today in printing.

Fig. 173. Bastarda script. Boethius, *De Consolatione Philosophiae*. France. Second quarter 15th century. 8½" x 6". Cornell University Library (MS B. 7, fol. 26v), Ithaca, New York.

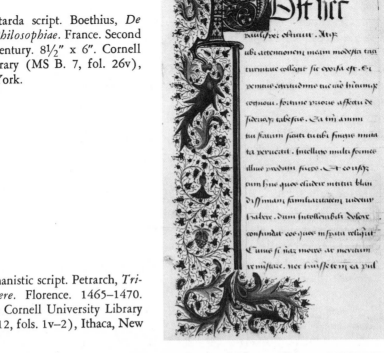

Fig. 174. Humanistic script. Petrarch, *Trionfi, Canzoniere*. Florence. 1465–1470. 10⅛" x 6¾". Cornell University Library (MS Pet. + Z12, fols. 1v–2), Ithaca, New York.

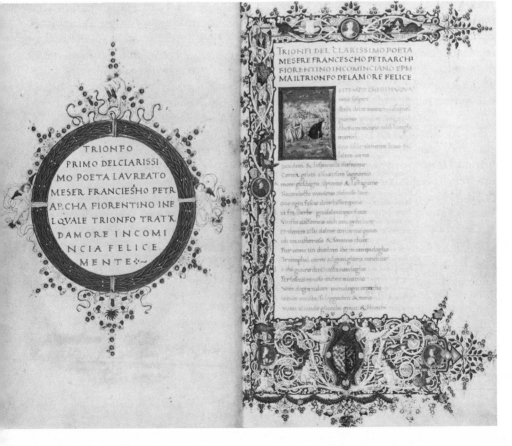

The process of copying an entire Bible or some other lengthy tome by hand was a difficult, time-consuming task. Frequently at the end of medieval manuscripts we find colophons in which the scribe wrote "deo gratias" as though with a sigh of relief that the book was finished. Occasionally he wrote a date and sometimes even his name. At the end of a Spanish Bible of 920, the scribe and illuminator stand beneath an omega, a symbol for "The End," and raise chalices in a toast to the completion of their labors. A colophon, written by a Spanish monk, Prior Petrus, in a twelfth-century manuscript of the Apocalypse indicates how painstaking a job it was to inscribe an entire book by hand, and, as a result, how precious the written and decorated word was to medieval man:

> A man who knows not how to write may think this no great feat. But only try to do it yourself and you shall learn how arduous is the writer's task. It dims your eyes, makes your back ache, knits your chest and belly together. It is a terrible ordeal for the whole body. So, gentle reader, turn these pages carefully and keep your finger far from the text. For just as hail plays havoc with the fruits of spring, so a careless reader is a bane to books and writing.

These Spanish manuscripts also demonstrate that most manuscripts of the first half of the Middle Ages appear to have been produced and decorated by monks in the scriptoria of monasteries. But a frontispiece to a Gothic Bible made for Blanche of Castile and her son, Louis IX, around 1226–1234 (pl. 21) illustrates that, with growing urbanization, the production of manuscripts shifted, to some extent, from the monasteries to the cathedral schools and lay ateliers. Below the representations of the queen and her youthful son, a cleric with tonsured head dictates to a scribe dressed in lay clothing. The cleric may be the author or the head of the scriptorium, however the transcribing is being done by a lay person. Throughout the remainder of the Gothic period, book production under the aegis of the universities or within lay ateliers becomes a major component of the book trade.

The demand for an increasing variety of books grew with the greater availability of education after the foundation of the universities and the spread of learning to more than just the members of a royal court or the upper hierarchy of the church. Ecclesiastical and liturgical texts were still written in Latin, but a growing body of popular religious tracts and secular literature was written in the various vernacular languages. In the fifteenth century numerous classical texts were also translated from Greek and Latin into the vernacular. The necessity of producing large numbers of books no doubt resulted in procedures for hastening the process of writing books. Dictation to numerous scribes rather than the individual copying a single exemplum or the use of several scribes to copy different parts of the book simultaneously were first tentative steps toward the mass production of manuscripts.

29. The Preparation of the Manuscript, the Process of Illumination, and Types of Text Decoration

The preparation of a handwritten and illuminated codex followed regularly established procedures. After the curing and cutting of the vellum to the appropriate size, the bifolios were folded and arranged into loose gatherings (see fig. 166, p. 202). As the hair side of the vellum was usually darker and slightly speckled, care was taken to arrange the bifolios so that these sides faced each other, thereby presenting a uniform appearance across the facing folios when the book was opened. As a result, the whiter, creamier sides also faced each other. The bifolios were then pricked with a fine instrument to indicate the dimensions and the number of lines of the text area, and fine lines in either silverpoint or colored ink were then drawn between these points. These lines then served as a guide for the scribe. The rulings also defined marginal areas around the text, narrow along the gutter or inner edge, wider at the top, and even wider along the outer edge and bottom of the folio.

The scribe then wrote the text, but left blank the spaces for capital letters of varying height and, if required in the plan of the book, spaces for painted miniatures. Small letters were written lightly in the space of the initials or in the adjacent margin as instructions for the illuminator; these were usually obscured by the subsequent decoration. Spaces or lines were left blank for headings written in red ink (*rubrics*), sometimes supplied by the scribe himself, sometimes by another, a *rubricator*. Catchwords with the first word or phrase on the following gathering were often written in the bottom margin of the last folio of the preceding gathering, although sometimes gatherings were given alphabetical or numerical signatures: all of these devices enabled the book to be easily assembled in its proper order.

In the treatise *In Praise of Scribes,* Johannes Trithemius described how an illuminated manuscript may have been prepared within a monastic scriptorium:

> If you do not know how to write, you still can assist the scribes in various ways. One of you can correct what another has written. Another can add the rubrics to the corrected text. A third can add initials and signs of division. Still another can arrange the leaves and attach the binding. Another of you can prepare the covers, the leather, the buckles and clasps. All sorts of assistance can be offered the scribe to help him pursue his work without interruption. He needs many things which can be prepared by others: parchment cut, flattened and ruled for script, ready ink and pens. You will always find something with which to help the scribe.

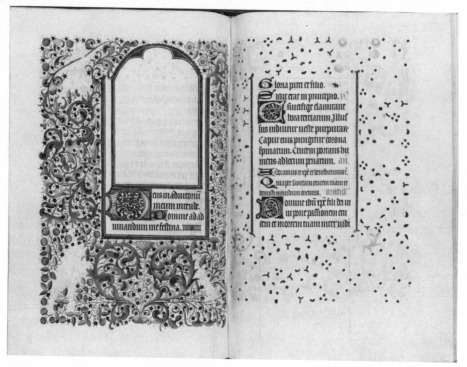

Fig. 175. Unfinished pages, book of hours. Provence. c. 1440. 9¾" x 6¾".
The Pierpont Morgan Library (MS 358, fols. 132v–133), New York.

At this point a manuscript consisting of text written on a stack of gatherings of loosely interleaved folios was ready to be illuminated. An unfinished illuminated book of hours of around 1440 in The Pierpont Morgan Library clearly shows the stages of execution that were then followed. Light drawings executed in silverpoint indicated the design of the decorative foliage, figures, and grotesque hybrid animals in the borders (fig. 175). Gold leaf was then applied over bole on decorative dots in the foliage and in the line endings, as well as on the one-line initials and vertical bars framing the text. Light, basic tonalities, of red, blue, or green were then painted on the appropriate areas of the decoration and, through a series of overpaintings, were built up, with modulated colors to indicate details, highlights, and shadows. A model book for the use of illuminators preserved at the University of Göttingen demonstrates numerous similar stages for the development of painted foliage and decorative backgrounds. The pigment used for this purpose was a gouache, an opaque mixture of pigments and cherry gum as a binding medium.

Apparently, in The Morgan Library manuscript, the painter of the foliage may not have been the person responsible for the marginal figures, for in many instances the marginal figures and miniatures are left blank in partially finished or completed foliate borders. In one case, a finished miniature appears on a page with partially finished marginal and text decoration (fig. 176). In this manuscript, at least, the illuminator responsible for the borders was also responsible for the initials, line endings, and text frames, for in every case where the work has been interrupted, all these elements are in the same stage of arrested development.

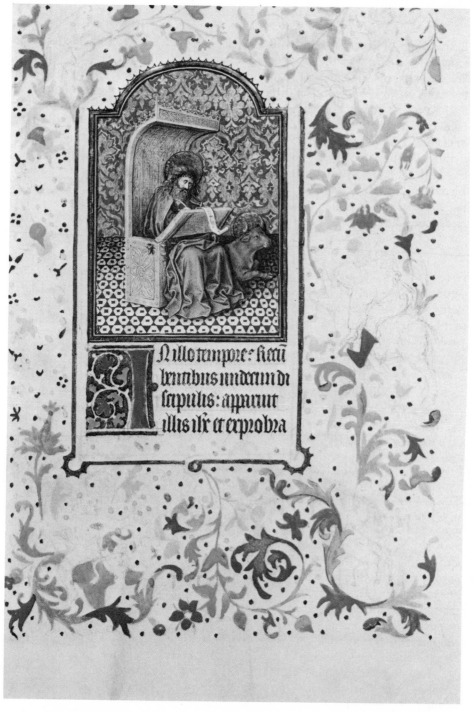

Fig. 176. "Saint Luke" and unfinished decoration, book of hours. Provence. c. 1440. 9¾" x 6¾". The Pierpont Morgan Library (MS 358, fol. 19), New York.

Examination of the distribution of the various stages of execution in this manuscript also reveals that the work was executed by bifolio and that sometimes the decoration on one side of a bifolio progressed farther than on the other side before the work was interrupted. The evidence in The Morgan Library manuscript points to the presence of at least several artisans, one of whom may have executed the borders and text decoration, and at least two identifiable artists who painted the miniatures and accompanying marginalia. There is no way of knowing, however, if this workshop was in any way affiliated with the scriptorium that provided the text with its blank spaces for initials, line endings, and miniatures. The Morgan Library manuscript is believed to have been produced in Provence around 1440, but it is possible that other manuscripts illuminated in different regions and periods were produced according to other ways of distributing the labor.

The artistry of skilled illuminators, or *historieurs* as they are sometimes referred to in French documents, was highly esteemed throughout the Middle Ages. Jacquemart de Hesdin, a miniaturist employed by the bibliophile Jean, Duc de Berry, killed a fellow artist because he stole his designs. But the duke thought so much of Jacquemart's services that he interceded with the king and obtained a pardon. Christine de Pizan, a poet in Paris in the first decade of the fifteenth century, praised the talents of a woman illuminator:

> Speaking of painting, I know at the present time a woman named Anastasie who is so expert and skillful in making borders for books and backgrounds for miniatures that there is no mention of a craftsman in the city of Paris, where there are the best in the world, who surpasses her in these matters.

Various forms of painted decoration were used in medieval manuscripts. Some were purely ornamental, others embodied narrative scenes in order to provide visualizations of the incidents depicted in the text. Miniatures of narrative scenes had existed in the scrolls of antiquity and were continued in Early Christian codices. Such a miniature is the representation of "Aeneas, Fatula, and Dido" in the Vatican Vergil of the fourth century (see fig. 168, p. 204). Enframed within a red border, this painting is a miniature version of a Roman fresco, presenting a vignette of the real world. Although sketchily painted like the catacomb frescoes, the solidly modeled figures cast shadows against walls and on the ground in the manner of Roman painting, from which they are derived. Subsequent miniatures continue this late antique style until about the sixth century with varying degrees of adherence to the principles underlying its inherent realism.

Important innovations in the decoration of books were made in northern Europe. Early Christian and early Byzantine manuscripts had not given special emphasis to opening letters or phrases of chapters or paragraphs of the text. In Anglo-Irish manuscripts of the end of the seventh century, however, the concept of embellishing the sacred text itself was developed. The opening phrase (*incipit*) of significant divisions of the text was rendered in large scale and was filled and

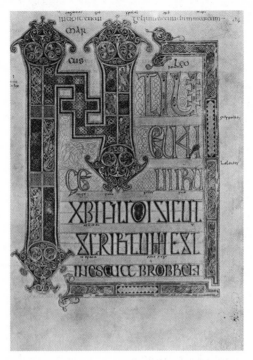

Fig. 177. *Initium evangelium* . . . , with decorative initials. Incipit of the
Gospel of Saint Mark, Lindisfarne Gospels. Northumbria. 690–698. 13½″
x 9½″. The British Library (MS Cotton Nero D. IV, fol. 94), London.

Fig. 178. *Beatus vir* . . . , with foliate initial. Incipit of Psalm 1,
Harley Psalter. Winchester. Last quarter 10th century. 11¼″ x 9½″.
The British Library (MS Harley 2904, fol. 4), London.

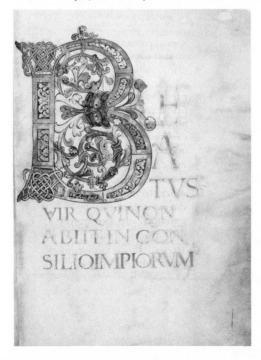

surrounded with intricate decoration. This ornament was based upon the abstract forms of geometric and zoomorphic art, which had supplanted the manifestations of Mediterranean culture during the period of the barbarian migrations.

A developed example of the illuminated incipit in this style is the *"Initium evangelium Jehsu Christi . . ."* (fig. 177), the opening phrase of the Gospel of Saint Mark in the gospel book produced at the Monastery of Lindisfarne in Northumbria between 690 and 698. The *INI* has been fused into an elaborate monogram, filled with intricate geometric interlace decoration and intertwined lacertines. The terminals of the *I*s are filled with spirals within spirals. The structure of the letters consists of gold bands forming a series of interior panels, so that the multicolored forms read like cloisonné enamel. Succeeding portions of the following words are written in a decreasing scale, but are encased in panels of dotted knotlike decoration. Lacertines of these same dots appear below the crossbar of the monogram. The *INI* is balanced by decorative panels framing the opposite side of the page so that the entire opening text is enclosed as though it were on display. The application of the pigment, particularly in the tightly woven interlace and dots surrounding the letters, is slightly raised in relief so that the light catches the edges and enhances their three-dimensional quality. Thus, in the glowing colors, subtle relief, and enframed jewellike treatment, the opening words become artifacts of barbarian metalwork serving a Christian purpose and imbuing the Word with light.

Once decorative initials were used in this manner to set off the beginnings of the gospels or important passages within them, they were soon varied to include a profusion of foliate and animal forms and used in many other contexts. An Anglo-Saxon psalter of the last quarter of the tenth century contains a magnificent foliate initial *B* (*Beatus vir,* fig. 178) introducing the first word of Psalm 1, followed by a decreasing scale of firmly executed gold epigraphic capitals. The *B,* made up of golden panels with colored acanthus leaves within, still retains animal heads and interlace patterns at the corners, which are derived from the Anglo-Irish tradition. The loops of the *B* terminate in a grotesque head that spews forth multicolored leafy scrolls heralding new traditions of foliate decoration in English Romanesque art.

We find, in fact, at this point in the development of Romanesque manuscript illumination, a repertoire of types of capital letters that conforms exactly with the types of carved capitals on the columns of Romanesque churches. In addition to decorative and foliate capitals we also have inhabited ones. In an English Romanesque Bible of the twelfth century (fig. 179) an elaborate spiraling vine emanating from a U-shaped dragon body with a horned human head contains within its tendrils a bird and a human figure being bitten by a dog. At first this seems to be an example of the capricious ferocity found among fighting, biting animals in carved inhabited capitals, and from a decorative point of view such an illustration derives directly from the zoomorphic barbarian tradition. But this particular representation also has meaning. The rubric above reads *"Incipit Liber Iob"* and the inhabited initial is the letter *V* (*Vir erat in terra*) introducing the Book of Job. Perhaps the figure enmeshed in the tendrils and beset by the dog is Job sub-

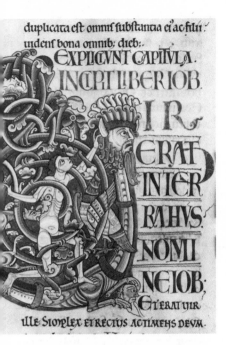

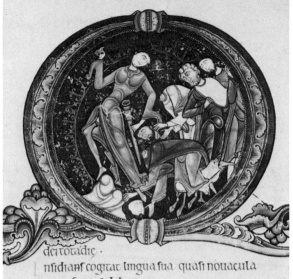

Fig. 179. *Vir erat . . .* , with inhabited initial. Incipit of the Book of Job, Bible. England. 12th century. Initial: 5½" x 4¼". Bodleian Library (MS Auct. E. inf. 1, fol. 304), Oxford.

Fig. 180. "Doeg Killing the High Priests." Historiated initial to Psalm 52, Winchester Bible. Winchester. c. 1150. Full page: 22¾" x 15¾". Winchester Cathedral Library.

jected to his tribulations. He pulls at the hair of the demonlike dragon, as though to free himself, while the equally ensnared bird may symbolize not only his predicament, but also the medieval belief that the body was the prison of the soul. Although not depicting a specific incident, this initial embodies the entire story of Job.

Historiated capitals became widely used in the Carolingian period and remained one of the principal vehicles for narrative scenes through the remainder of the Middle Ages. A mid-twelfth-century historiated initial in the Winchester Bible depicting "Doeg Killing the High Priests" (fig. 180) that prefaces Psalm 52 is a major example of English Romanesque painting. Because of the lively, prancing style of the figures within the *Q,* the artist has been named the Master of the Leaping Figures. The bending postures of the figures, echoing the shape of the latter, recall the correspondence of figure with frame that appears in some Romanesque sculpture. The rich reds, yellows, and greens, contrasting with a deep blue ground, glow with vibrant intensity on the vellum page. Historiated initials painted in the fifteenth century depicting "God Adored by the Angels" in a large Italian gradual (see fig. 172, p. 208) or the "Adoration of the Child" in a small Dutch book of hours (see fig. 182, p. 219) demonstrate a continuing penchant for brilliant colors, charming vignettes, and sometimes, fanciful decorations.

30. ECCLESIASTICAL BOOKS:
THEIR PATRONAGE AND THEIR MINIATURES

The Bible was originally the principal book from which the Christian ritual was derived. As the liturgy evolved and became more complex, however, passages from the Bible were excerpted and rearranged in different sequences to suit specific needs. The lectionary and evangelistary were rearrangements of the gospels according to the order in which they were read as the lessons in the Mass during the liturgical year. The sacramentary containing the ritual of High Mass was developed first; only later did the Missal containing additional elements for the celebration of Low Mass evolve. Because the chanting of the psalms was an important part of the daily ritual in early medieval monasteries, psalters, with just the psalms, were widely used. Benedictionals containing special prayers and benedictions and pontificals containing special services to be said by the pope or a bishop were also formulated. These liturgical books were not all invented at once, but came into being over the centuries to facilitate the celebration of the Mass.

In the early Middle Ages such manuscripts, even for the church, were rare and costly, and were probably commissioned only by the upper hierarchy of the clergy and the imperial court. Although now lost, codices of the Bible commissioned by Constantine may have served as an important source for the development of an Early Christian tradition of Bible illustration, which, in turn, strongly influenced Anglo-Irish, Carolingian, and Ottonian illumination. Books written on purple-dyed parchment, possibly for members of the Byzantine court, undoubtedly served as models for similar manuscripts produced for the Carolingian and Ottonian courts.

One of the earliest surviving examples of a pictorial representation of patronage is in the Bible of Charles the Bald of around 843 to 851 (fig. 181). Count Vivian, Lay Abbot of the monastery of Saint Martin at Tours and councilor to the Carolingian emperor, commissioned the book and then presented the finished copy to Charles. The full-page presentation miniature, an elaborate imperial portrait of the emperor flanked with attendants and graced with the sign of divine investiture, the hand of God above, also served to commemorate the donation of the manuscript, witnessed by clerics and members of the court

In the later Middle Ages a new repertoire of devotional books came into being. Evolving out of the practice of the daily chanting of psalms and the performance of services called the Divine Office eight times a day, breviaries were formulated for the clergy and books of hours for the laity. The increasing popularity of the book of hours corresponds with the trend toward private devotion, particularly in the fourteenth and fifteenth centuries, and many of these books were owned by lesser clergy or members of the mercantile burgher class. Frequently, books of hours contain the portraits and armorial devices of the persons

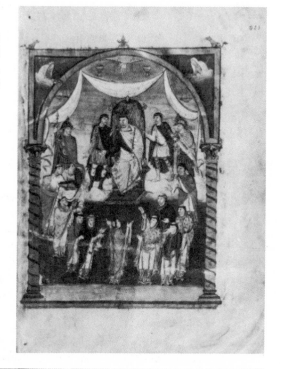

Fig. 181. "Count Vivian Presenting the Bible to Charles the Bald." First Bible of Charles the Bald. Tours. c. 843–851. 19½" x 13⅝". Bibliothèque Nationale (MS lat. 1, fol. 423), Paris.

Fig. 182. "Donors Kneeling Before the Virgin and Child" and historiated initial with "Adoration of the Child." Book of hours. Utrecht. c. 1460. 7¼" x 4⅞". Rijksmuseum Meermanno-Westreenianum (MS 10.F.50, fols. 13v–14), The Hague.

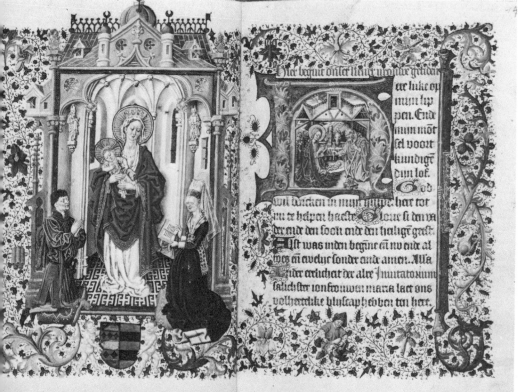

for whom the book was made. In a Dutch book of hours of around 1460 (fig. 182), a full-page frontispiece depicts a husband and wife, possibly members of the Lochorst and Morel families of Utrecht, kneeling before a standing Virgin and Child within a Gothic apse. As so frequently happens in medieval books, the arms below the original owners' have been altered, in this case to those of a lady who possessed the book in the seventeenth century. Such portraits of pious devotion, reinforced by armorial marks of ownership, brought the possessors into closer contact with their religion. The prevalence of these devotional books reveals that there was now a broader base of people who could read these books as well as a greater dispersal of wealth so that they could afford them. Because of the widespread demand for books of hours at the end of the Middle Ages, their production became a veritable industry in such cities as Paris, Bruges, and Utrecht.

To the books for the Mass and the Divine Office should be added the manuscripts that contained the chants. With the evolution of musical notation, and the desire to have the chants in separate books to be placed before the monks in the choir of the church, there evolved the gradual for the Mass and the antiphonal for the Divine Office. In the late Middle Ages many of these books of chants were produced in large format to enhance legibility and, as exemplified by the gradual illuminated by a mid-fifteenth-century illuminator known only as the Master of the Franciscan Breviary, they were often lavishly decorated (see fig. 172, p. 208).

A variety of styles of painting and kinds of miniatures adorned these ecclesiastical books throughout the Middle Ages. In Anglo-Irish gospel books, the individual gospels were frequently prefaced by a full-page *carpet page,* often with a cruciform design. The Lindisfarne Gospels contains six of these decorative pages executed with utmost precision and skill (pl. 18). In the page prefacing the Gospel of Saint Mark, the rectangular format encloses decorative panels filled with step patterns, tightly interlaced circular knots, and spiral-trumpet motifs. The bands with blue and yellow knot patterns form an interior square containing a circle with four arms, an abstracted form of an Irish cross. This circle encloses a regular grid of colored step patterns, but in the residual areas outside the circle is a mass of intertwined lacertines. These abstract geometric and zoomorphic forms, set within panels bounded by red, emulate the effect of cloisonné enamel in the same way that the facing incipit initials of the *Initium* reflect barbarian jewelry. This repertoire of barbarian metalwork patterns and the careful emulation of cloisonné work appear to function in the same way as the golden cover of the Lindau Gospels (pl. 17), where a cruciform shape was imposed upon a background of writhing snakes. Here the animal-headed terminals outside the rectangular format of the decoration and the lacertines tightly contained within the order imposed by the circle, cross, and square, all symbols of the imposition of divine order and perfection, perhaps reiterate the theme of the power and order of the church over the chaos of the world.

Equally significant is the role these carpet pages play in the Lindisfarne Gospels. One appears before the Prologue of Saint Jerome and one facing the incipit of each of the gospels. They therefore serve as painted emulations of sumptuous metalwork covers for the manuscript as a whole and for the individual books

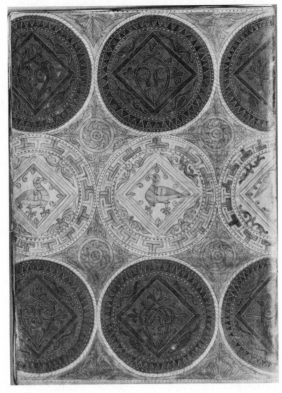

Fig. 183. Imitation Byzantine silk page introducing the Gospel
of Saint Matthew. Codex Aureus of Echternach of Henry III.
Echternach or Trier. 1053–1056. 17⅜″ x 12″. Germanisches
Nationalmuseum (MS 156142, fol. 18), Nuremberg.

within it. A similar purpose is served by painted copies of Byzantine silk fabrics
prefacing the gospels in the Ottonian Codex Aureus of Echternach now in Nuremberg
(fig. 183).

One of the most recurrent themes in medieval manuscript illumination is the
representation of the Evangelist prefacing his gospel. Ultimately derived from the
antique representation of authors or poets inspired by a muse, the Evangelist portrait usually depicted the apostle receiving inspiration from the apocryphal beast
that was his attribute. In a Carolingian gospel book prepared for Archbishop Ebbo
of Reims before 823, "Saint Matthew" (fig. 184) is seated in a landscape, hunched
over an open codex upon a lectern, while his attribute, the angel, hovers in the
upper right corner. In the bulky, volumetric treatment of the figure we find the
continuation of a classical mode of painting that had been revived at the court of
Charlemagne around 800. But in the streaky, vibrant manner of painting we find
an innovation perhaps derived from the linear style found in sketchy drawings in
the Utrecht Psalter, a style that was peculiar to Ebbo's monastery of Hautvillers.
The figures and their setting are consumed by nervous, energetic lines of pigment
that are shot with gold and hastily applied to the parchment. The result is a figure
scintillating with the electrifying impact of the heavenly message, which he in-

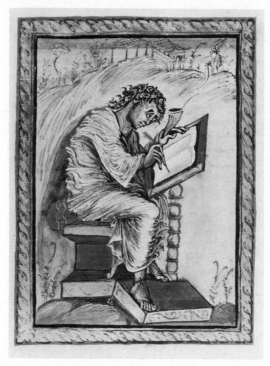

Fig. 184. "Saint Matthew." Ebbo Gospels. Hautvillers, near Reims. Before 823. 10¼" x 8¼". Bibliothèque Municipale (MS 1, fol. 18v), Épernay. (Photograph: Bibliothèque Nationale, Paris)

scribes with ecstatic fervor. Even the landscape and its sketchily rendered temples are vibrant with this instant of divine inspiration. Thus, revived classical forms were soon subjected to a new desire to capture the fervent, spiritual essence of the moment and were thereby transformed into a new mode of abstraction.

In the Romanesque period different forms of abstraction were imposed upon the Evangelist figures to achieve the desired effect. In the Corbie Gospels of around 1090 from northern France, "Saint John" (pl. 19) is placed within an arcade, linking him with the imperial tradition of the enthroned emperor, a compositional device that had been used for Evangelist portraits since the sixth century. Seated on a throne and holding a scroll, the Evangelist is seemingly contorted and twisted by the impact of the divine message whispered into his ear by his attribute, the eagle. The flattened form and violent zigzag placement of his body, further activated by the bold red stripes and repetitive curved silver hemlines of his garment, create a painted version of the compressed energy found in Romanesque sculpture. The concentric patterns of drapery on the torso, the constraint imposed by the arcade, the twisting of the eagle's head and of the saint's arms and legs evoke the sense of ecstatic inspiration found in the jamb figure of Isaiah at Souillac (see fig. 78, p. 98).

Representations of the Evangelist in later manuscripts, particularly in the fifteenth century, dwelled more upon physical actuality. The seated figure of "Saint Luke" in the Provençal book of hours of around 1440 (see fig. 176, p. 213) shows the Evangelist seated and quietly working at a lectern while his attribute, the ox, reposes beside him. Although this representation does not place the figure within an architectural setting, it nevertheless details a tiled floor, shaded toward the rear to give the effect of recessive depth, places the canopied throne at an angle in the implied space, and gives the saint a heavily modulated effect of weight and volume. Paintings with this greater emphasis on realism were consistent with the devotional attitudes of the late Middle Ages, for they made the scene more immediate to the worshiper's reality.

In contrast to the vestige of classical realism evident in the narrative miniature of "Aeneas and Dido" in the Vatican Vergil, a miniature of "Saint Edmund Led into Captivity" (pl. 20) in an English Romanesque manuscript of *The Life of St. Edmund* painted in the second quarter of the twelfth century also reduces the story and setting to an abstract schema. The figures are elongated and flattened. The background had been reduced to alternate blue and red panels of unequal size but juxtaposed in a balanced composition like a forerunner of a Mondrian abstraction. The groundline is indicated by wavelike curlicues and the tree dividing the composition between the colored panels is equally arbitrary. Here, as in other examples of Romanesque art, the interest was not so much in depicting an actual and recognizable scene as in seizing upon the essence of the narrative: Saint Edmund calm and dignified amid the hauling and beating of his assailants.

Biblical narrative in manuscripts, to judge from the numerous Carolingian Bibles that are believed to have been copied after now-lost Early Christian books, became prevalent as a phenomenon parallel to the proliferation of biblical cycles in mosaic and fresco in Early Christian basilicas. An Ottonian reflection of this tradition, in the Codex Aureus of Echternach, commissioned by the Emperor Henry III between 1053 and 1056 as a gift for the monastery at Echternach, presents full-page miniatures with three horizontal bands of narrative scenes (fig. 185). On a page relating the Incarnation, the "Annunciation" and the "Visitation" are depicted in the upper register, each scene neatly enclosed in its own architectural frame. The "Nativity" takes place below, also in an architectural setting, while to the right the shepherds among their flocks in a rudimentary landscape hear the news of the birth of Christ from four angels. The bottom register is entirely devoted to the "Three Magi Before Herod," showing them asking him of news of the birth of the Messiah, and the entire scene is unified by the palatial ensemble. Simple, direct presentations of the incidents against colored backgrounds and with a minimum of subsidiary detail, reinforced with an occasional identifying label (*pastores* for the shepherds) and a running inscription in the frames between the scenes, make the narrative clear. Lively miniatures from a similar Ottonian manuscript of a slightly earlier date may have served as the models for Bernward's bronze doors at Hildesheim (see fig. 85, p. 104).

A new variant of the biblical narrative and even of the biblical text gained currency in the mid-thirteenth century. A series of moralizations were derived from various biblical incidents and they were presented in pictorial form in paired medallions (fig. 186). These moralized Bibles did not actually contain the biblical

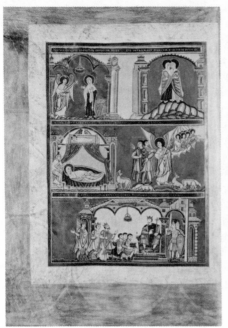

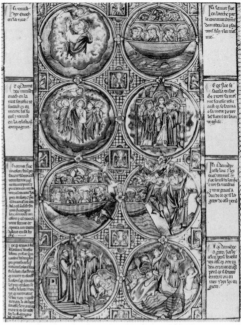

Fig. 185. "Annunciation," "Visitation," "Nativity" and "Annunciation to the Shepherds," and "Three Magi Before Herod." Codex Aureus of Echternach of Henry III. Echternach or Trier. 1053–1056. 17⅜" x 12". Germanisches Nationalmuseum (MS 156142, fol. 19), Nuremberg.

Fig. 186. "Story of Enoch and Noah." Moralized Bible. France. c. 1250. 13⅛" x 10¼". Österreichische Nationalbibliothek (MS 2554, fol. 3), Vienna.

Fig. 187. Jean Pucelle: "Crucifixion" and "Adoration of the Magi." *The Hours of Jeanne d'Évreux.* France. c. 1325–1328. Each page 3½" x 2⁷⁄₁₆". The Metropolitan Museum of Art, The Cloisters Collection, Purchase 1954 (54.1.2, fols. 68v–69).

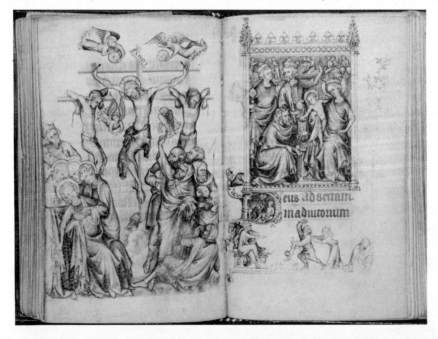

text, but rather a brief statement of the applicable incident and its moralization in a series of columns of text flanking the medallions. The medallions themselves were arranged either in two vertical rows, or in a central rectangular panel that was filled with geometric decorations similar to the arrangement of stained-glass windows. Indeed, the multiplication of incidents and images (a moralized Bible in Vienna contains 129 surviving pages, each with eight scenes, for a total of 1,032 medallions, another in Vienna contains 1,950 medallions) reflects the vast programs of stained glass, as at the Sainte-Chapelle, with which they are contemporary.

A page relating the story of Enoch and of Noah's ark in one of the Vienna Bibles illustrates the relationships between the paired medallions and their accompanying texts. The pairs in this manuscript read vertically rather than horizontally. The first depicts Enoch ascending into Heaven in a cloud as God blesses him. The medallion below represents a monk, a nun, and three saints, and the accompanying text amplifies the scene by telling us that as Enoch is received into Heaven, so shall Christ receive his elect. In the upper right medallion, Noah is shown in his ark with his family and pairs of animals. Below, a bishop and monks are shown flanking Christ in a church. The implication elucidated in the text is that as Noah found salvation by seeking refuge in the ark, so all those who love Christ can seek salvation in the church. In the bottom pair of medallions on the left, a bird flies away from the ark, two return, and a crow eats meat below the ship. Below, the moralization of this scene is explained in terms of proper behavior in the medieval monastery. Noah is equated with the priest who exhorts his flock to prayer, and he is also equated with the good monk who adheres to the Benedictine vow of *stabilitas loci,* never leaving the monastery during his life, represented by a dying monk with his soul departing from his mouth. The abbot receiving two monks reflects Noah receiving the two doves who returned home after a lengthy absence. The returning monks acknowledge their guilt and are about to receive a beating with the upraised rods. Below, another monk drinks in an inn while the sly innkeeper either gives him or relieves him of a bag of money: he is equated with the raven who lingers over carrion in the outside world. In the last pair of scenes Noah and his family give thanks for their deliverance from the peril of the flood, and below, this event is equated with prayers of thanksgiving for delivery from a variety of perils: salvation from wild animals on land, and from shipwreck and predatory fish at sea.

In keeping with increasing emphasis on private devotion in the Gothic period, books of hours, used for personal meditation at specific times during the day, were produced, first for the nobility, and then for a wider segment of the population. These devotional books were made appealing through their fine workmanship, small size, and profusion of decoration. The book of hours believed to have been made for Jeanne d'Évreux, Queen of France, by Jean Pucelle around 1325 to 1328 (fig. 187) illustrates many of these developments. Minute and refined, it was a fitting object for the queen of France. Only 3½ inches by 2⁷⁄₁₆ inches in size, it contained extremely delicately painted scenes in grisaille. With this device, however, the illuminator achieved a startling sense of relief, in marked contrast with the flattened forms in miniatures of the latter half of the thirteenth century. In fact, the style of painting and indeed many of the compositions reflect the effect and arrangement of scenes found in contemporary ivory carving, and it seems entirely likely that Pucelle was emulating the subtle effects of light and shadow in ivory reliefs. The "Crucifixion" and the "Adoration of the Magi" in *The Hours of Jeanne d'Évreux* are almost identical with their counterparts in the ivories examined above (see figs. 161, 162, pp. 194, 195), revealing the currency of these motifs in the ateliers of various trades in the fourteenth century. The "Crucifixion," reflecting the heightened emotionalism of the same scene in Duccio's *Maestà*, manifests an infusion of influences from Italian fourteenth-century art that was further accentuated by the illuminators and ivory carvers throughout the rest of the century.

By the end of the fourteenth century, books of hours were valued as precious works of art as much as for their devotional value. Jean, Duke of Berry, the brother of King Charles V of France, commissioned a series of books of hours in the last decade of the fourteenth and the first decades of the fifteenth century, each one more lavish than the last. This series culminated in the *Très Riches Heures* (the "Very Rich Hours"), which was still in the process of illumination at the time of his death in 1416. Documents record that this book was decorated by the three Limbourg brothers who had worked for the duke on a number of projects since around 1405. The devotional texts of the book are prefaced by twelve calendar scenes that accompany the list of the feast days of the saints for the liturgical year. The Limbourgs created remarkable elaborations of the usual representations of the labors of the months and the signs of the zodiac, which symbolized the celestial progress of the stars and the terrestrial sequence of the seasons, that illustrated such calendars.

The month of January was customarily illustrated by a banqueting scene or by persons warming themselves by a fire. In the *Très Riches Heures* (fig. 188) both are combined, for the Duke of Berry is shown seated before a screened fireplace at a table laden with golden plate, including a ship saltcellar recorded in the inventories of his possessions. His page announces "Approche, Approche" to the crowd of courtiers. Against the back wall hangs a tapestry of a battle scene. "January" therefore becomes a flattering portrait of the duke surrounded by his sumptuous worldly possessions and the members of his court.

The miniature for the month of "February" (fig. 189) depicts peasants warming themselves by a fire and going about their daily chores. The scene takes place in a remarkable landscape with barren trees under a sky leaden with impending snow. Snowy fields stretch across rolling meadows to a distant town in one of the first accurate portrayals of landscape in northern European painting. Although poor and living in humble surroundings, the peasants seem comfortable enough and we suspect that the miniaturist is continuing his flattery of the duke by informing us that all is well within his estate. This implication of the calendar scenes is continued in other representations of the months, for seven of the duke's castles are depicted in these scenes. In the month of August (fig. 190) lords and ladies in courtly costumes ride out to go falconing, while in the background

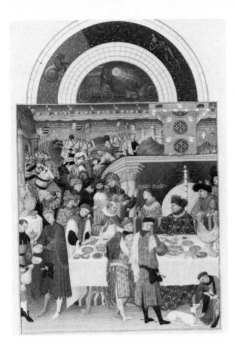

Fig. 188. Limbourg Brothers: "The Duke of Berry at Table, January." *Très Riches Heures.* France. c. 1415. 9⅜" x 6". Musée Condé, Chantilly. (Giraudon)

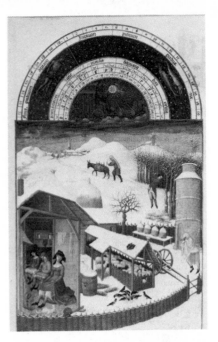

Fig. 189. Limbourg Brothers: "February." *Très Riches Heures.* France. c. 1415. 8¾" x 5⅜". Musée Condé, Chantilly. (Giraudon)

Fig. 190. Limbourg Brothers: "August" and Château d'Étampes. *Très Riches Heures.* France. c. 1415. 8¾" x 5⅜". Musée Condé, Chantilly. (Giraudon)

Fig. 191. Limbourg Brothers: "Temptation of Christ" and Château de Mehun-sur-Yèvre. *Très Riches Heures.* France. c. 1415. 6⅝" x 4½". Musée Condé, Chantilly. (Giraudon)

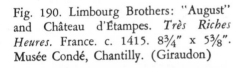

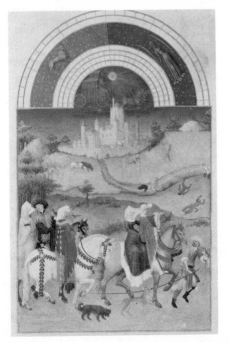

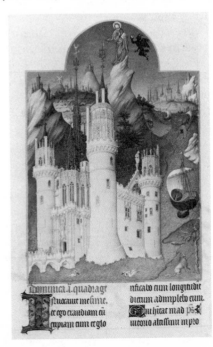

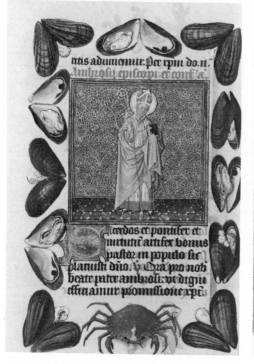

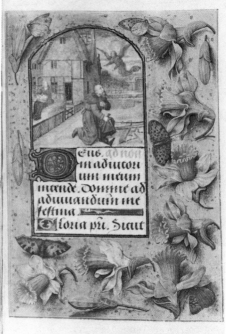

Fig. 192. "Saint Ambrose." *Book of Hours of Catherine of Cleves.* Utrecht. c. 1440–1445. 7%6" x 5⅛". The Pierpont Morgan Library (MS 917, p. 244), New York.

Fig. 193. "Joseph and the Angel." *Book of Hours of Engelbert of Nassau.* Flanders. c. 1477–1490. 5¼" x 3¾". Bodleian Library (MS Douce 219, fol. 153r), Oxford.

peasants harvest wheat and take a dip in a pond. On the horizon looms the duke's castle at Étampes.

Perhaps the highpoint of flattery in the miniatures of the *Très Riches Heures,* but touched with a note of caution, is to be found in the miniature of the "Temptation of Christ" (fig. 191). Here, Christ stands atop a sharp pinnacle and rejects the Devil's offer of all the Kingdoms of the World. The castle below, a recognized marvel of architectural delicacy in its day, described in the late fourteenth-century chronicles of Jean Froissart as "l'une des plus belles maisons du monde," is the duke's eighth castle at Mehun-sur-Yèvre. In this miniature it epitomizes the height of worldly splendor, and Christ's refusal to be tempted adds the ironic note of a *vanitas* theme: the empty vanity of power, wealth, and possessions, for they will all come to naught and Man cannot attain salvation through them. In fact the duke and his three illustrious illuminators all perished in an outbreak of the plague in 1416, leaving the *Très Riches Heures* unfinished. Also, at the time that work was progressing on this last manuscript for the duke, the conditions of his estates were far from ideal: the French had been defeated at the Battle of Agincourt in 1415, the duke's palace in Paris had been burned by the populace, and the peasants were revolting against their lords all over France. There may have been, therefore, in this marvelous sequence of perceptive miniatures, so full of realistic detail, a touch of nostalgia for a lost era that was disrupted by violent changes.

Further reflections of the increasing secularization of devotional books may be observed in the changing patterns of border decorations. In the thirteenth century prolonged staffs emanating from initial letters (see fig. 171, p. 207), which in the Romanesque period had served to contain dragons or rudimentary plant forms (see fig. 180, p. 217), grew into the adjacent margins and sprouted branches and leaves. In the fifteenth century these borders became dense friezes of penned branches filled with leaves, golden pods, and colored flowers. Acanthus leaves were added and integrated, providing broader areas of color to supplement the contrast of fine ink lines and glinting gold. The borders of the mid-fifteenth-century Dutch book of hours (see fig. 182, p. 219) and the unfinished book of hours (see fig. 175, p. 212) in The Morgan Library represent two later developments of this increasingly lavish decoration. These borders, unlike the drolleries and satirical or amplifying scenes of fourteenth-century manuscripts, served no other purpose than to make the manuscript more resplendent to the eye, and therefore valuable to the owner. Indeed, the books of hours produced for the Duke of Berry were no longer valued as just the embellished Word of God; they were regarded as *objets d'art* and were referred to as *joyaux* (jewels), along with actual bejeweled objects in the duke's inventories.

The desire for immediacy in devotion was accompanied by an increasingly secular outlook during the Gothic period. A variety of animals, grotesques, topsy-turvy and satirical scenes crept into the margins of devotional books. Hares chasing hounds made fun of the normal hunting scene, and clerics behaving in unseemly ways satirized the all-too-frequent instances of less than pious behavior. Reflections of these engaging drolleries were also carved in Gothic capitals and on the bosses at the juncture of rib vaults.

Reality, as well as fantasy and satire, intruded into the miniatures and borders of manuscripts. In the *Book of Hours of Catherine of Cleves* (fig. 192), a lavish manuscript made in the Netherlands around 1440 to 1445 for a niece of Philip the Good, traditional Dutch border decorations are interspersed with borders containing meticulously detailed birdcages, archery equipment, identifiable coins, and the shellfish surrounding the miniature of "Saint Ambrose." Laid out with stark simplicity against the plain vellum of the page, these objects appear real enough to remove. The predilection for illusionism that these borders manifest is carried even further by Flemish illuminators in the 1470s to the 1490s. In the *Book of Hours of Engelbert of Nassau* (fig. 193) jewels and flowers and many other objects are depicted against a gold or colored ground, often casting shadows upon it as though they existed in three dimensions before it.

In an extraordinary tour de force in a book of hours made for Mary of Burgundy between 1467 and 1480, perhaps by the same illuminator, the Master of Mary of Burgundy, a noble lady is shown seated before an open window (fig. 194) through which is visible a church interior with the seated Virgin and Child and a kneeling lord and ladies. The view through the window is the actual minia-

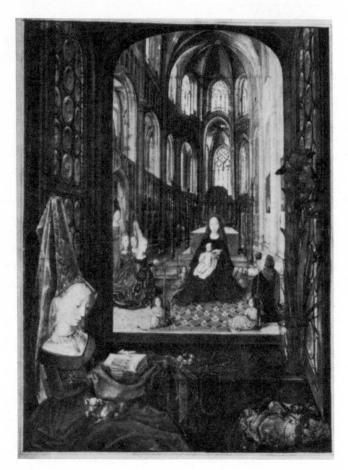

Fig. 194. "Virgin and Child in a Church and Mary of Burgundy Before an Open Window." *Book of Hours of Mary of Burgundy*. Flanders. c. 1467–1480. 8⅞" x 6⅝". Österreichische Nationalbibliothek (MS 1857, fol. 14), Vienna.

ture—a vista into a sacred realm—while the foreground—with open panes of glass, a sill with a vase of iris and a rosary, and the seated woman and brocaded cushion— is actually the border area around the miniature. This is part of our world. In this miniature we have the final intrusion of the aesthetic of the framed panel painting providing a window on another space, beyond the page of the illuminated manuscript.

Late medieval illuminators realized that they had altered the aesthetic of the page, for in several further examples they either treated the text area as a lettered panel placed before an illusionistic scene continuing behind it, or made it look like a tattered piece of parchment stretched before an architectural backdrop. In the *Hennessy Hours* (fig. 195), decorated in Brussels around 1540, the border around the text, a hunting scene, is actually the miniature, and the text becomes the enframed surface.

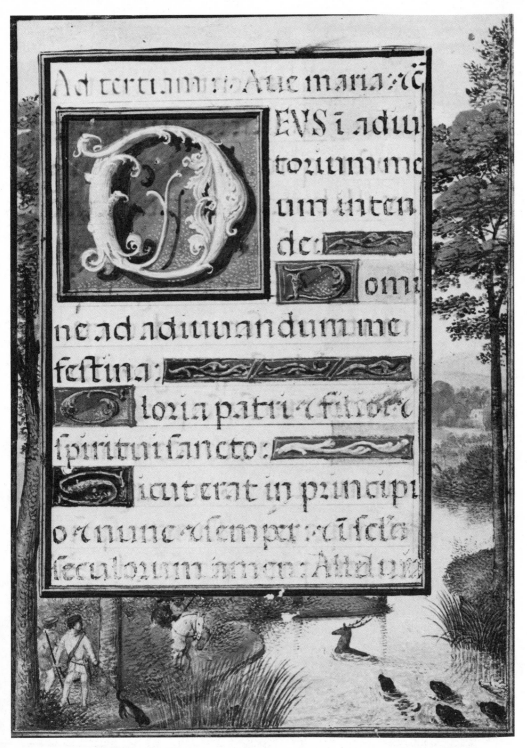

Ad tertiam: Auc maria xc
EVS i adiu
torium me
um inten
de. Domi
ne ad adiuuandum me
festina: Gloria patri z filio z
spiritui sancto: Sicut erat in principi
o z nunc z semper: z i scla
seculorum amen: Alleluia

Fig. 195. Border with "Hunting Scene." *Hennessy Hours.* Flanders.
c. 1540. 4½" x 3⅜". Bibliothèque Royale (MS II.158, fol. 80r), Brussels.

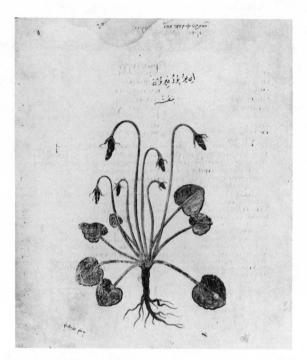

Fig. 196. "Violet." Dioscurides, *Materia Medica.*
Constantinople. 512. 15¼" x 13¼". Österreichische
Nationalbibliothek (MS med. gr. 1, fol. 148), Vienna.

31. SECULAR MANUSCRIPTS

The predominance of scriptural, liturgical, patristic, and devotional manuscripts
produced throughout the Middle Ages should not obscure the fact that numerous
secular texts were also copied and illustrated. A wealth of literary texts, exemplified
by the Vatican Vergil of the fourth century, mentioned above, and scientific books
existed in late antique times, and these continued to provide a storehouse of knowledge and a basis for further expositions for medieval scholars.

The large and luxuriously illustrated herbal, the *Materia Medica* of Dioscurides, prepared for the Byzantine princess Anicia Juliana in 512, was probably
copied from an earlier Greek manuscript. The Byzantine copy contains author
portraits in the firmly modeled classical style and numerous illustrations of plants
rendered accurately as botanical specimens. The miniature depicting a violet (fig.
196) shows the entire plant, flower buds, stems, leaves, and roots, as though laid
out on the parchment for examination. Undoubtedly, the realistic representation
of such plants, originally over four hundred of them were in the manuscript,
would have aided their identification by pharmacologists, who would have used
these plants for the mixing of medicines. According to Dioscurides, the violet
"has a cooling faculty . . . helps a burning stomach, and the inflammations of
the eyes . . . and they say that the purple part of the flower . . . does help the
epilepsies that are upon children."

A later version of the herbal compiled by the Arabian physician Albulkasem de Baldac, the *Tacuinum Sanitatis* (*Handbook of Health*), was in vogue at the end of the fourteenth century. In the prologue, the physician states:

> The *Tacuinum Sanitatis* is about the six things that are necessary for every man in the daily preservation of his health, about their correct uses and their effects. . . . Our intention in this book is to shorten long-winded discourses and synthesize the various ideas. Our intention also, however, is not to neglect the advice of the ancients.

In a miniature in one of the copies of this treatise in Vienna a lady is carrying a basket of picked spinach (fig. 197) on her head while other plants of the vegetable grow in profusion on the ground behind her. Botanical accuracy here has given way to a more generalized depiction of the plant and a presentation of it growing in its appropriate environment, an innovation that is continued in most of the other illustrations in other copies of this manuscript. The text below the miniature succinctly tells us of the properties and uses of spinach:

> *Nature:* Cold and humid in the first degree, of moderate warmth at other times. *Optimum:* Those leaves still wet with rain water. *Usefulness:* They are good for a cough and for the chest. *Dangers:* They disturb the digestion. *Neutralization of the dangers:* Fried with salted water, or with vinegar and aromatic herbs. *Effects:* Moderately nourishing. They are good for warm temperaments, for the young, at all times, and in every region.

With such information, the medieval physician believed, the user could administer this plant to maintain the proper balance of joy, anger, fear, and distress, and thereby preserve good health.

Fig. 197. "Spinach." *Tacuinum Sanitatis.* Italy. c. 1390. 13⅛″ x 9¼″.
Österreichische Nationalbibliothek (MS ser. nov. 2644, fol. 27), Vienna.

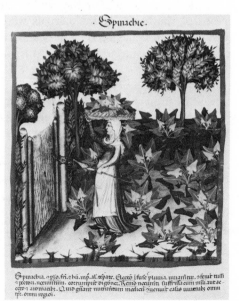

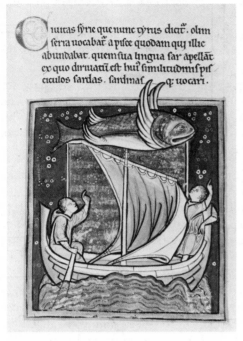

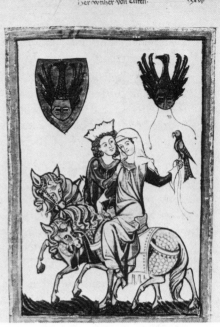

Cuitas fyrie que nunc tyrus dicat. olim ſerra uocabat a pifce quodam qui illic abundabat. quem ſua lingua ſar apellat ex quo diruatu eſt huiſ ſimilitudiniſ piſ ciculos ſardas. ſardinaſ q: uocari.

Fig. 198. "Serra." *Bestiary.* Lincoln?, England. c. 1185. 8½" x 6½". The Pierpont Morgan Library (MS 81, fol. 69), New York.

Fig. 199. "Werner von Teufen." Manesse Codex. Zurich?, Switzerland. c. 1315–1330. 15" x 9⅞". Universitätsbibliothek (MS Pal. germ. 848, fol. 69r), Heidelberg.

Similar traditions can be found in other books on natural history originally derived from classical manuscripts. The *Bestiary,* a medieval compendium of real and imaginary beasts, was based upon the Physiologus of the third or fourth century A.D. As recorded in medieval variants of the twelfth and thirteenth centuries, however, the descriptions of the habits of the animals were equated with moralizations concerning good Christian behavior. The discussion of the serra (fig. 198), the flying fish, in an English bestiary of around 1185 turns natural history into an object lesson:

> There is a beast in the sea which we call a Serra and its has enormous fins. When this monster sees a ship sailing on the sea, it erects its wings and tries to outfly the ship, up to about two hundred yards. Then it cannot keep up the effort; so it folds up its fins and draws them in, after which, bored by being out of the water, it dives back into the ocean.
>
> This peculiar animal is exactly like human beings today. Naturally the ship symbolizes the Righteous, who sail through the squalls and tempests of this world without danger of shipwreck in their faith. The Serra, on the contrary, is the monster which could not keep up with the righteous ship. It symbolizes the people who start off trying to devote themselves to good works,

but afterwards, not keeping it up, they get vanquished by various kinds of nasty habits and, undependable as the to-fro waves of the sea, they drive down to Hell.

You do not get anywhere by starting. You get there by pressing on.

Arising out of this tradition of natural history books, but based upon contemporary observations, were a series of treatises on hunting, the most famous ones being the *Book of the Hunt* by Gaston de Phébus and a treatise on falconry, *De Arte Venandi cum Avibus* (*On the Art of Hunting with Birds*), by the Holy Roman Emperor, Frederick II. An illustrated copy (pl. 22) prepared for Frederick's son, Manfred, around 1260, now in the Vatican Library, contains sensitive depictions of all manner of birds, with special emphasis on the care and training of falcons. A significant treatise on ornithology, many of its paintings of birds and comments on their habits are based upon empirical observation. By the end of the century copies had been translated into French and German.

In addition to these books on the natural sciences and other learned treatises on music, astronomy, a book on the properties of stones (*De Lapidario* by Alfonso X of Spain), and even a book on fishing in the lakes of the Austrian Alps made for the Emperor Maximilian I in 1504, numerous illustrated manuscripts of literary content began to appear. A copy of secular songs called *Carmina Burana* was illuminated in Germany in the twelfth century and it served as the basis for Carl Orff's choral and orchestral piece of the twentieth century. A German vernacular variation of the *Aeneid*, the *Eneide* by Heinrich von Veldeke, written and illustrated in the late twelfth century, shows the classical heroes dressed in medieval armor. A collection of German courtly love songs and poems (*Minnelieder*), perhaps produced in Switzerland around 1315 to 1330, contains 137 miniatures of well-known German nobles and poets in various knightly activities. One of the most frequent activities was, of course, the chivalric pursuit of a lady. "Werner von Teufen" (fig. 199) is shown with his lady on horseback on their way to go falconing, but Werner has delayed their hunt with gentle dalliance by chucking his lady under the chin as she coyly turns away. Falconing for the purpose of socializing with the opposite sex is also one of the themes in the "August" miniature of the later *Très Riches Heures* (see fig. 190, p. 227), and a major theme of fourteenth-century Gothic ivories on the subject of courtly love. In the late Middle Ages numerous courtly romances, epic tales, and treatises on the rules of chivalry were written and illustrated.

In the fifteenth century the demand increased also for translations of the ancient historians—Suetonius, Livy, and Tacitus—and, in France, for the works of the great Italian poets—Dante, Petrarch, and Boccaccio. The proliferation of these books in France and Flanders led to the beginnings of the northern European literary Renaissance.

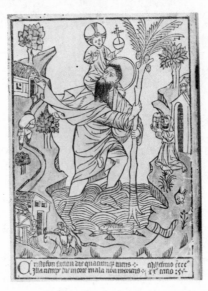

Fig. 200. Buxheim Saint Christopher. Germany. 1423. Woodcut,
11⅜″ x 8⅛″. The John Rylands Library, Manchester.

32. THE EARLY PRINTED BOOK

The invention of printing with movable type in the mid-fifteenth century and the subsequent foundation of presses throughout Europe did not immediately cut into the production of manuscripts or materially change the visual effect of the book. But several related innovations worked together to produce a more economical and faster means of mass-producing images and texts.

Paper had been a known but sparingly used substance for writing in Europe since the eleventh century, but large-scale production and use do not appear to have occurred until the fifteenth. Carved wooden blocks for the printing of images on textiles or on paper had been known in the Orient since A.D. 600, but the oldest surviving block for this purpose in Europe, the *Bois Protat,* seems to date from 1380 to 1400. This wood block marks, however, the beginning of an important development in the production of devotional images that was eventually to affect the nature of illustrations in printed books.

In keeping with the heightened emphasis on private devotion in the fifteenth century, the demand for inexpensive devotional images increased. Woodcuts of revered saints, such as the Buxheim Saint Christopher (fig. 200), dated 1423 according to its legend, were printed on paper and sold in the marketplace. The technique of making the wood block was difficult, for the design had to be drawn on the block and then the area around the lines had to be carved away so that the lines remained in relief. Once this was done, the relief design was inked and paper laid upon it and rubbed to produce an impression, and repeated impressions could be made with little additional effort. The most difficult part of the Buxheim design, however, was the inscription, for this had to be written in reverse on the block, and meticulous care exercised in cutting out the wood around the letters. In

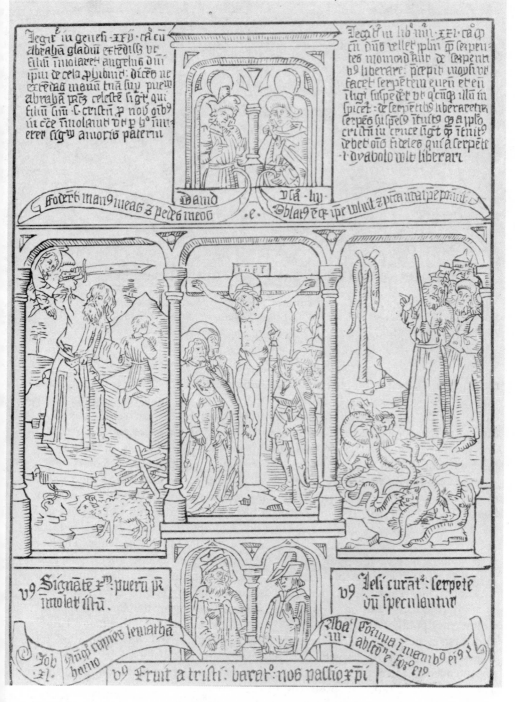

Fig. 201. "Sacrifice of Isaac by Abraham," "Crucifixion," and "Moses Raising up the Brazen Serpent." *Biblia Pauperum*. The Netherlands? c. 1460. 10¼" x 7⅞". The British Library, London.

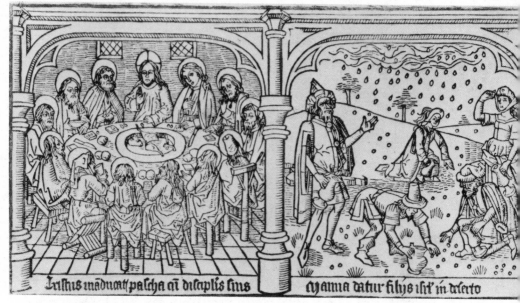

Fig. 202. "Last Supper" and "Gathering of Manna." *Speculum Humanae Salvationis*. The Netherlands. c. 1470–1480. Bayerische Staatsbibliothek (Xyl. 37, p. 36), Munich.

the Buxheim Saint Christopher and other early woodcuts bold, sweeping lines and simple graphic conventions, such as parallel lines to indicate shading, were employed. By the sixteenth century Albrecht Dürer had developed wood-block carving to the point that he could indicate a variety of tonalities and textures and imply volume and space. Frequently the devotional woodcuts, as in the case of the Saint Christopher, were later hand-colored with gouache or watercolor.

Among the books printed before 1500, in the period considered the infancy of printing and therefore called *incunabula,* was a special group known as block books. These made extensive use of wood blocks containing both illustrations and passages of text. The *Biblia Pauperum* (Bible of the Poor, fig. 201) is a block book believed to have been printed around 1460 in the Netherlands. Derived from a long manuscript tradition with pen-drawn illustrations, the *Biblia Pauperum* presented a triplet of scenes, two Old Testament scenes flanking a New Testament one. Thus, the "Crucifixion" is flanked on the left by the "Sacrifice of Isaac by Abraham" and on the right by "Moses Raising up the Brazen Serpent." Both scenes prefigure Christ's sacrifice that will save mankind. Above and below, Old Testament prophets comment on the significance and relationship of the scenes. These block books with didactic juxtapositions of biblical incidents were not intended so much for poor people as for the lesser clergy, who could use them as sources of inspiration in preaching to the populace.

A somewhat later incunabulum, the *Speculum Humanae Salvationis* (Mirror of Man's Salvation), used woodcut illustrations above four columns of text set in movable type (figs. 202, 203). The sequence of scenes is expanded, three Old

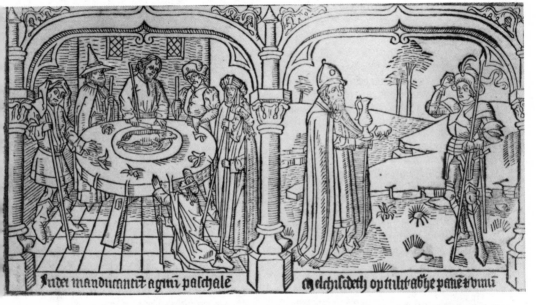

Fig. 203. "Eating of the Paschal Lamb" and "Abraham and Melchizedek."
Speculum Humanae Salvationis. The Netherlands. c. 1470–1480. Bayerische Staatsbibliothek (Xyl. 37, p. 37), Munich.

Testament scenes follow the New Testament incident, the "Last Supper" is followed by the "Gathering of Manna," the "Eating of the Paschal Lamb," and
"Abraham and Melchizedek," all prefigurations of the mystical and sacrificial
meal of Holy Communion.

The perfection of a technique of printing with movable type has been credited
to Johannes Gutenberg who printed a large two-volume Bible (fig. 204) in Mainz
between 1450 and 1455. Although it was difficult at first to make the type and to
hold it steady and aligned in the press, once the letters were cast and the technical
problems were solved, it was easy to prepare a page for printing. Once copy was
proofed to correct mistakes, hundreds of copies of a page could be run off in a day.
Although printed on paper, many copies of Gutenberg's forty-two-line Bible, so
named after the number of lines in the two columns of text per page, were decorated by hand to look like a manuscript. Elaborate foliate decoration was painted
in the borders and decorative or historiated initials in the text. Many incunabula
were decorated in this way, and many were even printed on vellum to retain the
feel as well as the effect of the manuscript.

After Gutenberg's invention the production of printed books increased by
geometric proportions every decade and soon a variety of moralizing, scientific,
and literary texts were being printed, as well as the usual sacred and devotional
books. By the sixteenth century the new process had made sufficient impact and
the price of printed books was sufficiently reduced that it became impracticable
to produce manuscripts except as luxury items.

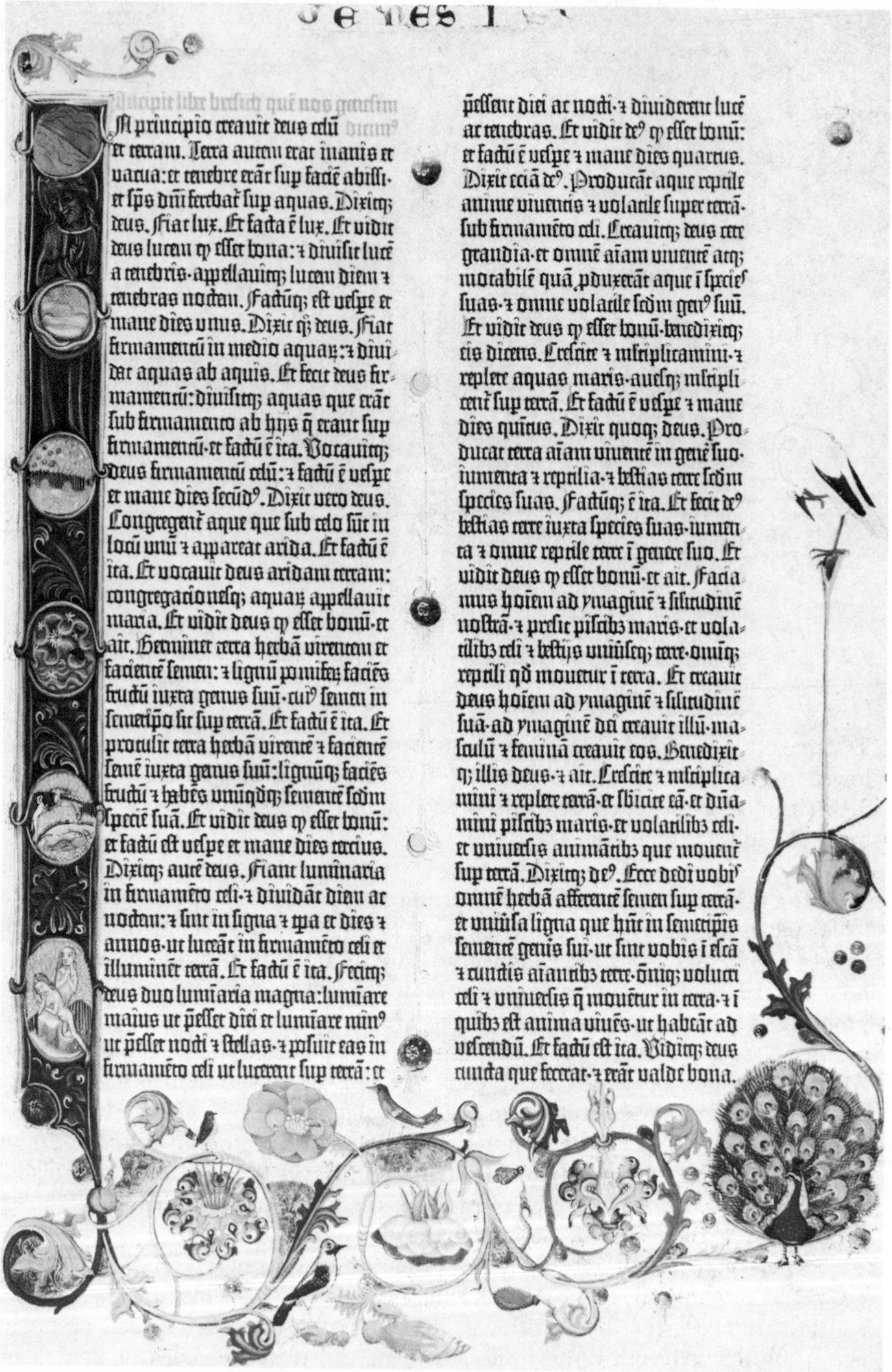

Genes I

Fig. 204. Genesis page. 42-line Bible printed by Johannes Gutenberg. Mainz. 1450–1455. 17⅛″ x 12¼″. Staatsbibliothek Preussischer Kulturbesitz (Inc. 1511, I, fol. 5r), West Berlin.

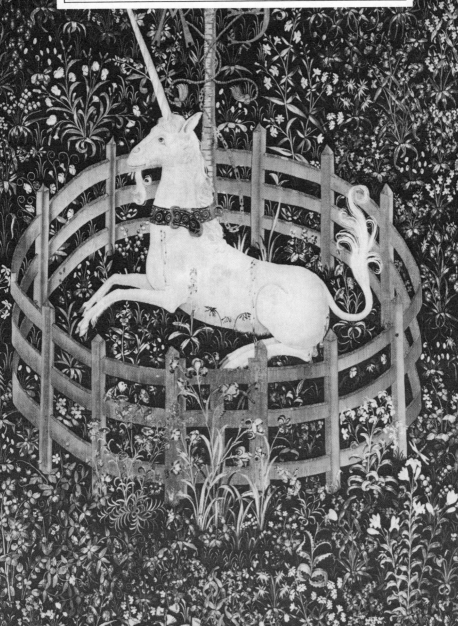

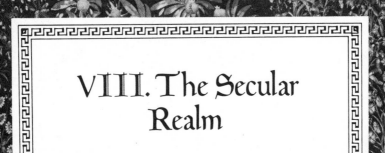

VIII. The Secular Realm

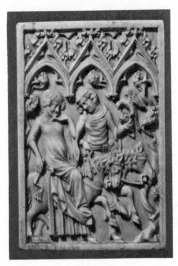

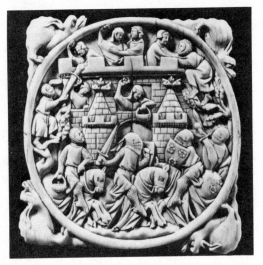

Fig. 205. Ivory writing tablet with courting scene. France. c. 1350. H. 3¾". Victoria and Albert Museum, London. (Crown Copyright)

Fig. 206. "Siege of the Castle of Love," ivory mirror back. France. c. 1350. 4½" x 4¼". Seattle Art Museum, Seattle.

33. THE COURTLY IMAGE

s secular themes became increasingly evident in the margins of Gothic manuscripts and in carved bosses and misericordes, so they were frequently depicted on ivory writing tablets, mirror backs, combs, and a variety of other objects for household use. Most prevalent was the theme of courtly love.

On a rectangular ivory writing tablet (fig. 205) with Gothic tracery similar to that found on contemporary devotional ivories, a lord and lady go falconing on horseback, but, as in the "Werner von Teufen" miniature in the Manesse Codex (see fig. 199, p. 234), he turns to caress the lady under the chin. The lady holds a whip in her right hand and she appears to be urging her mount onward; this may, however, also be interpreted as a gesture of encouragement, of spurring her companion onward. Variations of this scene were frequently used on round ivory mirror backs, undoubtedly destined for the dressing tables of noble ladies. Such gestures of endearment at the meeting of lovers, or during the amorous conversation, were all reflections of a strict code of behavior. Even a tryst during the hunt, an occasion when a knight and his lady would contrive to exchange glances, say an unnoticed word to each other, or even slip away from the rest of the hunting party for a moment together, was enacted, to a point, according to the restrained ritual embodied in the chivalric rules of courtly love.

A fitting complement to a noble lady's secular writing tablet might be a round carved mirror back containing further representations of the same theme. Frequently the circular form of these mirror backs, as in the case of a superb example now in the Seattle Art Museum (fig. 206), was squared off with grotesque hybrids called *wyverns*. The elaborate and furious battle scene depicted on this ivory is not as serious as one might think at first glance. The castle is defended by damsels, who pelt the assailants with roses. A knight scaling the wall at the right is being assisted by one of the ladies, while the knight climbing the tree at the left turns over his sword in surrender, even before mounting the battlement, to a lady who is about to hurl a rose at him. Below, another knight on horseback brings more ammunition, more roses in a basket. Two knights battle before the turreted gateway; one has three roses emblazoned on his shield and on the horse's trappings. The scene is thus one of the most popular allegorical representations on the theme of courtly love.

It has been said that this is an incident from the *Roman de la Rose,* the allegorical poem concerning chivalric behavior and pursuit of love begun by Guillaume de Lorris around 1230 and finished by Jean de Meun before 1270. This poem had a profound influence throughout the later Middle Ages. Certainly the theme is related, but the actual circumstances are far different, for in the poem Venus assists Love's barons in an assault on the Castle of Jealousy and Shame. It has even been proposed that deeply symbolic and religious overtones lie behind the imagery of some of these secular scenes. Although it is difficult to accept the thesis that the castle is really an evocation of the heavenly city of the Apocalypse, there is undoubtedly an interweaving of religious and secular iconography, stemming from such parallels as that between the cult of the Virgin and the exaltation of love in the literature of the day. The closest example occurs in the fourth chapter of the German poem *Die Minneburg,* written between 1325 and 1350, in which a youth is encouraged by the god of love to attack a castle, the Freudenburg, inhabited by a lady. Although the theme was a literary one, it was popularized in numerous medieval pageants, which enacted in almost every detail the "Siege of the Castle of Love" as depicted on the Seattle ivory.

Several remarkable ivory caskets (*Minnekästschen*), probably intended to contain a noble lady's jewels and other trinkets, are decorated with further elaborations on the theme of courtly love, as well as scenes from various literary romances. A casket in the Walters Art Gallery in Baltimore (fig. 207), probably carved in Paris in the first half of the fourteenth century, contains on its lid two central panels in which a joust takes place. Armed combat on the field of honor became a necessary ritual proof of strength and courage for the knight who wished to win his lady's favors according to the chivalric code. Two knights mounted on caparisoned horses joust at full tilt before the crenelated wall of a castle from which lords and ladies observe the contest. The shield of the knight on the right is emblazoned with three roses, recalling the battle in the Seattle ivory mirror back. In fact, the flanking scenes depict the "Siege of the Castle of Love": on the left two knights load roses into a catapult while another climbs a rope ladder up the ramparts. A fourth knight threatens to fire a rose with his crossbow, but a winged god of love is about to pierce him through the heart with an arrow. On the right, amorous couples embrace on the battlements of the castle while a knight and lady tilt with flowering branches below.

The other panels of this casket contain a repertoire of medieval romances and legends. On the front panel (fig. 208) Aristotle instructs the youthful Alexander

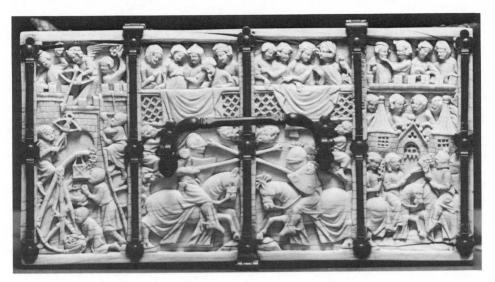

Fig. 207. "Joust and Siege of the Castle of Love," ivory lid of casket. France. c. First half 14th century. $9\frac{11}{16}$" x $4\frac{13}{16}$". Walters Art Gallery, Baltimore.

Fig. 208. "Aristotle and Alexander," "Aristotle and Phyllis," and "Fountain of Youth," ivory casket. France. c. First half 14th century. $4\frac{1}{2}$" x $9\frac{11}{16}$". Walters Art Gallery, Baltimore.

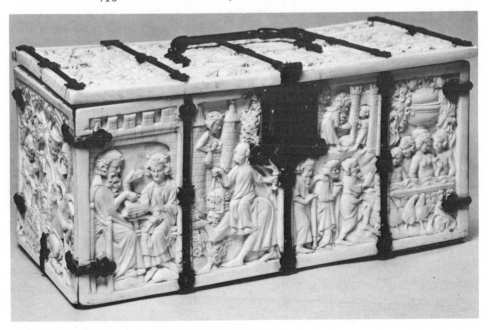

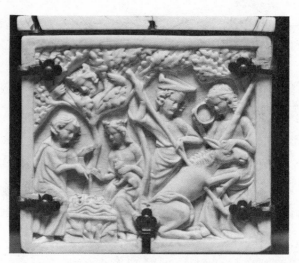

Fig. 209. "Tristan and Iseult" and "Capture of the Unicorn," end of ivory casket. France. c. First half 14th century. 4½" x 4¹³⁄₁₆". Walters Art Gallery, Baltimore.

the Great in the ways of love and women. But in the second scene all of Aristotle's wisdom has come to naught, for he is being ridden like an ass by his ladylove Phyllis, and thereby made to look like a fool. This theme became a widely used satire on the folly of love, which blinds even a wise man. The two remaining scenes depict the old and infirm seeking the "Fountain of Youth," which, when they find it in the last panel, restores their youth and their amorous ardor.

On one of the ends of the Baltimore casket (fig. 209) two scenes are paired. The first represents the tryst of Queen Iseult and the knight Tristan. They meet by a fountain beneath a tree, in which King Mark hides and spies on them. In this episode from the Arthurian romances, the couple saw the king's reflection, actually depicted in the carved ripples of the water, and contrived to speak to each other so as to deceive him further. A tree separates this scene from the incident on the right, which depicts the "Capture of the Unicorn." The unicorn was believed to be so swift that no hunter could catch him. But he would come willingly to a virgin and lay his head docilely in her lap, whereupon the hunter could kill him. This white, pure beast who willingly sacrificed himself through the intermediary of a virgin became therefore a symbol for Christ. The juxtaposition of the two scenes contrasts the maiden's purity with Iseult's deceit.

The remaining panels of the Baltimore casket relate other legends from the Arthurian romances: Sir Gawain fighting the lion and receiving a maiden in reward; Sir Lancelot crossing the Bridge of Swords; and Sir Galahad being given the key to the Castle of Maidens. All of these incidents are related in the twelfth-century compilation of the Arthurian legends by Chrétien de Troyes.

The references to contemporary courtly literature were arranged with an eye for their interwoven meanings and relationships in the same manner that biblical narratives were juxtaposed in the service of the religious message. Their frequent use presupposes a widespread familiarity with these secular themes by the fourteenth century.

34. THE TAPESTRY

Sumptuous woven and embroidered fabrics have always been held in high esteem as ceremonial garments or decorative trappings. Patterned silks were imported from Byzantium for the coronation cloak of Charlemagne, for the wrappings of the relics of Saint Siviard at Sens cathedral, or for the covers of books. Decorative pages in the Codex Aureus of Echternach, illuminated between 1053 and 1056, contain an array of heraldic birds and decorative medallions in imitation of a silk cover (see fig. 183, p. 221). These textile pages serve the same function as the simulated metalwork bookcovers in the carpet pages of the Lindisfarne Gospels. Later, in the fourteenth century, intricate embroidery (*opus anglicanum*) was widely used for bishop's copes, altar cloths, and a variety of liturgical vestments.

Elaborate decorative and narrative wall hangings became significant ecclesiastical and domestic furnishings in the Middle Ages, and fragments of tapestry dating from the ninth and tenth centuries indicate they had a long tradition. Frequently frescoes in Romanesque and Gothic churches simulated their effect. At Assisi, in the thirteenth century, simulated decorative wall hangings were painted beneath the frescoes of the life of Saint Francis (see fig. 154, p. 184). The earliest and most complete surviving narrative textile, however, is the embroidered *Bayeux Tapestry,* which was made shortly after 1066 to recount the events of the Norman invasion of England.

The *Bayeux Tapestry* (pls. 23, 24) is a strip of linen 230 feet long and 19½ inches high, embroidered with wool thread dyed in eight colors. It may have been commissioned by the half-brother of William the Conqueror, Bishop Odo of Bayeux. Although its original purpose is also obscure, it appears to justify the Norman invasion of England in 1066. In the first narrative scene, Edward the Confessor gives instructions to Harold the Saxon who then leaves for France, probably in 1064. Edward had agreed that Duke William of Normandy should be his successor to the English throne, and Harold already owed various kinds of allegiance to the duke. On a subsequent trip to France where William rescued Harold from imprisonment, Harold renewed his oath of fealty to the Duke of Normandy. Nevertheless, when Edward died, Harold proclaimed himself King of England. The tapestry shows William's invasion and the resulting death of Harold at the Battle of Hastings to be just retribution for Harold's breach of faith according to his oaths of feudal allegiance.

If the message of the tapestry was political and propagandistic, it nevertheless relates the epic with vivacious narrative, meticulous detail showing the preparations for the invasion and subsequent battle, and charming marginal animals and fables. A running inscription in irregular lettering explains the scenes and identifies some of the personalities. Thus the first scene is captioned "Edward Rex: ubi:

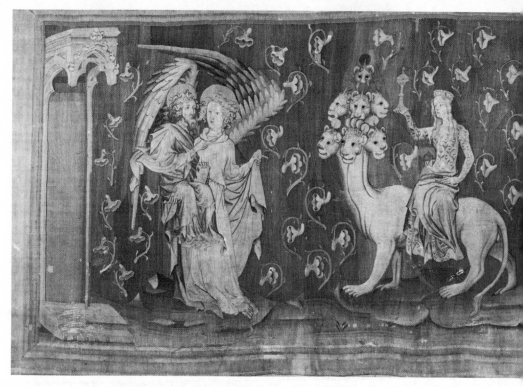

Fig. 210. "The Whore of Babylon Riding the Beast with Seven Heads."
Apocalypse Tapestry. Designed by Jean Bondol and woven by Nicolas de
Bataille. 1373–1381. Musée des Tapisseries, Angers. (Archives photo-
graphiques, Paris, S.P.A.D.E.M.)

Harold Dux Anglorum . . ."; and William embarking on the invasion is explained: "Willelm Dux in Magno Navigo, mare transivit et venit ad Pevenesæ"
(Pevensey on the English coast). The figural style is consistent with that found
in Anglo-Saxon illuminated manuscripts of the period, and it seems likely that the
tapestry was designed and embroidered in southeastern England between 1070
and 1077 when Odo died.

Wall hangings for a variety of religious and secular purposes became increasingly prevalent in northern Europe during the Gothic period. One of the most
extensive surviving sets of tapestries on a religious theme was made for Louis I,
Duke of Anjou, between 1373 and 1381 for the cathedral at Angers. Now housed
in the chapel of Louis's castle at Angers, only sixty-seven of the original ninety
scenes survive. It relates the visionary incidents described in the apocalyptic book
of The Revelation of Saint John. At repeated intervals throughout the tapestry
large figures of prophets are shown seated within an elaborate Gothic tabernacle
holding a scroll and a book, foretelling the Second Coming. In each scene Saint
John looks on while an angel explains the vision to him.

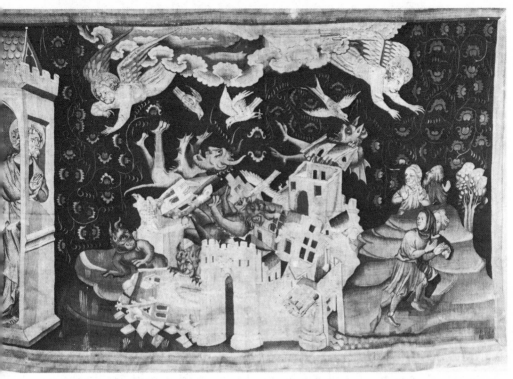

Fig. 211. "The Fall of Babylon." *Apocalypse Tapestry*. Designed by Jean Bondol and woven by Nicolas de Bataille. 1373–1381. Musée des Tapisseries, Angers. (Archives photographiques, Paris, S.P.A.D.E.M.)

In one panel, the angel shows Saint John "The Whore of Babylon" (fig. 210), the symbol of idolatry, "sitting on a scarlet beast of the sea, drunk with the blood of martyrs, which was full of blasphemous names, and it had seven heads and seven horns, and on her forehead was written a name of mystery: 'Babylon the great, mother of harlots and of earth's abominations.'" In contrast with the force of these descriptions, but in keeping with the delicate courtly style of the late fourteenth century, the Whore of Babylon appears as a youthful, charming Gothic princess and the beast with seven heads is as ferocious as a smiling household pet. "The Fall of Babylon" (fig. 211), however, is made more catastrophic with falling ramparts and crashing towers.

Perhaps some of the charm and grace of these representations derive from the source of their inspiration. Louis I, one of the brothers of King Charles V of France, commissioned the king's court painter Jean Bondol to make the initial designs for the tapestry. Bondol, in turn, borrowed many of his compositions from an illustrated manuscript of the Apocalypse that was in the king's library, and lent for the purpose. The designs were then woven in the workshop of Nicolas de Bataille. The finished ensemble, covering a large expanse of wall and divided into horizontal and vertical panels, has the coloristic effect of mural painting similar to the frescoes in the Arena Chapel, but with the added warmth and texture of woven fabric.

Sets of allegorical and secular tapestries were produced in great profusion during the fifteenth and sixteenth centuries. Although woven in the last years of the fifteenth century, a set of tapestries representing allegories of the five senses in the Musée de Cluny, usually referred to as *La Dame à la licorne* (pl. 25), uses the heraldic placement of the figures and the flower-strewn background of the *verdures* or *millefleurs* type of tapestry used throughout the century. In these tapestries a lady in richly brocaded dress stands or is seated on a verdant blue island in the middle of a rose-pink ground. A lion and a unicorn flank her, holding banners with three crescent moons on a diagonal blue stripe, the arms of the Le Viste family, which had commissioned the set. Occasionally the animals carry a shield with the same arms. Flowers and animals are freely strewn across the surface. In the tapestry depicting "Sight" the unicorn places its feet in the lap of the seated maiden and contemplates its image in the mirror held in her hand. In this scene the normally heraldic animal has assumed the role current in medieval legends of the unicorn that could be captured only by enticing it to lay its head in the lap of a virgin. A sixth tapestry, showing the lady choosing jewels from a coffret before a conical tent and with the motto "Mon seul desir," either may symbolize the donation of all of these tapestries to the lady in question, or may belong to yet another series of which the other pieces have been lost. In the consistency of their composition and subtle coloring this set of tapestries would have provided a charming decorative ensemble for a chamber in a late medieval palace.

Indeed, the records of one of the most prolific tapestry weavers in Flanders in the late fifteenth century, Pasquier Grenier, indicate that sets of tapestries were referred to as *chambres de tapisseries,* and the *Five Senses* tapestries and other sets representing pastoral scenes of woodcutters, grape harvesters, other laboring peasants, or hunting scenes were frequently referred to as *chambres de tapisseries de verdure*. Although some tapestries were allegorical, religious, or historical, and therefore instructive, their purpose was both decorative and functional. Placed on the stone walls of large rooms in medieval castles, they cut the drafts, muffled the echoes, and created an ambience of comfort and intimacy. When nobles traveled from one of their estates to another, they frequently took their tapestries with them. Documents show that Pasquier Grenier sold a chambre de tapisseries to Philip the Bold, Duke of Burgundy, "to take with him and serve him on his trip to Spain." Flemish and French tapestries were particularly valued as expensive gifts of esteem and were used as diplomatic gifts to curry favors. In Flanders their production was an economic asset, and the Burgundian court encouraged the tapestry-weaving industry as a mainstay of the economy after English competition cut into their cloth trade.

The famous series of tapestries of *The Hunt of the Unicorn* now hung in a reconstructed medieval room at The Cloisters re-creates the effect of, a chambre de tapisseries. Five panels and a fragment of another survived the harsh and

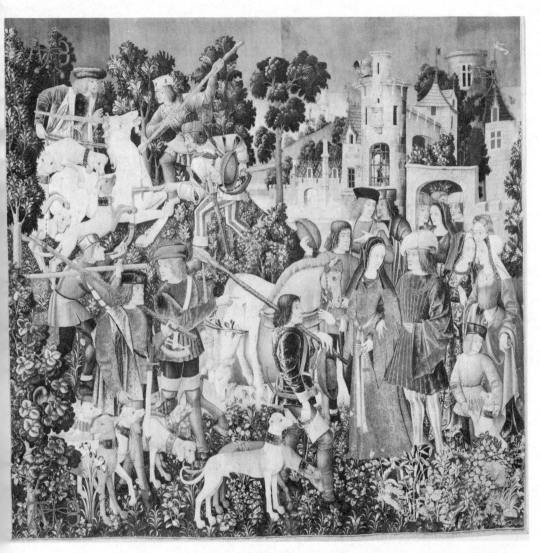

Fig. 212. "The Unicorn Is Brought to Anne of Brittany and Louis XII of France." *The Hunt of the Unicorn.* French or Flemish. c. 1499. Wool and silk with metal threads, 12′ 1″ x 12′ 9″. The Metropolitan Museum of Art, The Cloisters Collection (Gift of John D. Rockefeller, Jr., 1937).

degrading treatment they received over the centuries (at one point they were used to wrap potatoes, at another, they were remade into linings for curtains). This series was probably made for Anne of Brittany around 1499 in celebration of her marriage to Louis XII in January of that year. Her monogram, an *A* and an *E* linked with a cord, appears in the foliage of all the panels. The newlyweds may be portrayed as the noble couple to whom the captured unicorn is brought in one of the scenes (fig. 212). This event takes place after the unicorn's capture, which may have occurred much in the manner depicted on the Baltimore casket or the

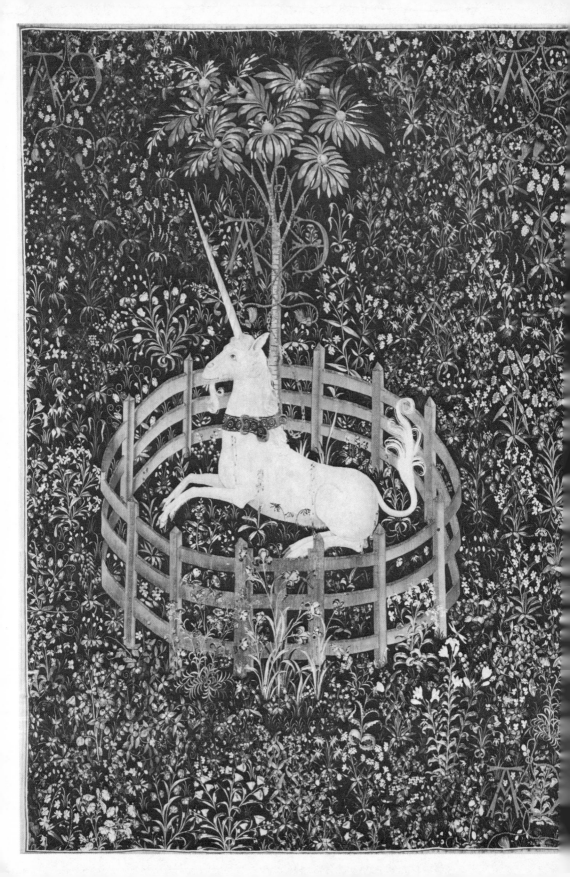

Musée de Cluny tapestry of "Sight." Because the taming of this wild and swift beast in the presence of a maiden was often equated with the Incarnation, this series of tapestries may also have religious connotations, although we must remember that the hunt was a favorite secular theme as well. Certainly the last tapestry, "The Unicorn in Captivity" (fig. 213), which has been determined not to be part of the original set but which was made for the same patron, served as a fortunate afterthought. It provided a possible Christian significance and a happy ending. The unicorn reposes peacefully within his fenced-in paddock recalling the Garden of Eden, and the still visible wounds remind us that he could be a symbol of the Resurrected Christ (particularly as the unicorn appeared dead in the previous panel). That he is leashed to a pomegranate tree may not only reflect the bond of marriage, which is a recurrent theme in the other tapestries, but also the mystical union with the church, for the pomegranate tree served as a symbol of fertility, and its fruit with its many seeds within one shell was a symbol of the church.

Whatever the original program, *The Hunt of the Unicorn* tapestries represent some of the finest works to have survived in this medium. The multitude of plants, most of them identifiable, are articulated with subtle modulations in a wide range of colored threads. Reflections of birds are recorded in rippling water, and even the larger vistas of distant fields and castles are touched with perceptive observation. The blue sky, which has been replaced, may originally have been slightly wider. It is believed that it contained the arms of France and was therefore cut off to prevent the destruction of the entire set during the French Revolution. Although "The Unicorn in Captivity" is properly a millefleur tapestry with the complete area filled with decorative foliage, the multitude of plants and the high horizon in the other scenes approximate the same effect. These tapestries therefore retain the decorative function of the medieval tapestry. Although filled with meticulous realism in the details, they are not yet the expansive, illusionistic, woven Renaissance paintings of later tapestries.

Fig. 213. "The Unicorn in Captivity." *The Hunt of the Unicorn.* French or Flemish. c. 1499. Wool and silk with metal threads, 12' 1" x 9' 9". The Metropolitan Museum of Art, The Cloisters Collection (Gift of John D. Rockefeller, Jr., 1937).

35. SECULAR ARCHITECTURE

With the growth of a fragmented feudal system in which lords of small areas constantly clashed with their neighbors, the nobles resorted to building fortified domiciles for protection. Usually the fortified enclosure was made large enough to hold the peasantry (and their flocks) of the surrounding countryside, who owed allegiance to the lord and who swore to bear arms for him in return for his protection.

By the eleventh century massive, square towers or keeps were built either in the middle of an enclosed area or near a back wall. They usually contained a main hall, a dungeon, and perhaps a chapel, and served as a last retreat in case the walls were breached in a siege. The twelfth-century keep at Rochester (fig. 214), built by William of Corbeil, Bishop of Canterbury, is an Anglo-Norman example of this kind of defensive structure. As a result of the crusades, beginning at the end of the eleventh century, Europeans became familiar with sophisticated Byzantine defensive structures that capitalized upon features of inaccessible high ground augmented with systems of perimeter curtain walls and dry moats. The crusaders emulated such structures at Krak des Chevaliers in Syria and introduced these complex plans to Europe. The sprawling castle complex atop the white cliffs of Dover (fig. 215), begun by Henry II in the second half of the twelfth century, made use of the irregular, precipitous terrain. The central, square keep was surrounded by two walls punctuated with square and rounded towers, which provided the opportunity for crossfire with bows and arrows on the besieging troops who might try to scale the walls. The outer curtain was preceded by a dry moat over which the road passed by means of a drawbridge to a massive two-towered gateway. Inside, a second moat surrounded the second wall with projecting towers and a second gateway with a drawbridge.

The fourteenth-century castle built for Jean, Duke of Berry, near Poitiers, the Château du Clain (fig. 216), depicted in the calendar scene for "July" in the *Très Riches Heures* reflects another standard format of defense, the triangular plan with round corner towers. Set within a lake that served as a moat, the castle presented a solid, unbroken exterior, but tracery windows and pinnacled gables looked into the interior courtyard. A flimsy wooden bridge, with a retractable section next to the castle wall, connected the castle to the land. On the right a series of less defensible buildings, one of which is a chapel, jutted out into the lake. The architectural detail of this castle was delicate and elaborate: machicolations and crenelations surrounded the upper cylinders of the turrets, and their conical roofs were surmounted by elaborate chimneys, gables, and spires.

These architectural fantasies were carried to their fullest extreme in the Duke of Berry's castle at Mehun-sur-Yèvre (see fig. 191, p. 227), mentioned previously as a symbol of worldly splendor. Here, broad windows penetrated the defensive

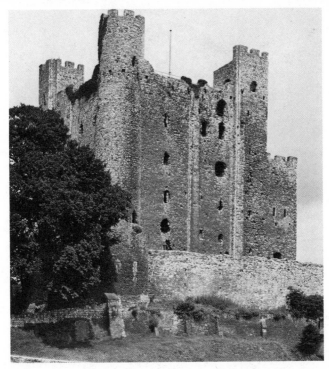

Fig. 214. Castle keep. Rochester. 12th century. (National
Monuments Record, England, Crown Copyright)

Fig. 215. Dover Castle. Begun second half 12th century. (National Monuments Record Air Photograph, Crown Copyright)

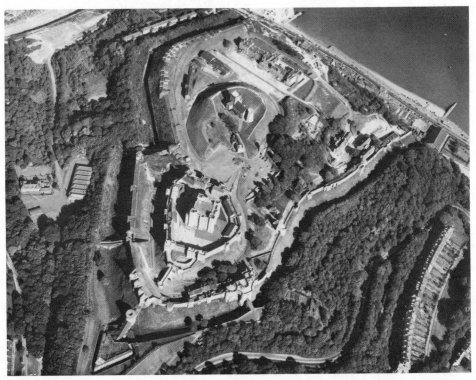

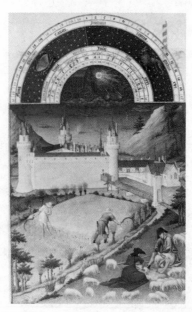

Fig. 216. Limbourg Brothers: Château du Clain, "July." *Très Riches Heures.*
France. c. 1415. 8¾" x 5¼". Musée Condé, Chantilly. (Giraudon)

walls, the upper portions were encrusted with tracery, and the entrance pavilion, covered with statuary below, dissolved into tracery lancets above. The building was an architectural jewel, not a fortress. Many of the châteaus in the Loire valley exemplify this transition from medieval stronghold to Renaissance hunting lodge and pleasure pavilion. The Château de Sully-sur-Loire (fig. 217), begun in 1360, consists of a rectangular pavilion with cylindrical corner turrets set on an island surrounded by a moat. But the walls of the towers and pavilion have been pierced by elegant Renaissance windows. Châteaus such as Chambord, built in the early sixteenth century, elaborated this basic form but made no pretense at being defensive refuges.

The domestic structures for the lesser populace, however, followed the indigenous traditions that had survived in their respective regions of Europe for hundreds of years. In northern Europe evidence of timber post-and-lintel constructions, covered with lashed poles and thatch, goes back centuries before Christ. By the Carolingian period upright and slanted beams were used as bracing for stone, brick, or rubble-filled walls, and such structures may have been used for the shops and barns of the Carolingian Abbey at Saint-Gall (see fig. 51, p. 61). This "half-timbered" construction proved to be the basis of much domestic building throughout the remainder of the Middle Ages and through the eighteenth century in Germany, France, England, and Scandinavia. Frequently, the timber trusswork formed pleasing geometric designs on the facades of the houses. The upper stories were often corbeled outward to gain more space. In towns and cities where space was at a premium, the corbeled upper stories, each one of a multistoried building projecting farther than the one below, almost shut out the light from the street below (fig. 218).

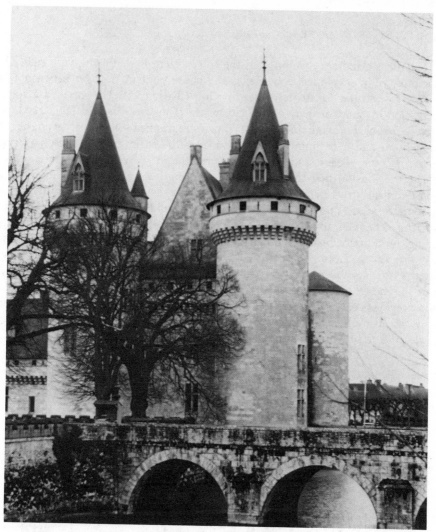

Fig. 217. Château de Sully-sur-Loire.
1360 and later. (R. G. Calkins)

Town houses were usually adapted to accommodate shops on the ground level with living quarters above. A twelfth-century merchant's house at Cluny (fig. 219), with one of the few surviving Romanesque domestic facades in France, contains a wide arched opening facing the street for the shop. Originally, the small door to the left opened onto a staircase leading to the second-floor apartment. The main living room was situated at the front of the house behind the monumental arcade of windows, and a corridor alongside a two-story courtyard led to a back bedroom. On the ground floor, the courtyard behind the shop area contained a well and opened onto the kitchen. Although this is a single-family house probably belonging to a wealthy tradesman, it followed a tradition of architecture that can be traced back to the apartment house blocks of ancient Rome and Ostia and was still the basic formula for many European town buildings into modern times.

Far more elaborate dwellings in the towns were built by the very rich. One of the most fully developed examples is the house built in Bourges between 1443 and 1451 by Jacques Coeur, treasurer to King Charles VII. He obtained a special dispensation to build on part of the city walls. The street facade (fig. 220) was relatively plain, but contained large square mullioned windows, even on the ground floor, and a monumental pavilion over the main entryway. Relief sculptures of Jacques Coeur and his wife were placed above the entrance, carved to create the illusion that the figures were leaning out of windows and watching the bustle in the street below. The gateway led into a large irregular courtyard and an elaborate facade (fig. 221) with many large windows and tracery balustrades. Projecting octagonal towers contained spiral staircases. This inner core of the building, built upon the city ramparts, contained numerous rooms, some with large stately fireplaces. Every fifteenth-century convenience for a comfortable, well-ordered existence was provided for, and Jacques Coeur's house was undoubtedly one of the most luxurious of the day. Like the Duke of Berry's castles at the end of the previous century, the profusion of chimneys, turrets, dormer windows, and steeply gabled roofs of different heights broke up the vastness of the ensemble and gave it a picturesque and intimate effect.

Fig. 218. Half-timbered houses. Colmar. 15th–16th century. (Editorial Photocolor Archives)

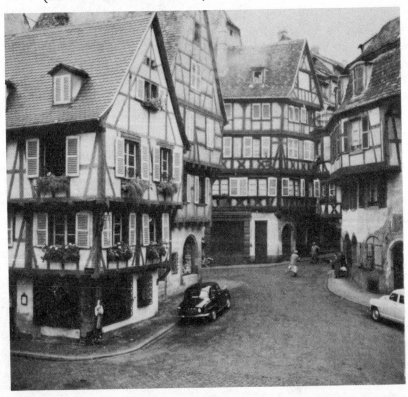

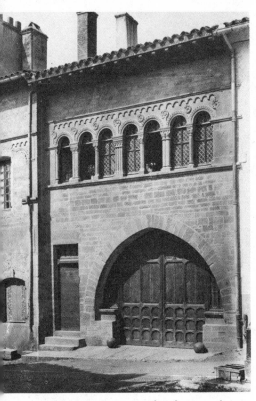

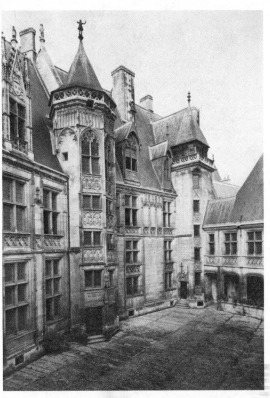

Fig. 219. Romanesque facade, town house. Cluny. 12th century. (Archives photographiques, Paris, S.P.A.D.E.M.)

Fig. 221. Courtyard and inner facade, house of Jacques Coeur. Bourges. 1443–1451. (Archives photographiques, Paris, S.P.A.D.E.M.)

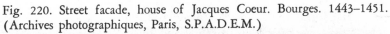

Fig. 220. Street facade, house of Jacques Coeur. Bourges. 1443–1451. (Archives photographiques, Paris, S.P.A.D.E.M.)

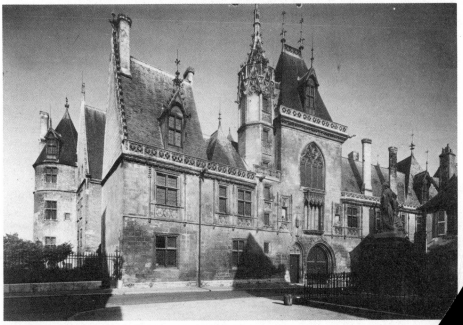

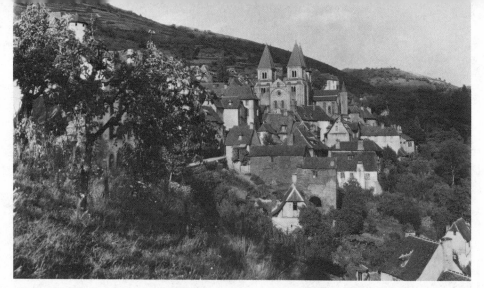

Fig. 222. View of Conques. (Archives photographiques, Paris, S.P.A.D.E.M.)

36. Medieval Towns and Cities

Villages in the medieval landscape were usually clustered about the castle of the lord who protected the surrounding peasantry from the harassment of brigands or of other nobles, or about the parish church that gave them spiritual sustenance. Sometimes, as at Conques (fig. 222) or at Vézelay, the church became the site of major pilgrimages, and such towns prospered from the trade that the throngs of pious engendered. But as the European economy was primarily rural and barely at a subsistence level for centuries after the dissolution of the connecting military and commercial links of the Roman Empire, the populace remained for the most part very close to land.

The forms of the early villages reflected the three main concerns of faith, protection, and proximity to crops and livestock. Sometimes the plans were circular, with the church and market square at the center, and the streets following an irregular radial direction outward to an encircling road or wall. Sometimes the plan was longitudinal, with castle and church perhaps near the center, and the houses of the peasantry were strung along a single road with individual plots of land behind them. Larger towns might be situated on the site of a previous Roman military camp and as a result assumed a more or less regular grid system emanating from two principal streets at right angles in the middle. Many of the larger towns were fortified: Dubrovnik in Yugoslavia, Carcassonne in France, Ávila in Spain, and Rothenburg ob der Tauber in Germany are some of the most complete surviving ensembles, although all have been subjected to various degrees of restoration.

Carcassonne (fig. 223), although largely restored in the nineteenth century, is undoubtedly one of the most spectacular of these walled cities. Situated on a hill overlooking the plain, a double wall with crenelations and round projecting towers, originally dating from the thirteenth century, surrounds the entire complex of the old town. A massive gateway was set at an angle to the wall to give better protection over the narrow drawbridge and entry in case of siege. At the opposite side

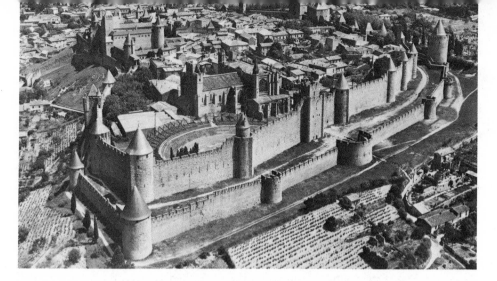

Fig. 223. View of Carcassonne. 13th century and later. (Archives photographiques, Paris, S.P.A.D.E.M.)

of the town, situated on a steep escarpment, was the keeplike castle. A walled pathway led down the steep hillside to provide a protected path of escape if needed.

Although some towns may have been begun on a regular plan, such as that dictated by the Roman *castrum,* as they grew in size, streets developed along the contours of the land and the meandering lines of footpaths caused by people and livestock. The narrow, winding streets of such picturesque old towns as Vézelay, Rothenburg, or Rouen inevitably led to a market square, or a square in front of a church or civic building. Having seen the church of Sainte-Foy at Conques from afar, the pilgrim would have followed the meandering street between closely built houses until he emerged into the square in front of the church, whose sculpted facade would have had the impact of a sudden revelation. This was true for the city as well, where the cathedral of Chartres was visible for miles around, but in the immediate area was largely lost to view amid the jumble of houses until one emerged before the *portail royal.*

With the further development of trade routes in the Gothic period, partially as a result of the crusades, many cities became powerful commercial centers. Maritime cities such as Venice, Genoa, and Pisa vied with each other for the control of Mediterranean trade routes, and the degree of their success was manifested by resplendent civic and ecclesiastical buildings. Chartres, the site of important relics and the center of the wheat-producing area of France, erected its cathedral as both a civic and an ecclesiastical monument. In northern Europe numerous cities on the Baltic and North seas, as well as on the important rivers flowing into them, banded together in the Hanseatic League to form a vast network of commercial links. Civic pride led to a virtual competition among the towns of the Hanseatic League for the most resplendent town hall, and this competition was also reflected in the buildings of the various guilds. In Bruges, the Guild of the Cloth Merchants (fig. 224), one of the most prosperous industries of northern Europe, constructed a guildhall between 1248 and 1482 with a tower 260 feet high. Now used as the marketplace, it was a symbol of the strength and wealth of the medieval trade guild and of thriving medieval commerce. These buildings assumed importance equal to the churches, and the squares in front of them became the commercial hubs of the cities.

The Italian city-states, fiercely independent and competitive throughout the Middle Ages, manifested similar developments in urban spaces and civic buildings. Florence and Siena, when they were not actually clashing on the battlefield, engaged in a competition for the largest and most resplendent cathedrals and for the town hall with the tallest tower. In both cities the ecclesiastical and civic functions were separated in different parts of the town, the cathedral and city hall each having its own urban space. In Siena a carefully planned semicircular plaza (fig. 225), the Piazza del Campo, fronted on the crenelated facade of the Palazzo Pubblico with its tenuously tall and elegant campanile, begun in 1298. The city council carefully enforced zoning ordinances so that the palaces facing the square maintained a series of appropriate and harmonious facades. The plaza itself became, and still is, the focal point for civic festivities.

An overriding concern of the Italian city-states, where successions of tyrants and benevolent oligarchies provided the populace with a gamut of good and bad government, was the provision of a just and able administration. In the council chamber of the Palazzo Pubblico in Siena, Ambrogio Lorenzetti was commissioned in the 1340s to paint a series of frescoes of *Allegories of Good and Bad Government* (fig. 226), and scenes of the results of each were constant reminders before the eyes of the city fathers. The effects of Bad Government are disastrous in the town: the city is set ablaze and armies of evil plunder and massacre the populace, and in the countryside crops and farms are destroyed. Under Good Government, however, the peasants peacefully harvest their crops, and nobles ride out in splendor to go falconing, while in the city nobles dance in the squares, farmers sell their produce and merchants their wares.

Lorenzetti's painting with its crowded houses, projecting upper stories and balconies, and multitude of square towers presents an accurate picture of the cityscape in fourteenth-century Siena. In nearby San Gimignano (fig. 227), a small, independent city-state, ninety-six square towers of varying heights once dominated the skyline. These were built by individual wealthy patrician families, and served both the competitive function of symbolizing the power and wealth of the family, and also the defensive function of protection during the incessant feuds, which frequently resulted in bloodshed. Not only the form but also the underlying symbolic role of these towers provide the continuing basis for the modern skyscraper.

The medieval town, with its multifarious interests, competing factions, and trade and craft guilds that generated wealth, gave rise to new attitudes that became increasingly independent of the concerns of the church. Although religion still played an important role and private devotion reached a high point in fervor in the fifteenth century, the complex economic and social changes elevated new secular and literary concerns to an almost equal status.

Fig. 224. Cloth Merchants' Guild Hall. Bruges. 1248–1482. (R. G. Calkins)

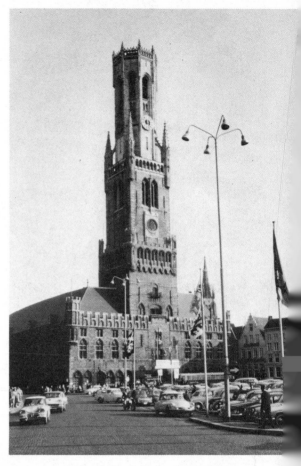

Fig. 225. Piazza del Campo and Palazzo Pubblico. Siena. Begun 1298. (R. G. Calkins)

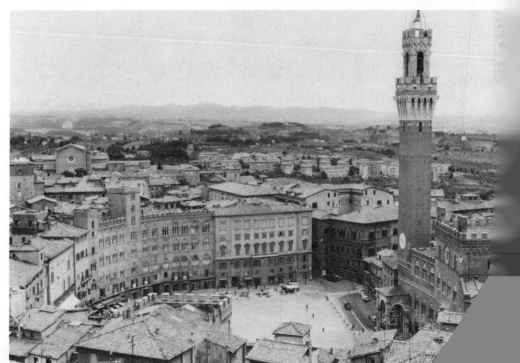

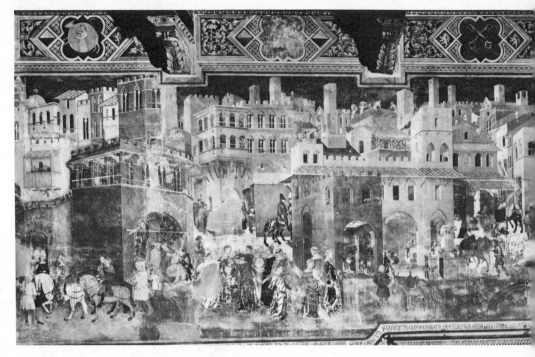

Fig. 226. Ambrogio Lorenzetti: "Effects of Good Government." *Allegories of Good and Bad Government*. Council Chamber, Palazzo Pubblico. Siena. 1340s. (Alinari)

Fig. 227. San Gimignano. (Alinari)

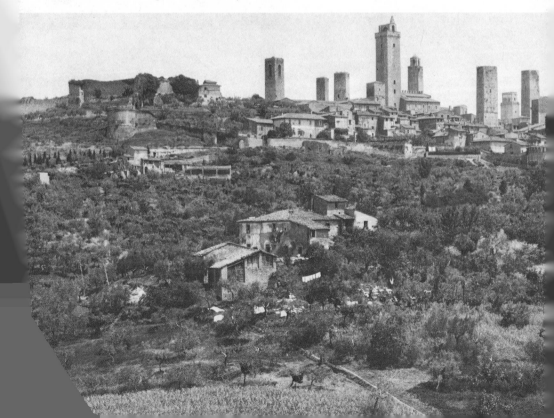

37. THE MEDIEVAL ARTIST AND ARCHITECT

In any discussion of medieval art one is confronted by the prevailing anonymity of the medieval artist. Only a relatively small number of artisans signed their works. For this reason art historians either have had to match documentary references to artists who are mentioned in guild memberships, inventories, tax records, letters of commissions, and contracts—with varying success—or, where no information is available, to invent names such as the Master of the Franciscan Breviary, after a characteristic work in his style, or the Master of Catherine of Cleves, after an object made for an identifiable patron.

This anonymity stems from the nature of medieval patronage and from the attitudes held by many of the artisans themselves. In the Middle Ages members of the church, court, or nobility commissioned works and specified most of the details, which the artisans then dutifully carried out. It was previously believed that artisans before the Gothic period were monks, but now the evidence suggests that a number of them were lay artisans who traveled about from one monastery to another. But whatever their station, monk or lay artisan, and whatever their trade, scribe, illuminator, sculptor, metalsmith, or architect, many artisans were apparently concerned with carrying out their commissions, building, maintaining, and embellishing the house of God and its artifacts without seeking or being given recognition for their labors. Documentary references to medieval works of art may specify for whom the work was made, but rarely mention who the artist was. Abbot Suger, who watched over every detail of the rebuilding and refurbishing of Saint-Denis, mentions that the enameled pedestal decorated with the four Evangelists that supported the cross for the high altar was completed by "several goldsmiths from Lorraine—at times five, at other times seven," but gives no indication of their identity. When names of artists do occur in documents, especially in the late Middle Ages, there is often no way of identifying their works. Only when artisans signed and dated their productions do we have a sure indication of identity and time, but the attribution of other, similar works to these artists or to their milieus must depend on careful stylistic analysis.

In the few cases where artisans did sign and date their works, we are provided with valuable insights into their status and attitudes. Normally such inscriptions are in the form of simple signatures and a date, as in the copy of the Apocalypse now in the Cathedral at Burgo de Osma in Spain, signed by the scribe "Petrus clericus" and a painter "Martinus" and dated 1086. Often the inscriptions are in the form of humble pleas, such as the one made by Tirolus Iafarinus on a metal Romanesque cross that the beholder might remember him in his prayers. Sometimes artists showed themselves at work. The lay artisan Engelramus represented himself and his son Redolfus on an ivory panel of a casket now in Leningrad, the illuminator Hildebert depicted himself in lay raiment with his apprentice Everwin in two manuscripts of around 1140, and in an early twelfth-century book Fra

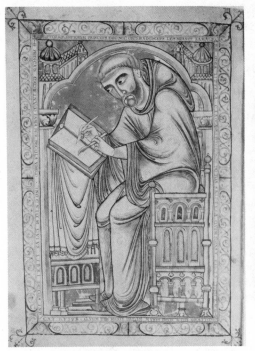

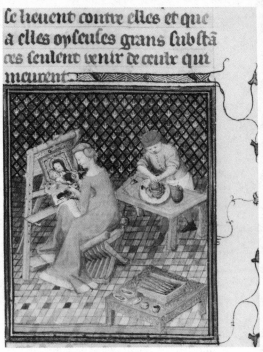

Fig. 228. Eadwine: "Self-Portrait." *Eadwine Psalter*. Christ Church, Canterbury. c. 1147. 18½" x 13". Trinity College Library (MS R. 17.1, fol. 283v), Cambridge.

Fig. 229. "The Artist Thamar and an Assistant." Boccaccio, *Le Livre des femmes nobles et renommées*. Paris. 1402. Bibliothèque Nationale (MS fr. 12420, fol. 86), Paris.

Rufilus, a monk, painted himself illuminating an initial inhabited by dragons and grotesques.

Some of the early inscriptions manifest an awareness of achievement. In a Bible made at León in 960, the scribe Sanctio and his master Florentius, both dressed in clerical habits, show themselves toasting each other and thanking God for the successful completion of the volume. We can detect an element of pride in the monumental "GISLEBERTUS HOC FECIT" carved beneath the feet of God (see fig. 84, p. 102) in the Autun tympanum of around 1130 and in the even stronger inscription by Gilabertus at Toulouse on some jamb figures from the portal of Saint Etienne, which translates something like "Gilabertus, not just any man, created me." But the height of self-esteem, and indeed a prefiguration of the new relationship of the artisan to society in the Gothic period, was achieved around 1147 by the English monk Eadwine, who not only provided the psalter he inscribed with a full-page "Self-Portrait" (fig. 228), which was rare enough, but also enframed it with the following inimitable conceit:

> Scribe, prince of scribes am I: neither my fame nor my praise will die quickly; demand of my letters who I am. The Letters: Fame proclaims you in your writing forever, Eadwine, you who are to be seen in this painting. The worthiness of this book demonstrates your excellence. O God, this book is given to you by him. Receive this acceptable gift.

The profound transformations that took place in Europe with the advent of the Gothic era, beginning slowly in the twelfth century and reaching full maturity in the thirteenth, had a considerable effect not only on artistic production but also on the relationship of the artist to society. The result was significant growth in the number of lay artisans as opposed to monastic ones. Thus, we find with increasing frequency representations of clerics and lay artisans working side by side, as in the case of the author dictating to a lay scribe or illuminator in the frontispiece of the Toledo Bible now in The Morgan Library (pl. 21) and a clerical scribe and a lay mural painter working in a miniature from a thirteenth-century pattern book in Vienna.

No doubt talented monks continued to produce works of art, but by the fourteenth century lay artisans were forming their own ateliers, becoming members of local craft guilds, and instituting rigorous systems of apprenticeship for the instruction of new members. Scribes and illuminators, among them Jean Pucelle, congregated in the sector of Paris around the Porte Saint-Denis, then known as the "Porte aux Peintres," and in the rue des Écrivains. Names of individual artists were recorded with increasing frequency in inventories and accounts, and as early as 1250 to 1270 the title *pictor regis* was created. In the middle of the fourteenth century, an artist appointed to the royal household, Gérard d'Orleans, accompanied his monarch Jean de France into prison in England after the battle of Poitiers, and, as mentioned above, the illuminator Jacquemart de Hesdin, who had killed a fellow artisan in a brawl, was pardoned through the intercession of his patron, Jean, Duke of Berry. The Limbourg brothers, the illuminators of the *Très Riches Heures,* were so sure of their position in the duke's household that they were able to present him with a practical joke, a block of wood painted to simulate a richly bound manuscript.

Along with an increased awareness of the value of quality and uniqueness, there developed a desire to show how things are done for the benefit of those who wish to learn a particular craft. One of the most important manifestations of this desire to instruct was an early twelfth-century treatise titled *De diversis artibus.* It was written by the Benedictine monk Theophilus, who, it is believed, was actually the German metalsmith Roger of Helmarshausen, active around Paderborn between 1110 and 1140. This treatise, like a number of earlier Byzantine manuals and later fifteenth-century manuscripts on the arts, was a compilation of recipes and technical instructions for painting, glassworking, and metalworking. Today, it provides valuable insights into the processes employed by medieval artisans in the fabrication of artifacts. Other insights into the actual artistic process may be found in contemporary representations of artisans at work (fig. 229), most often depicted in manuscript illustrations, in which we find painters, scribes, illuminators, architects, metalworkers, stone carvers, and polychromers at their task.

We also learn much of the artist's selective process and of his *modus operandi* from sketchbooks and model books that have survived. Among the most remarkable and revealing of these is the notebook of the thirteenth-century French draftsman Villard de Honnecourt, who not only sought to instruct, but also to record those

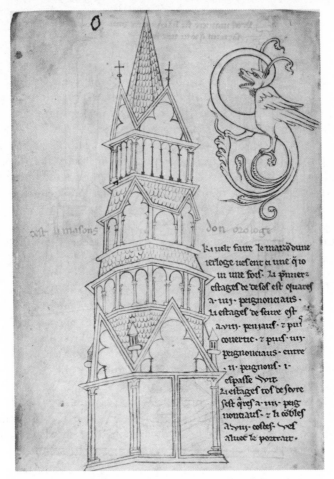

Fig. 230. Villard de Honnecourt: "Clock Tower."
Notebook. c. 1225–1250. 10½" x 6¼".
Bibliothèque Nationale (MS fr. 19093, fol. 6v), Paris.

things that he deemed noteworthy. Villard was struck by the design of a pleasing clock tower, which he sketched (fig. 230) between 1225 and 1250, accompanied by the following notation:

> This is a clock tower. Whoever wishes to build a clock tower should study this one that I once saw. The first story is square, with four small gables. The second story has eight panels and a roof, and, above that four smaller gables with a broad space between each arch. The topmost story is square with four gables with an eight-sided roof. Here is a picture of it.

Whether Villard de Honnecourt was an architect as many scholars believe, or merely an artist, he is representative of a large number of medieval artisans and architects who emerged from relative anonymity with the building of the High Gothic cathedrals. It is true that we have records of some earlier identifiable designers of buildings—Isidorus of Miletus and Anthemius of Tralles at Hagia Sophia in the 530s, and Odo of Metz at the palatine chapel at Aachen for Charlemagne around 800—but we do not know who actually designed the choir at

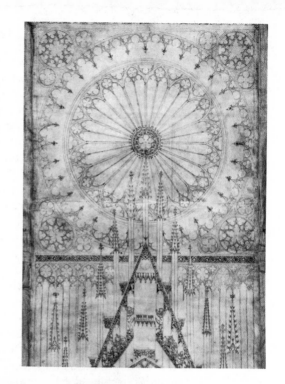

Fig. 231. Michael de Fribourg: design for gable, rose, and Apostles Gallery. Strasbourg Cathedral. c. 1365. Musée de l'Oeuvre de Notre Dame, Strasbourg. (Cliché Franz, Strasbourg)

Fig. 232. Facade (detail). Strasbourg Cathedral. Late 14th century. (Archives photographiques, Paris, S.P.A.D.E.M.)

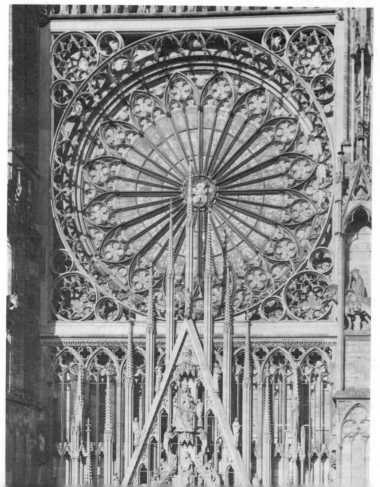

Saint-Denis or who was in charge of the construction at Chartres. Nevertheless, the establishment of a strong guild system among the masons, and the designation of master masons who were in charge of the vast logistical operations involved in building a cathedral, resulted in a new identity for these architects. The hiring of William of Sens, later mortally crippled in an accident at Canterbury, is recorded in the commentaries of Gervaise of Tilbury on the reconstruction of Canterbury Cathedral. Jean d'Orbais was one of four master masons in charge of the *chantier* at Reims in the thirteenth century. Robert de Luzarches began the construction of the nave at Amiens in 1220, and was followed by Thomas de Cormont in 1236, and he, in turn, by his son, Regnault de Cormont, between 1240 and 1260.

In Italy practitioners of various arts were commissioned to create architecture. Giotto, the painter, was accorded the ceremonial title of City Architect of Florence and was asked to design the campanile of Florence Cathedral. Lorenzo Maitani, a sculptor, was put in charge of the Opera del Duomo of Orvieto Cathedral and designed its facade; Giovannino dei Grassi, a manuscript illuminator and sculptor, was made the Master of the Works of Milan Cathedral at the end of the fourteenth century; and Lorenzo Ghiberti, a metalworker and sculptor, assisted Filippo Brunelleschi in the construction of the first Renaissance dome, which was placed upon the Gothic underpinnings of Florence Cathedral in the early fifteenth century.

Many architects achieved an international reputation. William of Sens was invited to England to help in the reconstruction of Canterbury Cathedral after a disastrous fire in 1174. Hans of Cologne traveled to Spain where he designed the tracery towers of Burgos Cathedral. A consortium of German and French architects were asked for advice on structural problems of Milan Cathedral. And members of the Parler family established an international artistic and architectural dynasty throughout northern Europe: Peter Parler designed the cathedral of Saint Vitus in Prague for Charles IV of Bohemia; his son, Wenzel, gave advice on the construction of the tower of the Stefansdom in Vienna; and his brother, Michael de Fribourg, designed the Apostles Gallery of Strasbourg Cathedral (figs. 231, 232).

It is indicative of a change in attitude toward architectural design that we find in Michael de Fribourg's design of around 1365 for the west facade at Strasbourg a careful working out of every detail on paper in advance of the construction. In contrast, Villard's drawings were less precise and more ad hoc in nature, frequently copying an extant example to serve as a model. Nevertheless, he demonstrated the beginning of an attitude of manipulating designs and working out multiple solutions to problems that were the forerunners to the working out of complete designs to be faithfully copied by the masons. The competition held for the design of the dome for Florence Cathedral in 1417, won by Brunelleschi, marks the maturing of this developing architectural practice into what became standard Renaissance and modern procedure in architectural planning.

But the previous medieval process tells us much about the inherent nature of medieval art and architecture. A miniature in a manuscript of the history of the abbey at Cluny (fig. 233) shows how the just proportions of the building of Cluny III were achieved. The monk Gunzo, who advised Hézelon of Liège, the

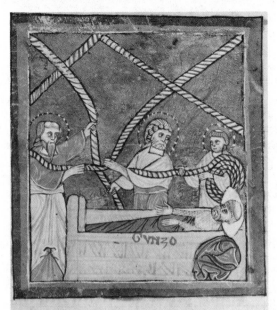

Fig. 233. "Dream of the Monk Gunzo." *History of Cluny*. c. 1190.
Bibliothèque Nationale (MS lat. 17716, fol. 43), Paris.

Fig. 234. "God the Creator as the Architect of the Universe."
Moralized Bible. France. c. 1250. 13⅛" x 10¼". Österreichische
Nationalbibliothek (MS 2554, fol. 1), Vienna.

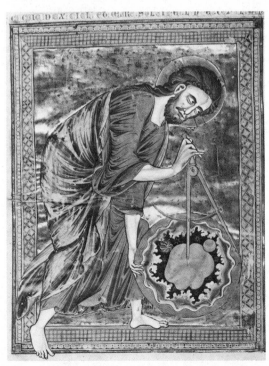

architect designated by Abbot Hugh to plan the reconstruction of the abbey, had a dream in which Saints Peter and Paul, the patron saints of the abbey, appeared and demonstrated with ropes how to lay out a square and rotate its diagonal to achieve measurements reflecting the perfect numbers of musical harmonies and of the golden section. Although this was a mechanical process of arriving at difficult geometric proportions and arithmetical measurements, the essential point is that the perfect proportions and just relationships of the parts to the whole were divinely inspired and reflected the perfection of musical harmonies and therefore of the cosmos. During the Middle Ages God the Creator was often regarded as the Architect of the Universe (fig. 234). He was frequently depicted holding dividers of the sort that masons used, measuring the just proportions of the heavens and earth, the sun, the moon, and the stars, creating them according to the divine harmonies.

Throughout much of the Middle Ages art, as well as architecture, was considered to be a reflection of the divine order and a bearer of the divine message. Medieval art mirrored Christian faith at all levels in its emphasis on religious narrative and symbolism. Much of it was didactic, reminding the worshiper of the incidents of the Bible and the precepts of the Faith, while some of it served as political propaganda in the service of the church and empire. But beneath the religious and imperial iconography, beneath the more subtle meanings of particular choices of symbols or forms, there lurks the artist himself, the anonymous servant of God who occasionally made his presence felt, stated his name, and made his claim on posterity. In such personalities as Gislebertus, Eadwine, and Villard de Honnecourt we find an emerging identity, an assertion of individuality, and an awareness of the importance of the artist in a historical and social sense. In them we find the precursors of the Renaissance, the beginning of the transformation of the medieval *artisan* into the Renaissance *artist*.

Selected Bibliography

1. GENERAL

Bishop, Morris. *The Middle Ages*. New York: American Heritage, 1970.

Braunfels, Wolfgang. *Monasteries of Western Europe, The Architecture of the Orders*. London: Thames & Hudson, 1972.

Calkins, Robert G. *A Medieval Treasury: An Exhibition of Medieval Art from the Third to the Sixteenth Century*. Ithaca, N.Y.: Office of University Publications, Cornell University, 1968.

Davis-Weyer, Caecilia. *Early Medieval Art 300–1150* (Sources and Documents in the History of Art). Englewood Cliffs, N.J.: Prentice-Hall, 1971.

Dehio, G., and Bezold, G. von. *Die Kirchliche Baukunst des Abendlandes*. 7 vols. Stuttgart: J. G. Cotta, 1884–1901.

Delort, Robert. *Life in the Middle Ages*. London: Phaidon, 1974.

Durandus, William. *The Symbolism of Churches and Church Ornaments: A Translation of the First Book of the Rationale Divinorum Officiorum*. Translated by John Mason Neale and Benjamin Webb. London: Gibbings & Co., 1893.

Egbert, Virginia W. *The Medieval Artist at Work*. Princeton: Princeton University Press, 1967.

Evans, Joan. *Art in Medieval France 987–1498*. Oxford: Clarendon Press, 1969.

———, ed. *The Flowering of the Middle Ages*. New York: McGraw-Hill, 1966.

———. *Life in Medieval France*. 3rd ed. London: Phaidon, 1969.

Focillon, Henri. *The Art of the West in the Middle Ages*. Edited by Jean Bony. 2 vols. London: Phaidon, 1963.

Hawthorne, John G., and Smith, Cyril S., tr. and eds. *On Divers Arts: the Treatise of Theophilus*. Chicago: The University of Chicago Press, 1963.

Holt, Elizabeth G. *A Documentary History of Art*. I. *The Middle Ages and the Renaissance*. Garden City, N.Y.: Doubleday, 1957.

Katzenellenbogen, Adolf. *Allegories of the Virtues and Vices in Medieval Art from Early Christian Times to the Thirteenth Century*. New York: W. W. Norton, 1964.

Kitzinger, Ernst. *Early Medieval Art in the British Museum*. London: The Trustees of The British Museum, 1960.

Krautheimer, Richard. *Studies in Early Christian, Medieval, and Renaissance Art*. New York: New York University Press, 1969.

Ladner, Gerhart B. *Ad Imaginem Dei: The Image of Man in Medieval Art*. Latrobe, Pa.: The Archabbey Press, 1965.

Martindale, Andrew. *The Rise of the Artist*. New York: McGraw-Hill, 1972.

Morey, Charles R. *Medieval Art*. New York: W. W. Norton, 1942.

Pevsner, Nikolaus. *An Outline of European Architecture*. 7th ed. Harmondsworth: Penguin Books, 1974.

Rice, David T., ed. *The Dawn of European Civilization: The Dark Ages.* New York: McGraw-Hill, 1966.

Schiller, Gertrud. *Iconography of Christian Art.* 2 vols. Greenwich, Conn.: New York Graphic Society, 1972.

Wixom, William. *Treasures from Medieval France* (exhibition catalogue). Cleveland: The Cleveland Museum of Art, 1967.

Zarnecki, George. *Art of the Medieval World.* Englewood Cliffs, N.J.: Prentice-Hall, 1975.

2. EARLY CHRISTIAN ART AND ARCHITECTURE

Beckwith, John. *Early Christian and Byzantine Art* (The Pelican History of Art). Harmondsworth: Penguin Books, 1970.

Gough, Michael. *The Origins of Christian Art.* New York: Praeger Publishers, 1974.

Grabar, André. *Christian Iconography. A Study of Its Origins.* Princeton: Princeton University Press, 1968.

————. *Early Christian Art from the Rise of Christianity to the Death of Theodosius* (The Arts of Mankind). New York: Odyssey Press, 1968.

————, and Nordenfalk, Carl. *Early Medieval Painting.* Geneva: Skira, 1957.

Krautheimer, Richard. *Early Christian and Byzantine Architecture* (The Pelican History of Art). 2d ed. Harmondsworth: Penguin Books, 1975.

MacDonald, William. *Early Christian and Byzantine Architecture.* New York: George Braziller, 1965.

The Metropolitan Museum of Art. *The Age of Spirituality* (exhibition catalogue). New York, 1978.

Oakeshott, Walter. *The Mosaics of Rome from the Third to the Fourteenth Centuries.* Greenwich, Conn.: New York Graphic Society, 1967.

Volbach, Fritz. *Early Christian Art.* New York: Harry N. Abrams, 1961.

3. BYZANTINE ART AND ARCHITECTURE

Beckwith, John. *The Art of Constantinople, an Introduction to Byzantine Art.* 2d ed. New York: Phaidon Press, 1968.

Demus, Otto. *Byzantine Art and the West.* New York: New York University Press, 1970.

————. *Byzantine Mosaic Decoration: Aspects of Monumental Art in Byzantium.* London: Routledge & Kegan Paul, 1953.

————, and Diez, E. *Byzantine Mosaics in Greece: Hosios Lucas and Daphni.* Cambridge, Mass.: Harvard University Press, 1931.

Grabar, André. *The Golden Age of Justinian from the Death of Theodosius to the Rise of Islam* (The Arts of Mankind). New York: Odyssey Press, 1967.

Kitzinger, Ernst. *Byzantine Art in the Making: Main Lines of Stylistic Development in Mediterranean Art, 3rd–7th Century.* Cambridge: Harvard University Press, 1977.

Krautheimer, Richard. *Early Christian and Byzantine Architecture* (The Pelican History of Art). Harmondsworth: Penguin Books, 1975.

Rice, David T. *The Appreciation of Byzantine Art* (The Appreciation of the Arts). London: Oxford University Press, 1972.

————. *Art of the Byzantine Era.* New York: Frederick A. Praeger, 1967.

Runciman, Steven. *Byzantine Style and Civilization.* Harmondsworth: Penguin Books, 1975.

Simson, Otto von. *The Sacred Fortress.* Chicago: The University of Chicago Press, 1948.

4. BARBARIAN, CAROLINGIAN, AND OTTONIAN ART AND ARCHITECTURE

Beckwith, John. *Early Medieval Art*. New York: Frederick A. Praeger, 1964.

Bruce-Mitford, Rupert. *The Sutton Hoo Ship-Burial, A Handbook*. 2d ed. London: The Trustees of The British Museum, 1972.

Crossley-Holland, Kevin, trans. *Beowulf*. London and Basingstoke: The Macmillan Co.; New York: Farrar, Straus & Giroux, 1968.

Grabar, André, and Nordenfalk, Carl. *Early Medieval Painting*. Geneva: Skira, 1957.

Hinks, Roger. *Carolingian Art*. Ann Arbor: The University of Michigan Press, 1962.

Hubert, Jean, Porcher, Jean, and Volbach, W. F. *The Carolingian Renaissance* (The Arts of Mankind). New York: George Braziller, 1970.

————. *Europe of the Invasions* (The Arts of Mankind). New York: George Braziller, 1969.

Ross, Marvin C., and Verdier, Philippe. *Arts of the Migration Period in the Walters Art Gallery*. Baltimore: The Walters Art Gallery, 1961.

5. ROMANESQUE ART AND ARCHITECTURE

Adams, Henry. *Mont-Saint-Michel and Chartres*. Garden City, N.Y.: Doubleday, 1933.

Beckwith, John. *Early Medieval Art*. New York: Frederick A. Praeger, 1964.

Collon-Gevaert, Suzanne, Lejeune, Jean, and Stiennon, Jacques. *A Treasury of Romanesque Art: Metalwork, Illuminations and Sculpture from the Valley of the Meuse*. London: Phaidon, 1972.

Conant, Kenneth J. *Carolingian and Romanesque Architecture: 800 to 1200* (The Pelican History of Art). Harmondsworth: Penguin Books, 1959.

Dodwell, Charles. *Painting in Europe, 800–1200* (The Pelican History of Art). Harmondsworth: Penguin Books, 1971.

Evans, Joan. *Cluniac Art of the Romanesque Period*. Cambridge: Cambridge University Press, 1950.

Focillon, Henri. *L'art des sculpteurs romans*. Paris: Presses Universitaires de France, 1964.

Forsyth, Ilene H. *The Throne of Wisdom, Wood Sculptures of the Madonna in Romanesque France*. Princeton: Princeton University Press, 1972.

Gauthier, Madeleine M. *Émaux limousins champlevés des XIIe, XIIIe, et XIVe siècles*. Paris: G. Le Prat, 1950.

Grabar, André, and Nordenfalk, Carl. *Romanesque Painting*. Geneva: Skira, 1958.

Grivot, Denis, and Zarnecki, George. *Gislebertus, Sculpteur d'Autun*. Paris: Éditions Trianon, 1960.

Grodecki, Louis, Mütherich, Florentine, Taralon, Jean, and Wormald, Francis. *Le siècle de l'An Mil* (L'Univers des formes). Paris: Gallimard, 1973.

Henderson, George. *Early Medieval* (Style and Civilization Series). Harmondsworth: Penguin Books, 1972.

Lasko, Peter. *Ars Sacra 800–1200* (The Pelican History of Art). Harmondsworth: Penguin Books, 1972.

Mâle, Émile. *L'art religieux du XIIe siècle en France*. Paris: Librairie Armand Colin, 1924.

Porter, Arthur K. *Romanesque Sculpture of the Pilgrimage Roads*. 10 vols. Boston: Marshall Jones, 1923.

Röhrig, Floridus. *Der Verduner Altar.* 3rd ed. Vienna: Verlag Herold, 1955.
Saalman, Howard. *Medieval Architecture.* New York: George Braziller, 1965.
Schapiro, Meyer. *Romanesque Art.* New York: George Braziller, 1976.
Stenton, Frank, ed. *The Bayeux Tapestry, A Comprehensive Survey.* London: Phaidon Press, 1957.
Stokstad, Marilyn. *Santiago de Compostela in the Age of the Great Pilgrimages.* Norman, Okla.: University of Oklahoma Press, 1978.
Swarzenski, Hanns. *Monuments of Romanesque Art.* 2d ed. Chicago: The University of Chicago Press, 1974.
Taralon, Jean, ed. *Treasures of the Churches of France.* New York: George Braziller, 1966.
Vielliard, Jeanne, ed. *Le Guide du pèlerin de Saint-Jacques de Compostelle.* Mâcon: Imprimerie Protat Frères, 1963.

6. GOTHIC AND SECULAR ART AND ARCHITECTURE

Adams, Henry. *Mont-Saint-Michel and Chartres.* Garden City, N.Y.: Doubleday, 1933.
Bowie, Theodore. *The Sketchbook of Villard de Honnecourt.* Bloomington, Ind.: Indiana University Press, 1959.
Branner, Robert, ed. *Chartres Cathedral* (Norton Critical Studies in Art History). New York: W. W. Norton, 1969.
———. *Gothic Architecture.* New York: George Braziller, 1965.
———. *St. Louis and the Court Style in Gothic Architecture.* London: A. Zwemmer, 1965.
Cuttler, Charles. *Northern Painting from Pucelle to Breugel: Fourteenth, Fifteenth and Sixteenth Centuries.* New York: Holt, Rinehart & Winston, 1968.
Fitchen, J. *The Construction of Gothic Cathedrals.* Oxford: Clarendon Press, 1961.
Frankl, Paul. *Gothic Architecture* (The Pelican History of Art). Harmondsworth: Penguin Books, 1962.
———. *The Gothic: Literary Sources and Interpretations Through Eight Centuries.* Princeton: Princeton University Press, 1960.
Freeman, Margaret. *The Unicorn Tapestries.* New York: E. P. Dutton, 1976.
Frisch, Teresa G. *Gothic Art 1140-c. 1450* (Sources and Documents in the History of Art). Englewood Cliffs, N.J.: Prentice-Hall, 1971.
Gimpel, Jean. *The Cathedral Builders.* New York: Grove Press, 1961.
Hartt, Frederick. *History of Italian Renaissance Art.* Englewood Cliffs, N.J.: Prentice-Hall, n.d.
Harvey, John. *The Gothic World, 1100-1600: A Survey of Architecture and Art.* New York: Harper & Row, 1969.
———. *The Master Builders: Architecture in the Middle Ages.* New York: McGraw-Hill, 1971.
Henderson, George. *Gothic* (Style and Civilization Series). Harmondsworth: Penguin Books, 1967.
Jantzen, Hans. *High Gothic: The Classic Cathedrals of Chartres, Reims, Amiens.* New York: Random House, 1962.
Katzenellenbogen, Adolf. *The Sculptural Programs of Chartres Cathedral.* Baltimore: The Johns Hopkins Press, 1959.
Loomis, Roger S. "The Allegorical Siege in the Art of the Middle Ages." *American Journal of Archaeology,* ser. 2, 13, no. 3 (1919): 255-269.

Mâle, Émile. *L'art religieux de la fin du moyen âge en France*. Paris: Librairie Armand Colin, 1949.

———. *The Gothic Image*. New York: Harper Brothers, 1958.

Martindale, Andrew. *Gothic Art from the Twelfth to the Fifteenth Century*. New York: Frederick A. Praeger, 1967.

The Metropolitan Museum of Art. *Masterpieces of Tapestry from the Fourteenth to the Sixteenth Century* (exhibition catalogue). Paris, 1973.

———. *The Secular Spirit, Life and Art at the End of the Middle Ages* (exhibition catalogue). New York: E. P. Dutton, 1975.

———. *The Year 1200* (exhibition catalogue and background essays). 2 vols. New York, 1970.

Natanson, Joseph. *Gothic Ivories of the 13th and 14th Centuries*. London: Alec Tiranti, 1951.

Oertel, Robert. *Early Italian Painting to 1400*. London: Thames & Hudson, 1968.

Panofsky, Erwin. *Abbot Suger on the Abbey Church of St. Denis and Its Art Treasures*. Princeton: Princeton University Press, 1946.

———. *Gothic Architecture and Scholasticism*. New York: Meridian Books, 1957.

Sauerländer, Willibald, and Hirmer, Max. *Gothic Sculpture in France 1140–1270*. New York: Harry N. Abrams, 1972.

Simson, Otto von. *The Gothic Cathedral, Origins of Gothic Architecture and the Medieval Concept of Order*. 2d ed. New York: Random House, 1962.

Stoddard, Whitney S. *Monastery and Cathedral in France*. Middletown, Conn.: Wesleyan University Press, 1966.

Stubblebine, James, ed. *Giotto: The Arena Chapel Frescoes* (Norton Critical Studies in Art History). New York: W. W. Norton, 1969.

Tintori, Leonetto, and Meiss, Millard. *The Painting of the Life of St. Francis at Assisi*. New York: W. W. Norton, 1967.

Von der Osten, Gert, and Vey, Horst. *Painting and Sculpture in Germany and the Netherlands: 1500–1600* (The Pelican History of Art). Harmondsworth: Penguin Books, 1969.

White, John. *Art and Architecture in Italy: 1250–1400* (The Pelican History of Art). Harmondsworth: Penguin Books, 1966.

7. MANUSCRIPTS AND INCUNABULA

Alexander, J. J. G. *The Decorated Letter*. New York: George Braziller, 1978.

———. *Italian Renaissance Illuminations*. New York: George Braziller, 1977.

Arano, Luisa C. *The Medieval Health Handbook: Tacuinum Sanitatis*. New York: George Braziller, 1976.

Avril, François. *Manuscript Painting at the Court of France: The Fourteenth Century (1310–1380)*. New York: George Braziller, 1978.

Calkins, Robert G. "Stages of Execution: Procedures of Illumination as Revealed in an Unfinished Book of Hours." *Gesta*, 17 (1978):61–70.

Dodwell, C. R. *The Canterbury School of Illumination 1066–1200*. Cambridge: Cambridge University Press, 1954.

Farquhar, James D., and Hindman, Sandra. *Pen to Press*. Baltimore: Department of the History of Art, The Johns Hopkins University, 1977.

Harthan, John. *The Book of Hours*. New York: Thomas Y. Crowell, 1977.

Herbert, J. A. *Illuminated Manuscripts*. London: Methuen, 1911.

John, James J. "Latin Paleography." In *Medieval Studies,* edited by James M. Powell, pp. 1–68. Syracuse, N.Y.: Syracuse University Press, 1976.

Lognon, J., and Cazelles, R. *The "Très Riches Heures" of Jean, Duke of Berry.* New York: George Braziller, 1969.

Lowe, E. A. *Handwriting, Our Medieval Legacy.* Rome: Edizioni di Storia e Letteratura, 1969.

Metz, Peter. *The Golden Gospels of Echternach, Codex Aureus Epternacensis.* New York: Frederick A. Praeger, 1957.

Mütherich, Florentine, and Gaehde, Joachim E. *Carolingian Painting.* New York: George Braziller, 1976.

Nordenfalk, Carl. *Celtic and Anglo-Saxon Painting: Book Illumination in the British Isles 600–800.* New York: George Braziller, 1977.

Oakeshott, Walter. *The Artists of the Winchester Bible.* London: Faber & Faber, 1945.

Plummer, John. *The Hours of Catherine of Cleves.* New York: George Braziller, 1966.

————. *Liturgical Manuscripts for the Mass and Divine Office* (exhibition catalogue, The Pierpont Morgan Library). New York, 1964.

Porcher, Jean. *Medieval French Miniatures.* New York: Harry N. Abrams, 1959.

Rickert, Margaret. *Painting in Britain: The Middle Ages* (The Pelican History of Art). 2d ed. Harmondsworth: Penguin Books, 1965.

Robb, David M. *The Art of the Illuminated Manuscript.* Cranbury, N.J.: A. S. Barnes, 1973.

Scheller, R. W. *A Survey of Medieval Model Books.* Haarlem: De Erven F. Bohn, 1963.

Soltész, Elizabeth. *Biblia Pauperum, Facsimile Edition of the Forty-Leaf Blockbook in the Library of the Esztergom Cathedral.* Budapest: Corvina Press, 1967.

Trithemius, Johannes. *In Praise of Scribes: De Laude Scriptorum.* Translated by Roland Behrendt. Lawrence, Kans.: Coronado Press, 1974.

Weitzmann, Kurt. *Late Antique and Early Christian Book Illumination.* New York: George Braziller, 1977.

White, T. H. *The Bestiary, A Book of Beasts.* New York: G. P. Putnam's Sons, 1954.

Williams, John. *Early Spanish Manuscript Illumination.* New York: George Braziller, 1977.

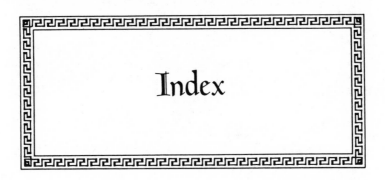

Index

Page references for illustrations are in **boldface** type.

Library of Congress Cataloging in Publication Data

Calkins, Robert G.
    Monuments of medieval art.

    Reprint. Originally published: New York : Dutton, c1979.
    Bibliography: p.
    Includes index.
    1. Art, Medieval.   I. Title.
N5970.C34   1985   709'.02   84-21504
ISBN 0-8014-9306-4